Books for review to the Reviews editor, Marx Memorial Library.
m.jump@marx-memorial-library.org.uk

m.jump@marx-memorial-library.org.uk
theory & struggle continues the series

Marx Memorial Library Newsletter and *Praxis*

ISSN 2057-0988 Print ISSN 2514-264X Online
ISBN 978-1-899155-49-1

Design/Production Tom Greenwood

PRAXIS
PRESS

praxispress@me.com
redletterspp.com

CONTENTS

REVIEWS

EDITORIAL

Welcome to the 2025 Issue of Theory and Struggle. The past year has been marked by particularly rapid changes, following elections in so many countries of the world, including Britain and the US. Former alliances have been thrown into question, accompanied by new threats to the prospects for stability and environmental sustainability for the future. This year's articles and review articles address a number of these challenges.

Perhaps unsurprisingly given the wider context, a number of articles explore contentious questions that have been, and continue to be, the subject of debate among Marxists. These include questions of political economy along with debates about the causes of conflicts and about ways forward in the Middle East and China. It is important to emphasise that articles in Theory and Struggle represent the views of their authors, not necessarily the views of Marx Memorial Library and Workers' School. We welcome considered responses from our readers, exploring alternative approaches from a Marxist perspective.

Meanwhile the inclusion of Round Table discussions has enabled us to explore different viewpoints within this particular Issue of Theory and Struggle already. The Round Table discussion on 'Combatting the pro-war narrative' explores perspectives from different components of the Peace Movement, internationally. The Round Table on 'Trade union strategies in post-Tory Britain' explores the opportunities and continuing threats to the Labour Movement from different trade union perspectives, in the contemporary context. And the Reviews section includes a number of contributions, addressing varying approaches to the environmental crisis.

This has also been a year of change for Theory and Struggle's own production and distribution processes, with the move to Praxis Press. Although Theory and Struggle's collaboration with Liverpool University Press was very successful for a number of years, this became problematic due to increasing financial challenges. We look forward to working with Praxis Press in more financially viable ways in the coming period. Meanwhile we should like to express our appreciations to our former colleagues at Liverpool University Press. It has been a pleasure to work with them over these past years.

There have been changes in the team at Theory and Struggle, as well. Last year we welcomed Tom Greenwood as our new designer. This year we should like to add our warmest welcome to Sonya Andermahr, who has joined Ann Field, Kate Hudson and Jonathan White, our Associate Editor, on the copy editing and proof-reading team. Our warmest appreciations to them. And our warmest appreciations to Emily Mann who carried out these responsibilities so effectively over the past decade.

Marjorie Mayo
Editor of Theory and Struggle

'RED FRIDAY', 31 JULY 1925: UNITY CONSTRUCTED AND DECONSTRUCTED

Roger Seifert read PPE at Oxford, before taking a MSc and PhD at London. He was professor of industrial relations at Keele (1993-2008) and Wolverhampton (2008-2018). He specialises in strikes, public sector industrial relations, trade unions, the role of the state, and labour history.

Abstract

This paper discusses the events surrounding Red Friday (31 July 1925) when the Conservative government backed away from a confrontation with the Miners' Federation of Great Britain (MFGB) supported by the Trades Union Congress (TUC). It discusses some of the issues concerning miners' wages, coal owners' profits, the role of government, and the solidarity behind that moment in time. It then schematically focusses on the defeat of the miners left to fend for themselves after the collapse of the 1926 general strike, and why that solidarity evaporated. It ends with some sense of how these events reflect on schisms inside the labour movement between reformists and Marxists.

Keywords
Red Friday, solidarity, Left schisms

'Red Friday', on 31 July 1925, was a victory for the unity of the working-class movement as the Conservative government gave way to the miners' demands backed up by other unions. The case is made that the solidarity necessary to support the miners was partly based on self-interest of other workers and partly determined by a Marxist approach to the nature of class struggle. Namely, that it requires workers and the leaders of their organisations, industrial and political, to appreciate that if the state-backed employers come for me in the evening, then they will come for you in the morning. The constant dilemma is why the words of the 1915 American Wobblies anthem (Industrial Workers of the World), 'solidarity for ever', are not always heeded.

Such unity was forged over years of hard graft by communists in the National Minority Movement[1] (NMM) and in the leadership of the Miners' Federation of Great Britain[2] (MFGB), the forerunner of the NUM. It was the communists who fought for unity and understood its importance in the face of a state-backed employers' offensive to cut wages. They were the most ardent defenders of its representation of class solidarity that transcended

---

[1]   The National Minority Movement "is not itself a Union but consists of militant members of the existing Trade Unions, associating together in this Movement to make the Unions real militant organisations for the class struggle", Constitution and Structure (London, NMM:1924), 2.

[2]   Robin Page Arnot, The Miners: Years of Struggle: A History of the Miners' Federation of Great Britain from 1910 Onwards. (London: Allen & Unwin, 1949).

the mere here-and-now and put down a marker for all future struggles. Unity, aka solidarity, is the watchword of the working-class movement - its best slogan and its best practice.

When most citizens are exploited and oppressed by a small minority, democratic and undemocratic alike, their main means of counterattack is fighting together. Ruling minorities use violence, ideology as false consciousness, and divide and rule to stay in power, but have been overthrown by people mobilised in a common cause, identifying common interests, and acting purposefully.

Allen Hutt[3] provided the defined relevance of 'Red Friday' based on the deeds and words of leading communists such as Rajani Palme Dutt and Wal Hannington as well as close allies such as A.J. Cook[4] through the pages of Labour Monthly and Workers' Weekly.[5] Hutt traces the split inside the movement between communists and increasingly rightward leaning social democratic supporters of the Labour Party leader, Ramsay MacDonald.

The Daily Herald reported on 31 July 1925 this interchange between the Conservative Prime Minister, Stanley Baldwin, and the miners' leaders: 'Miners: "but what you propose means a reduction of wages"; Prime Minister: "yes, all the workers in this country have got to face a reduction of wages" Miners: "what do you mean?"; Prime Minister: "I mean all the workers of this country have got to take reductions in wages to help put industry on its feet"'.[6]

The years before ....

Miners' wages were the immediate issue that sparked the series of disputes leading up to events in July 1925. Since the 1880s they were decided by the combined forces of the MFGB, the government, the coal owners, and indeterminant market outcomes. The 1921 settlement was 'fundamentally different from the old pre-war arrangements for regulating wages'.[7] The old system broadly linked average selling prices to wages. Across the country there were variations on the sliding scale by which wages rose and fell with prices, but not quite. The weakness of the supply and demand model, which was unique to coal mining, was that in good times when wages rose miners traded time off (and so less production) with rising wage levels. They preferred to stay away from work if they could afford it, while the coal owners wanted maximum production and lower wages all of the time.

The 1921 settlement shifted the basis for district-by-district wage levels from prices to profits. It acknowledged, without formally endorsing, the notion of the 'living wage' with a fail-safe, that 'wages are never to fall below 20 per cent on the "standard wages".[8] Supple explains 'there was by no means a complete reversion to laissez-faire: the National Wages Agreement of July 1921 provided universal guidelines for district settlements, for the division of proceeds between wages and profits, and for the levels of minimum and subsistence wages'.[9]

---

3   Allen Hutt, Post-War History of the British Working Class (London, Victor Gollancz, 1937).

4   Paul Davies, A.J. Cook 1883-1931, (Bristol, AJ Cook memorial committee: 1983).

5   Founded in February 1923 by the CPGB, it was the forerunner of the Daily Worker, later the Morning Star

6   Hutt, 110.

7   J.W.F. Rowe, Wages in the coal industry, (London, P.S. King & Son: 1923), 137.

8   Rowe, 139.

9   Barry Supple, The history of the British coal industry, volume 4, The Political Economy of Decline, 1913-1946, (Oxford: Clarendon Press, 1987), 215.

By the summer of 1922 wages had fallen back and union leaders appealed directly to the government for support. The MFGB, as many other sectoral-based unions, were eager for modernisation – more investment and greater efficiency thereby securing jobs and wages.

The owners were uninterested, and union policy was to call upon government to intervene and provide subsidies for change. As coal was the main national energy source, the MFGB argued that government should underwrite its constant supply through a wages' guarantee. State intervention and eventually ownership and control were a major part of these early socialist demands.

In January 1923 the French occupied the Ruhr allowing for a temporary increase in demand for British coal, and pari passu slightly higher wages for some miners. At the year's end the MFGB asked the employers for a formal review of wages and the 1921 settlement. This was refused and the union gave three months' notice of the termination of the agreement. The upturn in demand and the 1924 minority Labour government gave the MFGB some cause for optimism. As a result, a better wage deal was brokered with the intervention of Manny Shinwell (mining minister) and MacDonald himself, alongside a Court of Inquiry (Buckmaster). Not unusually, 'although its recommendations led to a settlement, the hearings of the Buckmaster Court were somewhat confused. The Inquiry's hoped-for clarification was clouded not merely by the almost hysterical perplexity which was the customary accompaniment of any attempt to explain the industry's wage system to laymen, but by disagreement between the two sides as to what the grounds of their controversy were'.[10]

The election of December 1923 ended in a messy outcome with the tensions between Protectionism and Free Trade a proxy for refining imperial preference. The limitations of the 1918 Versailles peace treaty had already been exposed by J.M. Keynes,[11] and the political leaders from across the narrow spectrum of party politics myopically headed for the disastrous 1929 slump and subsequent tragic 1930s recession. Mass unemployment loomed as first the return to the Gold Standard and then wage cuts threatened domestic demand levels. It pitched organised trade unionists against cost-cutting employers backed by the state. Ideologies in the form of 'conventional wisdom' took hold as the BBC started to broadcast into every home reactionary Christian values dressed up as British common sense. The newly formed CPGB[12] quickly asserted a different set of popular anti-capitalist formulations. Such matters set the stage for murky cross-party allegiances and dark schisms within the labour movement.

The election resulted in 258 Conservative MPs, 191 Labour, and 159 Liberals. As Taylor noted, 'the outcome was a tangle' and the Liberals eschewed any coalition, thus paving the way for a minority Labour government. On 22 January 1924 MacDonald became the first Labour Prime Minister and although 'the revolutionary left was almost passed over... it marked a social revolution despite its moderation: working men in a majority, the great public schools and the old universities eclipsed for the first time'.[13]

This mattered little in practice. The Labour government showed no great ambition; they collectively lacked the know-how and motivation to make change happen.

---

10   Supple, 217.

11   J.M. Keynes, The economic consequences of the peace, (London: MacMillan, 1919).

12   James Klugmann, History of the Communist Party of Great Britain, volume 1, Formation and early years, 1919-1924, (London: Lawrence & Wishart, 1969).

13   A.J.P. Taylor, English History 1914-1945, (Oxford: Clarendon Press, 1965), 208-9.

Unsurprisingly, it was around employment and labour markets, unemployment remained over one million, that Labour floundered. The social democrats in office had no answer, not even a sniff of a remedy, as their appreciation of the workings of a capitalist economy was as vague as it was naive. Indeed, they rejected early feelers in Keynesian-style state control over domestic demand even within the straitjacket of orthodox Treasury economics. It was this soft underbelly of Labour in government that further exposed the rift with the trade-union movement. Even though the TUC and TGWU leadership were moderates inclined to support all things MacDonald suggested, they reared up when it came to wage cuts and job losses.

Strikes continued at pace among engine drivers, dockers, and London tramwaymen. Taylor noted, 'Here was fine trouble in the making. The unions provided most of the money for the Labour party, yet Labour in office had to show that it was fit to govern.'[14] Ernest Bevin at the TGWU swallowed it up, and the TUC put it in its back pocket as another 'ugly memory'. Much of this is familiar in 2025 and much stoked the fires of bitter resentment that soon created the conditions for harsher lessons to come.

The June 1924 General Election returned a Conservative majority mainly predicated upon the collapse of the weakened Liberals and the red-scare scandal of the fake Zinoviev letter.[15] Conservatives won 48.3% of the vote with 419 of the 615 MPs. This victory, now with Churchill back in the fold, laid the basis for further crises at home and abroad.

By the end of 1924 the coal market had collapsed. The owners called upon the union to negotiate change, and on 18 March 1925 the Joint Sub-committee met with ten from each side. There were to be thirteen such meetings until June ... all were in private, but notes record that all were antagonistic, bad tempered, and tediously circular. The MFGB in the shape of Herbert Smith not only rejected the suggestion of wage cuts with longer hours but scorned the entire edifice of the owners' case rooted in poor management and outdated ownership structures. By the end of June, the owners gave notice of ending the agreement and proposed drastic wage cuts.

When Churchill restored the Gold Standard (the six years of suspension under the 1919 Act was over) he was supported by both political and economic elites deluded in their wish to return to pre-war imperial dominance. The dollar-sterling exchange rate was shifting, and all conventions suggested a return at the old rate of parity, but as Galbraith wryly noted 'why would even Churchill do such a stupid thing?'[16] By over-valuing sterling British goods would be less competitive in overseas markets, and this triggered a slump in trade for staple exports such as coal. The Gold Standard move was partly to protect the financial advantages of the City of London, and their voices, as with Thatcher in the 1980s, were those most heeded in the corridors of power. On 28 April 1925 Churchill announced the disastrous return to the Gold Standard at the old rate.[17]

Critically, the MFGB had not only rejected the employers' offer but refused to meet again until it was withdrawn. As part of their strategy to involve the government, the miners formed a de facto Quadruple Alliance with the railwaymen in the National Union of

---

14   Taylor, 213.
15   Taylor, 219.
16   J.K. Galbraith, The Age of Uncertainty, quoted from the 1977 BBC series.
17   J.M. Keynes, The economic consequences of Mr. Churchill. (London: L. and V. Woolf, 1925).

Railwaymen (NUR), transport workers in the Transport and General Workers Union (TGWU), and seafarers in the National Union of Seamen (NUS). The government was drawn into the dispute and announced another Court of Inquiry under H.P. Macmillan, which was boycotted by the union. It focussed on wages, arguing against wage cuts and for a socially based minimum wage. That was the rub – the sector was a mess, with conservative backward looking owners, and an international coal market in anarchic disarray.

Supple concludes 'the Macmillan Report's combination of well-meaning vagueness and its sympathy for the miners had, if anything, brought a breakdown in negotiations nearer'.[18] This was the starting gun for both 'Red Friday' and the 1926 General Strike, as John Murray later noted, 'the march to the General Strike really began at that moment. For it was the return to the Gold Standard which started the clamour for a lowering of production costs to boost exports; and a lowering of production costs meant only one thing to the industrialists of 1925 – yet another cut in wages'.[19] This challenge to the largely moderate leadership of the trade unions (there were fewer strike days in 1925 than at any time since the war) meant that even Bevin, eager as usual to work with employers to modernise industry, stopped short of agreeing wage cuts. As Taylor rightly suggests, 'the coal industry was almost inevitably the field of conflict'.[20] With over a million workers it remained the largest industrial sector and as such every other worker knew that their jobs were linked to coal production and miners' wages.

The day went well ...
On 30 June 1925 the coal owners gave one month's notice to end the existing agreement. The offer was a drastic cut in wages; the MFGB rejected it outright, and the owners announced a lock out to start on 31 July. The TUC ordered an embargo on coal movements with the leaders of the railway and transport unions giving unbridled backing for the miners' cause. The government, having dithered, climbed down and offered up a deal twenty-six hours before the deadline. The proposal was for a nine-month subsidy to maintain both wages and profits, and the ubiquitous royal commission to modernise the sector. This was 'Red Friday' a victory for trade-union solidarity. The lock-out was cancelled, and the commission under Sir Herbert Samuel, a former Liberal minister, was set up with three members none of whom knew anything about the coal industry.

Hutt noted, 'I am sure that those who remember those days will agree that their first reaction was one almost of incredulity. The news seemed too good to be true. As its significance was grasped a mood of real exaltation seized hold of the movement'.[21] The TUC's announcement of the victory spoke of the 'immense stimulus to every trade unionist' and furthermore 'the manifestation of solidarity which has been exhibited by all sections of the trade union movement is a striking potent for the future and marks an epoch in the history of the movement'.[22]

The CPGB leadership had earlier warned of a state-backed employers' offensive starting with the miners and urging unity in support. Workers' Weekly was the prime organ of argument and throughout the first half of the year pushed the case for an alliance of miners with the railway, transport, and metal workers. On January 10, for example, Harry Pollitt urged trade union unity to 'solidify the struggle against the bosses', and on 14 February the paper published an open letter to the railwaymen to help 'Organise the common struggle'. This call

18   Supple, 224.
19   John Murray, The General Strike of 1926, (London: Lawrence & Wishart, 1951), 33.
20   Taylor, 239.
21   Hutt, 112.
22   cited in Hutt, 112.

for unity was the drum beat of struggle with a piece on 28 March on the necessity of 'mass action', and articles by Gallacher, Watkins, Hannington, Pollitt, and Cook all stressed the need to 'prepare for the coming struggle' (9 May), 'Organise! Organise! Organise!' (6 June), and the 'fight for solidarity' (15 August).

Arthur Horner moved the motion for unity across the unions at the CPGB's seventh congress at the end of May. As Klugmann notes 'all the most militant sections of the workers, including in a major role the Communist Party and the NMM, put support for the miners at the centre of their endeavours '.[23] He concludes 'never before had the Government been confronted by so united and militant a TUC leadership. And the effect was instant. The Cabinet was recalled ... early on Friday, July 31, the Government agreed to offer a nine-month subsidy in return for which the owners were to withdraw their notices '.[24]

G.D.H. Cole noted a few years later that, 'The Triple Alliance had perished in the fiasco of 1921; and the miners now appealed to the whole Trade Union movement. Urged on by the militants, the Trades Union Congress was induced to threaten a General Strike in their support; and the Baldwin government, not ready to face such a movement, bought off the miners with a temporary subsidy in aid of wages -- which incidentally was so arranged as to present large profits to the coal-owners'.[25]

In her biography of Arthur Horner, Nina Fishman suggests that it was Cook who 'took the initiative in meeting the TGWU and other unions to revive the Triple Alliance on a more formal basis. He also cultivated closer relations with the TUC General Council'. The formation of the GC in 1921 was seen by those involved, including Cole and Robin Page Arnot at the Labour Research Department (LRD), as a positive move in establishing a permanent body capable of influencing government policy on economic matters. Fishman argues that 'The NMM and CPGB leadership viewed the Council optimistically as a potential centre of working-class power in a revolutionary situation ... delegates to the TUC at Scarborough in the first week of September were full of self-congratulation about the satisfactory conclusion to "Red Friday", as it had been immediately described'.[26] In Klugmann's view 'a victory had been won; this was indubitable. Red Friday was and remains a red-letter day in working-class history. But, and it was a big but, the real issue was what was to follow'.[27]

The morning after ... the government prepares, the official labour movement does not

Murray argues that, 'the General Council, following "Red Friday", abdicated from any responsible spirit of preparedness, while the government, urged on by the fire-eaters, Churchill, Birkenhead and Joynson-Hicks, vigilantly and steadily mounted guard.' [28]

The actual thinking behind Baldwin's decision to backdown has been interpreted in different ways – as a victory for organised labour under communist direction; as a breathing space to allow the forces of reaction to regroup; and as an instinctive British-style compromise in keeping with One Nation Toryism. 'Red Friday was a moment of high drama

---

23   James Klugmann, History of the CPGB vol 2 The General Strike 1925-1926, (London: Lawrence & Wishart, 1969), 28.

24   Klugmann, General Strike, 30-31.

25   G.D.H. Cole, British Trade Unionism Today: a survey, (London: Methuen & Co, 1939), 71.

26   Nina Fishman (2010) Arthur Horner: a political biography, vol 1, 1894-1944; (London: / Lawrence & Wishart, 2010), 102-104.

27   Klugmann, General Strike, 31.

28   Murray, 48.

in troubled times.' [29] Current convention deems that the government was not confident that it could use existing emergency powers, despite goading from the press, to deal with the miners. As a consequence, the 'Red Friday' retreat allowed time to hone the cutting edge of state apparatus ready for the next 'trial of strength'.

A volunteer-based strike-breaking organisation, for example, was set up at the end of September. The Organisation for the Maintenance of Supplies, backed by army and corporate leaders with support from the Home Secretary, allowed secret training of these 'shock troops' to take place as replacements for striking lorry and train drivers, as well as how to operate telephones and telegraphs. As Hutt argues 'this cool and calculating preparation by the Government had absolutely no parallel on the side of the Labour movement'.[30] The sound and fury from the TUC were undiminished at its 1925 Scarborough conference. Class struggle was supported, the overthrow of capitalism cheered, and workshop organisation endorsed. But when it came to specifics in defence of the movement little was said and done as the composition of the General Council itself shifted to the right with the election of Ernest Bevin and re-election of J.H. Thomas -- seen as class enemies by the communists.[31]

A month later the Labour Party conference in Liverpool represented the triumph of the right wing under MacDonald. Here its liberal tendency won through with the expression that Labour was above class conflict because it served the nation. Three factors emerged from this landmark concourse -- the exclusion and future persecution of communists, a programme based on national renewal through Parliamentary means without nationalisation, and a pact with the Liberals to help form the next Labour government. The MFGB pressed ahead with its own industrial alliance of unions in transport and heavy industry for both offensive and defensive purposes. It was described as a '[s]upreme war council of industrial allies' better equipped than the TUC for any future class conflict. The alliance, however, foundered from the start as the NUR in particular began to undermine it from within despite the realities that more and more employers were demanding wage cuts. The CPGB warned as early as January 1926 that the capitalist class would not allow a repeat of 'Red Friday', and throughout 1925 and 1926 the coal industry was the centre of class struggle, and 'The Communist party backed them all the way and its membership grew in all the coalfields'.[32]

A programme of action was in preparation with the gearing up of the TUC's GC, the alliance itself, and the formation of factory committees. The official labour leadership waited for the Samuel Report which recommended wage cuts and/or longer hours for the miners, while vaguely referring to capital re-organisation of the sector with or without state subsidies. The Commission divided the labour movement along the existing fault lines --- the left denounced its one-sided attack on workers, while the right social democrats welcomed a report that favoured modernisation of British industry with a possible interventionist twist from the state.

The germs of a general strike were apparent from this; the TGWU complained that stopping the movement of coal fell disproportionately upon its members and therefore wanted the TUC to broaden the scope of solidarity thus paving the way for a more

29   R. Maguire, (2004) 'Reassessing the British Government's Emergency Organisation on 'Red Friday', 31 July 1925'. Contemporary British History, 18 (1), 1-24 at 2.

30   Hutt, 116.

31   Harry Pollitt, The Workers' Charter, (London: NMM, 1930?), 16.

32   Noreen Branson and Bill Moore, Labour-Communist relations, part 1, 1920-1935, Our History pamphlet 82, (London: CP History Group, 1990), 35.

generalised strike. Bevin was instrumental in this brand of unity with the union's biennial conference in Scarborough formally endorsing such an arrangement.

The government's retreat on 31 July 1925, while a pragmatic short-term response, was predicated on the fear of further feeding the growth of communist militancy within the NMM's rank-and-file.[33] The government took their 'reds under every bed' scaremongering to new depths with the prosecution of twelve leading communists. They were imprisoned for sedition, but this fed, rather than reduced, the communist influence inside the unions and beyond. It also further deepened the schisms within the labour movement and created the standard divisions familiar between communists and social reformers that persist today and will tomorrow.

Schisms and lessons

The chasm in analysis and policy between the Leninists in the CPGB and NMM and those inside the Labour Party and TUC backing MacDonald's brand of social democracy was ever more apparent: class struggle based on unity in practice and a socialist objective, against class collaboration in the name of national renewal and anti-communism. Communist historians such as Klugmann and Branson and Moore took up the story referencing Arnot's works on the MFGB with approval and acknowledging the role of Cook in forging trade union unity using the NMM as an example of what could be achieved. Cook himself said, 'once again ringing through industrial areas of Britain in every mine, workshop and factory – is that blessed word unity'. But he also warned that 'the forward march of trade unionism... is again in danger of receiving another check in 1925'.[34]

Arnot's history of coal mining trade unions emphasised the role of wages as the material basis for both the formation and development of the MFGB and the militancy among some miners required to underpin its bargaining position. The 'wages movement' was the spur to unity in the late 1880s.[35] The complexity of the wages system was interwoven with the need for a living wage and exacerbated by the export trade, but 'the impact of the economic crisis upon the coal-mining industry was particularly severe for another reason than the loss of export or the erosion by other sources of energy and other fuels of coal's one-time unchallenged supremacy. This other reason was found in the peculiar structure of the capitalist ownership of the collieries'.[36]

More pertinently, the solidarity shown on 'Red Friday' came from work throughout 1924 when, for example, 'A.J. Cook spent his week-ends addressing meetings in the coal-fields in order to build up the moral unity of the miners. Cook's campaign for unity, extending beyond the mining industry, began to rouse echoes in other trades, especially where the Minority Movement had made headway'.[37] Arnot makes it clear that Churchill's blunder in the return to the Gold Standard laid the basis for a unity of unions with TUC support that, for the moment, encompassed all political groups within the movement. Even though the government's retreat was dubbed 'Red Friday', 'the miners, however, through the mouth

---

33   Mary Davis and John Foster, The Transport and General Workers Union: representing a mass movement; UNITE history volume 1, 1880-1931, (Liverpool University Press, 2021), 57-59.

34   A.J. Cook, 'The problem of the hour – is unity possible?' Labour Monthly, vol 7(7) July 1925, 410-11.

35   Robin Page Arnot, A History of the Miners Federation of Great Britain 1889-1910, (London: George Allen & Unwin, 1949), 95-101.

36   Robin Page Arnot, The miners in crisis and war: a history of the MFGB from 1930 onwards, (London: George Allen & Unwin, 1961), 23.

37   Robin Page Arnot, (1955) A history of the Scottish miners, (London: George Allen & Unwin, 1955), 163.

of the MFGB chairman, warned that it was not a 'glorious victory' but that 'it is only an armistice'. Nonetheless, Red Friday was a 'glorious victory' for unity of purpose in the trade union world'.[38]

This ambiguity surrounding 'Red Friday' is part hindsight given the speed with which it was followed by the general strike, and part the awareness at the time that class struggle, genuine class on class confrontation with no fudge, was in the wake of the Russian revolution and defeat of German imperialists, a possible and practical way in which to rebalance the social and economic worlds of Britian in the 1920s.

The state, from a Leninist perspective, is an instrument of class rule.[39] The democratic struggle was endlessly suborned by the powerful vested interests represented by large corporations, social elites around the monarchy, and fought over in the press, in educational institutions, and overlain with ruling class cultural mores. In the case of July 1925, the state gave way in the face of a clear and present danger from the combined forces of organised labour. The response, when it came, was ferocious as class war was meted out to the miners and their allies, both political and industrial. As Fishman reports in October 1925, during the nine-month truce, police, under instructions from the Home Secretary, raided the offices of the CPGB, YCL, and NMM,[40] and arrested and imprisoned several leading communists.[41]

The left consensus was that 'Red Friday' was not definitively a working-class victory. Cook saw what was what: '[T]his is the first round. Let us prepare for the final struggle', and the TUC agreed that another effort to cut wages was coming over the hill. The Workers Weekly went further; 'what has been achieved is the imposition on the capitalist class of an unstable truce, which cannot lead to industrial peace but only to renewed class conflict [as] ... the capitalist class will prepare for a crushing attack upon the workers'.[42] Soon after Tom Mann, speaking at the NMM's August conference asked: 'are we prepared to meet the opposing forces when the next round begins? ... the miners will require a much more highly disciplined regimentation of the organised forces of the workers when the next battle begins'.[43]

While the Conservative-dominated papers raged at Baldwin's retreat in the face of union threats, those on the miners' side saw it through a different lens of class conflict. John Hamilton wrote 'the history of the mining industry is one of repeated epic struggles between colliers and mine-owners. Every tiny reform, advance in wages, or improved working conditions, have had to be forced by prolonged agitation and strikes... the miners have learnt the lesson of solidarity; the smashing of that solidarity is the owners' aim'.[44]

Contemporary views, from those at the heart of the matter show the bitter herbs in the workers' political diet after the defeat of the General Strike. On 12 May 1926 the TUC GC called off the general strike without conditions, and while Baldwin shrank from full throated class war, the employers took their revenge on union activists. Such leading cadres had shown their ability to empower millions of workers ready and willing to heed the call

---

38   Arnot, Scottish Miners, 164-5.
39   V. I. Lenin, State and Revolution, Selected Works (London: Lawrence & Wishart: 1969 [1917]), 264–351.
40   Fishman, 107.
41   R. Hayden, 'British Communists Jailed for Sedition'. Current History (1926), 23 (4), 575-580.
42   cited in Hutt, 113.
43   cited in Hutt, 114.
44   John Hamilton, A History of the Miners' Struggle, (London: Plebs League, 1926?), 2; 15-16.

of the TUC, back the miners, and fight the employers, strike breakers, and the state. That story is for next year's centenary, but for now the miners fought on to defeat by vindictive coal owners after another six months. The near starvation in the coal fields was a grim testament to the breakdown of unity with or without the TUC and allowed the miners to endure further wage cuts and a return to district agreements. An LRD pamphlet suggested that 'for if the coal shortage is seriously endangering British industry, it means that the miners have only to hold on, to hold hard, to intensify and redouble their efforts in order to bring victory'.[45] This view is almost identical to that taken by Arthur Scargill at Orgreave on 18 June 1984 when he sought but failed to keep the miners fighting for another few days to close the coking plant.

As the coal shortage grew so, 'the whole of the capitalist class, and particularly the Bankers, have been hit pretty hard already by the unexpectedly long resistance of the Miners'.[46] A year later Hannington argued that the employers' demands for an extension to the working day, apart from further impoverishing those in work, would create more unemployment among the miners, 'previous to the 1926 stoppage there were already some 200,000 miners refused employment. The Eight Hour Day not only sounded the death knell to their hopes of re-employment but added half as much again to their number'.[47] The fight back mattered; 'the march unquestionably proved the success of militancy in the face of right-wing official opposition. The enthusiasm displayed on the road and in London showed the response of the masses to real action. It showed that even those at the very head and control of the Labour movement were unable to prevent the workers' support for men who were prepared to act as well as talk'.[48]

Some miners demanded a return to a national wage agreement, nationalisation, and a single unified miners' union. Nat Watkins, for example, secretary of the National Miners' Minority Movement argued for 'ONE MINERS' UNION now. Our task is not so difficult as at first sight it might appear, for already the Minority Movement has prepared a scheme of re-organisation'.[49] Out of this the case for nationalisation developed apace with both Arthur Horner[50] and Harry Pollitt[51] noting the concrete realities of private ownership and the long history of coal owner intransigence, greed, failure to modernise, and attacks on the union and key activists. Earlier, George Hardie (Keir Hardie's younger brother) and MP for Glasgow Springburn wrote, 'to attempt ... to assess the value of the coal miner and his product to the community, and as the producer of our basic power in industry, I plead that he be treated not as some one apart from his fellow-workers in above ground occupations, but as an important unit in the industrial field of labour whose reward and conditions of employment should be equal to the best obtainable by others'.[52]

On that was built the basis for the unity that triumphed on 'Red Friday', and was fought over ever since as summed up by Cook, 'Ever since last July when "Red Friday" wiped out the stain of "Black Friday" and brought joy to the heart of every worker, the capitalist class

45   The coal shortage: why the miners will win, LRD, October 1926. White papers, 24, 5.
46   The Miners' Struggle and the Big Five Banks: how victory can be secured, LRD, November 1926, White Paper 26, 6.
47   Wal Hannington, The March of the Miners: how we smashed the opposition, (London: NUWCM, 1927), 3.
48   Hannington 1927, 33.
49   Nat Watkins, An open letter to all miners on the next big step – one miners' union, (London: NMM, 1927?), 14.
50   Arthur L. Horner, Coal and the Nation: a square deal for miners, (London: CPGB. 1943).
51   Harry Pollitt, Miners' Target, (CPGB, London: CPGB, 1943).
52   George Hardie, Coal and the Miner, (Glasgow: Reformers' bookstall, 1924?), 1.

of Britain, backed by a strong Tory government, has been preparing to retrieve its position; while many of the Labour leaders, almost afraid of the growing power of Labour industrially, knowing the activities of the Government and their preparations, remained inactive'.[53] So, 'solidarity for ever' only becomes a concrete reality when sectional self-interest is overcome by both the theory of class society and the struggle of united working-class movement.

---

53   A.J. Cook, The Nine Days: the story of the general strike as told by the miners' secretary, (London: LRD, 1926), 3.

BROKEN BRITAIN

MICHAEL ROBERTS

Michael Roberts is a Marxist economist and author of several books, including The Great Recession: a Marxist View (2009, Lulu Press); The Long Depression: Marxism and the Global Crisis of Capitalism (Haymarket, 2016); with Guglielmo Carchedi World in Crisis: a global analysis of Marx's law of profitability (Haymarket, 2018) and Capitalism in the 21st Century: Through the Prism of Value (Pluto, 2022). He blogs regularly at: thenextrecession.wordpress.com

Abstract

The British economy is broken. National output per person has stagnated for five years; prices of goods and services are up over 20% on average since the COVID pandemic ended; living standards have fallen, and inequality of incomes and wealth has widened. Public services are exhausted; housing for most is unaffordable; the health service is under huge pressure. Yet private equity firms and privatised utilities are draining the economy dry as they make bumper profits. Will the new Labour government do anything to mend this broken economy?

Keywords

British economy, Labour's economic strategy

Falling behind

The British economy is broken. National output per person has stagnated for five years; prices of goods and services are up over 20% on average since the COVID pandemic ended; living standards have fallen, and inequality of incomes and wealth has widened. Public services are exhausted; housing for most is unaffordable; the health service is under huge pressure. Yet private equity firms and privatised utilities are draining the economy dry as they make bumper profits. Will the new Labour government do anything to mend this broken economy?

The UK economy is now the ninth-largest world economy (in terms of output at prices adjusted for purchasing power) and sixth when output is calculated at exchange rates. The British economy has been in steady decline since the end of WW1. The relative decline in the UK economy is revealed by its long-term fall in productivity growth compared to other imperialist economies, particularly in the 21st century.

From the 1980s, Britain has increasingly become what we could call a 'rentier economy'[1], ending most of its manufacturing base and relying mostly on the City of London financial sector and accompanying business services, providing a conduit for the redistribution of capital from the Middle East oil sheikhs, Russian oligarchs, Indian entrepreneurs and American techs.

Throughout this period, British capitalism declined relative to its peers among the G7 economies and other larger European states. But particularly after the Great Recession, and after the decision to leave the EU and the COVID pandemic, the British economy went into a downward spiral that so far it has not been able to stop. Real GDP growth is still more than 20% below its pre-2008 trend.

---

1   www.thenextrecession.wordpress.com/2013/01/28/the-rentier-economy/

The UK economy was the hardest hit of the top G7 economies in the year of the COVID. Real GDP fell by 9.9%, which the then Conservative finance minister Rishi Sunak admitted was the worst contraction in national income in 300 years! The economic think-tank, the Resolution Foundation, reckons that the UK economy may have 'experienced the weakest growth for 65 years outside of one (a recession).'[2]

What is also not noted is that Britain's population growth is at its fastest rate in a century (three-quarters driven by immigration of 6m people since 2010)[3]. If population growth is excluded, the UK has barely seen any economic growth, with GDP per person only just above the level of 2007 and real consumer purchasing power still lower than in 2007.

Productivity disaster

Indeed, productivity growth (that's output per worker per hour) has been terrible. Productivity has slowed to under 1% a year. Before the 2008-09 economic crisis, Britain's output per hour worked grew steadily at an annual pace of 2.2% a year. In the decade since 2007, that rate has dropped to 0.2%. If the previous trend had continued, the UK's national income would be 20% higher than it is today.

The UK's independent Institute for Fiscal Studies (IFS) finds that growth in output per worker has fallen to the lowest pace since 1850: 'The recent decline in potential output per worker in the UK is unprecedented since the late 19th century. And the slump in productivity growth is unprecedented in the last 250 years.'[4]

In effect, UK productivity has flat-lined for a decade. So now productivity levels are as much as one-third below those in the US, Germany and France. As Andy Haldane put it a few years ago, 'the average French worker achieves by Thursday lunchtime what the average British worker achieves only by close of business on a Friday.'[5] Indeed, excluding London, the UK's average productivity level is below that of the poorest state in the US, Mississippi.[6] The productivity gap between the top- and bottom-performing companies is materially larger in the UK than in France, Germany or the US. This productivity gap has also widened by far more since the crisis – around 2-3 times more – in the UK than elsewhere. This long and lengthening tail of 'stationary' companies explains why the UK has a one-third productivity gap with international competitors and a one-fifth productivity gap relative to the past.[7]

Productive investment crawls

Why is productivity growth so poor, especially among the key big British multi-nationals? The answer is clear: reduced business investment growth.[8] Business investment growth has been on a steady trend downwards since the end of the Great Recession.

Total UK investment to GDP has been lower than most comparable capitalist economies and has been declining for the last 30 years. The UK's investment performance is worse than

2   www.resolutionfoundation.org/press-releases/britain-needs-a-new-economic-strategy-to-end-its-stagnation-and-close-its-8300-living-standards-gap-with-its-peers/
3   www.independent.co.uk/news/uk/politics/uk-population-growing-at-its-fastest-rate-for-a-half-a-century-2305202.html
4   www.ifs.org.uk/publications/uk-economic-outlook-navigating-endgame
5   www.bankofengland.co.uk/-/media/boe/files/speech/2018/the-uks-productivity-problem-hub-no-spokes-speech-by-andy-haldane
6   www.ft.com/content/e5c741a7-befa-4d49-a819-f1b0510a9802
7   www.thersa.org/globalassets/reports/2020/can-good-work-solve-the-productivity-puzzle.pdf
8   www.ippr.org/articles/rock-bottom?s=09

every other G7 country. Compared to Japan, the US, Germany, France, Italy and Canada, the UK languished in last place for business investment in 2022, a spot now held for three years in a row and for 24 out of the last 30 years. Businesses aren't choosing to invest in the UK. The UK ranks a lowly 28th for business investment out of 31 OECD countries. Countries like Slovenia, Latvia and Hungary all attract higher levels of private sector investment than the UK as a per cent of GDP.[9]

Then there is Brexit. It is estimated that the post-Brexit trading relationship between the UK and EU, as set out in the 'Trade and Cooperation Agreement' (TCA) that came into effect in January 2021, will reduce long-run productivity growth by 4 per cent relative to remaining in the EU.[10] The great boom in world trade since the 1990s came screeching to a halt after the Great Recession of 2008-9 and since then world trade has basically stagnated. And that has been expressed in the UK, which now has its largest trade deficit in its history. And it is not just trade. Foreign investment has been declining, something British capital has increasingly relied upon since 1980s. The UK is getting less productive investment by foreign companies into the economy. The number of foreign direct investment (FDI) projects landing in the UK has fallen by 6% year-on-year for the past two years, hitting a low of 1,555 in 2023. This represents a significant 16% decline since the pandemic. [11]

An unequal rentier economy

Britain was once the 'workshop of the world'. But that was a long time ago – in the 19th century up to the depression of 1873-97, to be exact. Britain lost its manufacturing dominance by the beginning of the First World War. The UK's share of global manufacturing output had risen from 9.5% in 1830, to 22.9% in the 1870s. But it fell to 13.6% by 1913, 10.7% by 1938, and 4.9% by 1973. And in 2024, Britain dropped out of the world's top ten leading nations for manufacturing for the first time in its history.[12] Indeed, Britain has fallen behind Mexico and Russia.

Britain still has some manufacturing base: in pharmaceuticals; aerospace; autos (all foreign-owned) and in arms. But Britain has become primarily a rentier economy, relying less on the creation of new value through production and productive investment and more and more on making income from re-distributing value production and in speculation in financial assets. Income for Britain's capitalist sector comes increasingly from interest, capital gains, real estate rents and foreign capital income flows. British capitalism is increasingly a conduit for international capital and income flows, without producing any of its own. As Tony Norfield puts it, 'Britain's status as an imperialist power rests on two economic foundations: huge foreign investments and a UK-based banking system that acts as broker for the global capitalist economy.'[13]

Rachel Reeves, Labour's Chancellor of the Exchequer echoed that view when she said that the City of London and its financial activities 'are the crown jewel in the UK economy powering growth in all parts of the country.'[14] And yet UK financial institutions mainly engage in speculation in financial assets or lending on homes, but provide very little in credit

9   www.ippr.org/media-office/revealed-investment-in-uk-is-lowest-in-g7-for-third-year-in-a-row-new-data-shows
10   www.obr.uk/forecasts-in-depth/the-economy-forecast/brexit-analysis/
11   www.ft.com/content/e33f9e7f-7ed2-4ac9-90bc-6c8843e6d078
12   www.thelondoneconomic.com/business-economics/britain-falls-out-of-top-ten-manufacturing-nations-for-first-time-379944/
13   Tony Norfield, The City: London and the Global Power of Finance (Verso, 2016)
14   www.standard.co.uk/news/politics/london-new-york-city-economy-growth-brexit-rachel-reeves-chancellor-b1174735.html

to small businesses. At the same time, there is a relentless advance of US asset managers and private equity into all parts of the UK economy, with the sole aim of making quick profits rather than investing long term.[15]

Nothing more confirms the decline of UK capitalism and its failure to invest and raise productivity than the profitability of British capital. It is a story of long-term decline since the 1950s. The decline was partially reversed for a while under the so-called neoliberal policies of the Thatcher regime (at the expense of labour's share of national income), but the decline resumed with a vengeance in the 21st century.

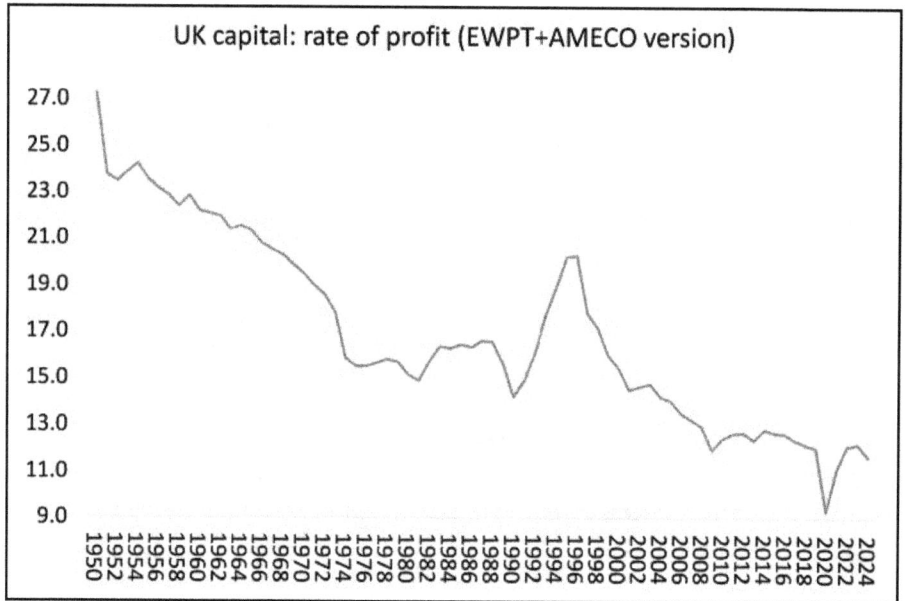

Source: EWPT, AMECO, author's calculations

Declining living standards

And what is the result of this poor productivity, productive investment and falling profitability for the living standards of most British households? The UK is only one of six countries in the 30-nation OECD bloc where earnings after inflation are still below 2007 levels and the UK is the worst of the top seven G7 economies.[16]

The callous austerity policies of the Conservatives after the Great Recession of 2009 in cutting public services and freezing wages have torn up the social safety net. Rates of basic benefits are now lower relative to wages than at any time since the inception of the Beveridge settlement, which established the welfare state in the 1940s. Basic protection against unemployment in the UK is also the lowest in the OECD.[17] 'The result is that a higher percentage of Britons live below the poverty line than in Poland!', according to Tom Clark.[18]

15   www.thenextrecession.wordpress.com/wp-content/uploads/2024/12/the-relentless-advance-of-american-asset-managers-in-europe.pdf
16   www.ft.com/content/4ac7e454-5a0c-4094-90af-fb54404d45a0
17   www.tuc.org.uk/research-analysis/reports/benefit-levels-uk
18   www.bitebackpublishing.com/books/broke

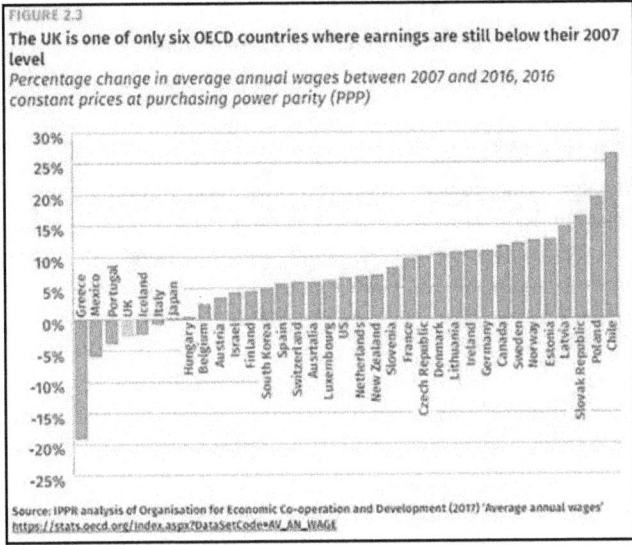

High inequality

And these are averages. Britain is now the second most economically unequal of the larger developed countries (after the US); 50 years ago it was one of the most equal.[19] The UK has the 9th most unequal incomes of 38 OECD countries, which means one of the highest levels of income inequality in Europe, if still less unequal than the US.

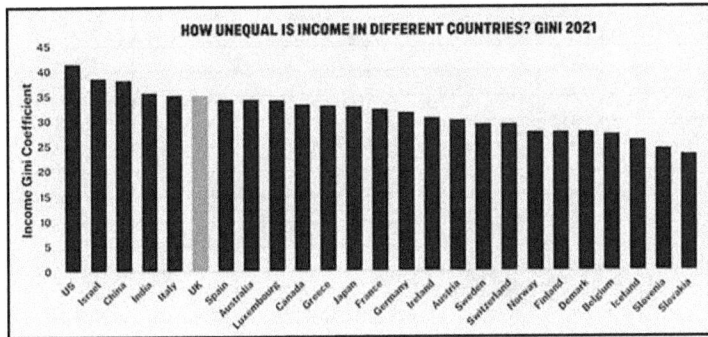

Source: World Inequality Lab

The UK's wealth inequality is much more severe than its income inequality, with the top fifth taking 36% of the country's income and 63% of the country's wealth, while the bottom

fifth have only 8% of the income and only 0.5% of the wealth, according to the Office for National Statistics.[20] The UK also has the widest regional disparities in wages in the whole of Europe. People in north-east of England have an average standard of living less than

---

19   www.equalitytrust.org.uk/scale-economic-inequality-uk/
20   www.equalitytrust.org.uk/scale-economic-inequality-uk/https://www.ons.gov.uk/
           peoplepopulationandcommunity/personalandhouseholdfinances/incomeandwealth/
           bulletins/wealthingreatbritainwave5/2014to2016

half that of the average Londoner. Wealth is also unevenly spread across Great Britain. The South-East is the wealthiest of all regions with median household total wealth of £503,400, over twice the amount of wealth in households in the North of England.[21]

Austerity and poverty

Poverty rates now higher than at any other time in the 21st century. The Social Metrics Commission (SMC) finds that a staggering 16 million people in the UK are living in families in poverty. 5.2 million are children, 9.2 million are working-age adults and 1.5 million are pension-age adults. So nearly one in four (24%) people in the UK now judged to be in poverty.[22]

Welfare cuts have caused 190,000 excess deaths from 2010 to 2019.[23] According to the Office for National Statistics, life expectancy at birth for 2020/22 is "back to the same level as 2010 to 2012 for females" and "slightly below" that benchmark for males—a whole decade, in other words, of zero or negative progress.[24] 'The most deprived areas of England,' government demographers report, registered 'a significant decrease' in life expectancy in the second half of the 2010s.[25] Looking ahead to 2040 (and comparing against a 2019 baseline), analysts at Liverpool University and the Health Foundation foresee an increase of some 700,000 in the number of working-age Britons living with a major long-term illness, overwhelmingly accounted for by a further rocketing of already-heavy rates of chronic pain, diabetes and anxiety/depression in poorer communities.[26]

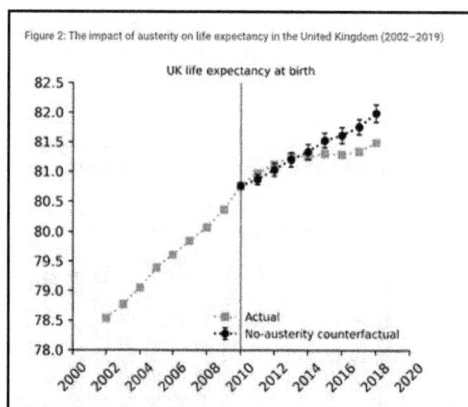

Figure 2: The impact of austerity on life expectancy in the United Kingdom (2002–2019)

Source: ONS

Child poverty rates have rocketed. In 2022/23, the number of children living in poverty increased by 100,000 from 4.2 million in 2021/22 to 4.3 million children.[27] That's 30% of children in the UK. The rate of child poverty in the North East of England increased by 9 percentage points in the seven years between 2015 and 2022. Substantial increases can also be seen in the Midlands and the North West.

---

21   www.ons.gov.uk/peoplepopulationandcommunity/personalandhouseholdfinances/
      incomeandwealth/bulletins/totalwealthingreatbritain/april2018tomarch2020
22   www.wpieconomics.com/poverty-rates-now-higher-than.../
23   www.eprints.lse.ac.uk/123915/1/WP_139.pdf
24   www.x.com/jdportes/status/1803538092680233328
25   www.ons.gov.uk/peoplepopulationandcommunity/healthandsocialcare/healthinequalities/
      bulletins/healthstatelifeexpectanciesbyindexofmultipledeprivationimd/2018to2020
26   www.health.org.uk/publications/health-inequalities-in-2040
27   www.actionforchildren.org.uk/blog/uk-poverty-stats-children-in-poverty/

The rise of 'food banks' has been a feature of the last ten years. The official tally of people whose households had turned to foodbanks in the last 12 months stands at 3m.[28] And families with 'very low food security' now stand at 3.7 million, a total that has shot up by a full two-thirds in 2024 alone.

Destruction of the NHS

One of the greatest achievements of the labour movement was the establishment of a National Health Service (NHS), free at the point of use. After 70 years, this great public service is now in tatters; starved of funds and staff and services increasingly hived off to the profits of the private sector. NHS funding faces the biggest real terms cut since the 1970s, warns the Institute for Fiscal Studies.[29]

The NHS has privatised 60% of NHS cataract operations to private providers. Private clinics received £700m for cataracts from 2018-19 to 2022-23 and 30-40% of money vanishes in profits.[30] And a new analysis by We Own It reveals that £6.7 billion, or £10 million each week, has left the NHS's budget in the form of profits on all private contracts given by the NHS in the last decade or so. We Own It analysis shows that out of the £6.7 billion total profits that have left the NHS, £5.2 billion, or 78%, were on contracts for services.[31] Britons now have access to fewer hospital beds and dentists relative to the population than in most other big economies, according to OECD data. And the waiting list for operations is at a record level. The NHS in England needs an extra £38bn a year to cut backlogs now.[32] But the Labour government does not propose to inject public funds into the NHS. Instead, it looks to bring the private health sector to fill the resources gap. Another example of the 'private-public partnership'.

Housing crisis

Then there is housing. In the 30 years from 1989, 3 million fewer houses were built than in the previous 30 years, despite a strong increase in demand.33 This mismatch between supply and demand has contributed to a serious affordability crisis. In 1997, the ratio of median house price to median income across England and Wales was 3.6 and in London it was 4.0. By 2023 the median house in London cost 12 times the median earnings and even in the least unaffordable region, north-east England, the ratio was 5.0.34 This rise means only younger people whose parents – even grandparents – were homeowners can now be

28   www.gov.uk/government/statistics/households-below-average-income-for-financial-years-ending-1995-to-2023

29   www.guernseypress.com/news/uk-news/2024/03/04/jeremy-hunt-warned-of-2bn-real-term-cuts-to-nhs-funding/

30   www.inkl.com/news/boom-in-cataract-surgery-in-england-as-private-clinics-eye-huge-profits#:~:text=Its%20analysis%20of%20data%20from%2037%20of%2042,hospitals%20and%20private%20clinics%20from%20%C2%A3218m%20to%20%C2%A3437m.

31   weownit.org.uk/blog/analysis-nhs-has-lost-10-million-week-private-profits-2012#:~:text=A%20new%20analysis%20by%20We%20Own%20It%20reveals,the%20NHS%20from%20January%202012%20to%20May%202024.

32   www.theguardian.com/politics/article/2024/jun/20/nhs-will-need-extra-38bn-a-year-by-2030-thinktank-warns#:~:text=The%20NHS%20in%20England%20will,political%20parties%20have%20been%20warned

33   https://cep.lse.ac.uk/pubs/download/ea061.pdf

34   www.ons.gov.uk/peoplepopulationandcommunity/housing/bulletins/housingaffordabilityinenglandandwales/2023

reasonably optimistic of being able to buy. Rents have been rising at the fastest pace in three decades and three times the rate in France and Germany.35 'Rough sleeping' in England is up by 60 per cent over the last two years, and the number of families stuck in (terrible) temporary accommodation has doubled since 2010. [36]

A decisive increase in the social housing stock - for example returning the affordable housing stock to 2010 levels relative to population - would require nearly 400,000 more social homes – the current stock is just 75,000.[37]

Failing the youth

As for education, that is also in deep trouble. Britain has gone from providing free tertiary education in the 1960s to huge fees funded by crippling loans. The pressure is on for cuts in school funding and UK universities have slipped in international rankings, while many face bankruptcy and closure as overseas students (and their fees) dwindle.

Then there are the prisons. We lock up lots of people in the UK and now jails are running out of space 'within days', say prison governors in England and Wales. 'The entire criminal justice system stands on the precipice of failure.'[38] Instead of putting young people in jail, maybe there should some places for them to go. But two-thirds of council-funded youth centres in England have been closed since 2010.[39] That's because local councils have suffered cuts of 20% in real terms since 2010, leaving a gap of over £6 billion to be found over the next two years.[40]

Water safety

Finally, there are the utilities. In Europe, only the UK has privatised water and the private equity owners of these water companies have drained the public for billions, while destroying the quality of water and the environment. Last March it was revealed that raw sewage was discharged into waterways for 3.6m hours in 2023 by England's privatised water firms, more than double the figure in 2022.[41]

Securonomics

In her recent Mais Lecture (Mais is a business school in the heart of City of London), speaking to the representatives of big business and finance, Rachel Reeves set out her view of what to do to mend broken Britain.[42] There will be more public investment but only 'where it can unlock additional private sector investment, create jobs, and provide a return for taxpayers.' Labour's industrial strategy will be 'mission-driven and focused on the future.

35   www.ft.com/content/6002df2b-581d-4f09-a10b-41ebeb2bcf9d
36   www.gov.uk/government/statistics/rough-sleeping-snapshot-in-england-
        autumn-2023/rough-sleeping-snapshot-in-england-autumn-2023
37   Resolution Foundation
38   www.bbc.co.uk/news/articles/cx777w9vgv9o#:~:text=The%20Prison%20
        Governors%E2%80%99%20Association%20%28PGA%29%20says%20police%20
        officers,precipice%20of%20failure%2C%E2%80%9D%20it%20says%20in%20a%20letter.
39   www.unison.org.uk/news/2024/06/closure-of-more-than-a-thousand-youth-centres-
        could-have-lasting-impact-on-society/
40   www.bbc.co.uk/news/uk-england-46443700
41   www.theguardian.com/environment/2024/mar/27/water-companies-in-england-
        face-outrage-over-record-sewage-discharges
42   www.labour.org.uk/updates/press-releases/rachel-reeves-mais-lecture/

We will work in partnership with industry to seize opportunities and remove barriers to growth.' Such is the purpose of 'securonomics', as Reeves calls her economic strategy.

But can securonomics put the Humpty Dumpty of a broken Britain back together again? The key should be a sharp rise in productive investment to restore economic growth that will deliver more income for all and more revenues for government to invest to meet the social needs in health and social care, education, transport, communications and housing – all of which are flailing and failing in broken Britain. But where is the extra investment to come from? The UK's investment to GDP ratio is pathetically low (around 17% of GDP compared to the G7 average of 23%) and investment by the big corporations is even lower at 10% of GDP. As for public investment, that ratio is as low as 2% of UK GDP.

A recent LSE study called for an increase in public investment of 1% pt of GDP, or a rise of £26 billion a year at current prices.[43] But what are Rachel Reeves and Labour proposing? They plan just £7.3 billion 'over the course of the next Parliament', through a National Wealth Fund 'making transformative investments across every part of the country'. The Corbyn-led Labour party proposed £25 billion. The Reeves-Starmer leadership proposes just a quarter of that and a fraction of what even the LSE economists reckon is needed. Indeed, what is needed for a proper transformation of industry and public services is more like £60 billion a year over next five years, or a rise of at least 2-3% points of GDP each year. Instead, Labour's plan actually implies a fall in public investment as a share of GDP over this parliament!

Reeves' hope is that this tiny increase in public investment will attract 'three pounds of private investment for every one pound of public investment, creating jobs across the country.' But even if it did (and that is very doubtful) then the total increase would still be far short of what is needed to turn the UK economy around.

The 'black hole'

Back in October 2023 at the last Labour conference before the general election of July 2024, Reeves said: 'If we want to spur investment, restore economic security and revive growth, then we must get Britain building again.' She set out a 'once-in-a-generation set of reforms to speed up the building of 'critical infrastructure' for energy, transport and housing, including a promise to fast-track planning applications for battery factories, life sciences and 5G technology. Labour's proposals were described as a 'clear, grown-up policy that will help deliver infrastructure projects we need to stay competitive, return to growth and stop the curse of chopping and changing'. However, immediately after the election, Reeves announced the the government would delay 'unfunded' road and hospital schemes as the chancellor seeks to fill what is claimed was an estimated £22 billion fiscal 'black hole' that was bequeathed by the last Conservative government.

But this a black hole of her own digging from the political choices that the government has made. The government could fill the hole and still sustain existing public spending by borrowing more in the form of government bonds. But that would increase the deficit on the government budget and raise the level of public debt – already at a record high. The government wants to appear as financially prudent to financial investors ie the City of London and foreign investors. Government long-term borrowing costs have surged to the highest level in more than a quarter of a century. So Reeves is refusing to borrow to invest.[44]

43   www.lse.ac.uk/granthaminstitute/wp-content/uploads/2024/01/Boosting-growth-and-productivity-in-the-UK-through-investments-in-the-sustainable-economy.pdf

44   www.finance.yahoo.com/news/uk-debt-costs-hit-highest-110016621.html?fr=sycsrp_catchall

Unfortunately for the Chancellor, since October, the British economy has continued to struggle with virtually no growth, while inflation remains above the Bank of England target. Government debt has been rising sharply and as a result, government bond yields have jumped sharply and the pound has slumped, worsening government finances. Now the government is considering yet more tax rises and spending cuts in a March budget. But that's only likely to worsen the potential for growth.

Taxation: cuts for the rich

Labour could raise taxes on high incomes and corporate profits to reduce the so-called 'black hole'. But the government has already ruled out any rise in income tax rates or taxes on company profits. Indeed, they have pledged not to raise the corporation tax on big business – at 25%, already the lowest in the G7 – in order not to 'deter' investment.

The Labour government has ruled out an annual wealth tax on the very rich, which could raise more than enough to cover any 'black hole'. Researchers from Warwick University and the London School of Economics, funded by the Economic and Social Research Council, reckon that a one-off wealth tax of 1% a year for five years on those having more than £1m in property and financial assets (net of debt), would raise £260 billion.[45] Alternatively, setting the threshold at £2 million per person or £4 million per household would raise £80 billion over five years and affect just 626,000 people (or less than 1% of the adult population), the report said. Applying a 1-2% wealth tax on assets over £10 million could raise up to £22 billion per year, thus filling the 'black hole'.

This is not the only taxation measure that Labour could take to fund more public investment for social objectives. Labour could equalise capital gains tax to income tax rates, raising up to £15.2 billion a year. It could apply national insurance to investment income, raising up to £8.6 billion a year. The Taxing Wealth Report 2024 suggests that wealth is under-taxed by £170 billion a year when total tax revenues in the UK in the tax year 2022/23, ending in March 2023, amounted to £899 billion.[46] There are also possibilities in simply collecting the taxes not paid. Businesess, small and large, avoid or evade tax to the tune of £25-100 billion a year because of tax loophoes exploited by lawyers and the lack of Inland Revenue staff to investigate and prosecute. But the government has many more staff chasing social benefit fraud estimated at just £4 billion a year.

Tax rises for the rest

Instead of deciding to tax the very rich just a bit more, the Labour government has instead attacked the incomes of the poorest in their effort to fill their 'black hole'. The child support benefit, capped by the Tories at two children, is to be maintained. And now the winter fuel allowance for pensioners is to be means-tested. That means more than 10 million pensioners will no longer receive the money during the winter months to help with hugely rising heating bills. The reduction in winter fuel payments will save just £1.5bn a year and yet the government says if it does not make this cut, public finances will be in disarray. But research carried out by Labour in 2017 – when the Tories proposed means-testing winter fuel payments – suggested the move would kill 4,000 pensioners.[47] UK pensioners have the lowest state pension in the developed world.[48] And an estimated 880,000 eligible pensioners fail to claim pension credit to which they are entitled. This is the real 'black hole'.

45   www.lse.ac.uk/News/Latest-news-from-LSE/2020/L-December/Wealth-Commission-report
46   www.taxresearch.org.uk/Blog/2024/03/20/the-introduction-to-the-taxing-wealth-report-2024/
47   www.independent.co.uk/news/uk/politics/starmer-tuc-warning-austerity-far-right-winter-fuel-payments-b2609121.html
48   www.ftadviser.com/pensions/2018/02/13/uk-state-pension-worst-in-the-developed-world/

Meanwhile, following the Tories, the government intends to raise defence and armaments spending to meet the NATO target of 2.5% of GDP a year.[49] The UK's defence spending at £65bn a year (plus £3bn a year pledged to Ukraine), as a percentage of GDP is already relatively high compared to other NATO countries— it's ranked nine out of 32 member states according to estimates for 2024.[50]

Investing for the future?

The UK needs 'significantly higher' growth to avoid tough budget measures, the IMF has warned. Keeping to Labour's self-imposed 'fiscal rules' would mean austerity throughout this parliament up to 2029 unless the UK triples its expected average real growth rate.[51] The UK needs £1 trillion of fresh investment over the next decade if the government is to hit its economic growth targets, a City taskforce has said.[52] In order to achieve at least 3% annual growth, the UK would have to attract around £100 billion of investment per year, divided between key sectors. That includes £20-£30 billion towards the UK's housing stock, £50 billion for the energy sector and £8 billion for water projects. It also calls for £20-£30 billion worth of venture capital for growing companies that are beyond the startup stage and need more sustainable funding to expand.

Public investment could really make a difference. The Office for Budget Responsibility (OBR) reckoned: 'a sustained 1 per cent of GDP increase in public investment could plausibly increase the level of potential output by just under ½ a percent after five years and around 2½ per cent in the long run (50 years).'[53] But where will Labour's Securonomics policy concentrate its own timid investment strategy? The answer is in financial services, the automotive industry (wholly owned by foreign companies), life sciences and 'creative sectors' (film, design, theatre, fashion etc). These are supposedly the sectors where the UK has an edge.

But what about the broken public services in Britain? Reeves has only about £10 billion 'to spare' on improving public services. The Nuffield Trust reckons that the current spending plans of the new Labour government for the NHS will mean a further period of austerity.[54]

Total health spending annual growth of 0.8% would result in the next four years being the tightest in NHS history under the Labour pledges – tighter even than the former Tory coalition government's 'austerity' period, which saw funding grow by just 1.4% real terms a year between 2010/11 and 2014/15.

49   www.reuters.com/world/uk/uks-starmer-committed-increasing-defence-spending-25-gdp-2024-07-09/

50   www.fullfact.org/news/uk-gdp-defence-spending/

51   www.reuters.com/world/uk/imf-raises-uks-2024-gdp-growth-forecast-reeves-readies-budget-2024-10-22/#:~:text=The%20International%20Monetary%20Fund%20on%20Tuesday%20raised%20its,minister%20Rachel%20Reeves%20prepares%20her%20first%20annual%20budget.

52   The Capital Markets of Tomorrow report - www.capitalmarketsindustrytaskforce.com/wp-content/uploads/2024/09/Capital-Markets-Of-Tomorrow-report.pdf

53   www.obr.uk/public-investment-and-potential-output/?s=09

54   www.nuffieldtrust.org.uk/resource/how-much-spending-on-the-nhs-have-the-major-parties-committed-to-in-their-election-manifestos

No social housing

What about housing? UK's current housing problems can be traced to Thatcher's government with the selling off social housing, turning building societies into banks, and making the barriers to mortgages lower. All these contributed to a housing market that is no longer functional. The UK has the highest homelessness in the OECD - which has been on an upward trajectory since 2010. Seven years after the horrendous Grenfell tower block fire caused by unsafe cladding sold by developers, thousands of flats across the country have not been made safe.[1]

There is a chronic shortage of social rent homes in England. In the last ten years,there has been a net loss of 260,000 'social rent' homes. These homes are genuinely affordable because they have rents linked to local income, secure tenancies, and any rent increases are more predictable than in the private rented sector. England alone needs at least 90,000 social rent homes built each year for ten years. This would be enough to house every homeless household and clear most social housing waiting lists.

The new Labour government says it will aim to build 300,000 new homes a year through the next five years. This sounds good, even though it is far fewer than needed and way fewer than Labour governments built in the 1950s and 1960s. But how is this to be done? It is certainly not going to be through a National Building Corporation that will employ building workers and architects directly to build good houses and flats to be owned by local council at reasonable rents for tenants to get the huge waiting lists down.

Instead, the whole housing plan will depend on private developers building homes for sale with minimal monitoring for 'affordable homes'. As Rachel Reeves put it, 'We need the private sector to build homes. We're not going to be in the business of building these homes directly.'[2] So no homes at reasonable rents owned by local councils, but homes for sale with less than half being 'affordable'.

Back in the 1950s and 1960s most new homes were built by the public sector (local authorities) for rent, with four times the current level. Now the Labour leaders are more concerned with removing planning regulations in local areas so that private developers can build where and how they want. And who are these developers? They are the likes of Blackstone, an American investment company, which in the past year bought new rental homes in Britain worth about £1.4 billion from the housebuilding company Vistry.[3] In addition, BlackRock, the biggest investment manager in the world, has been brought in by Reeves to 'advise' on housing expansion.[4]

Public ownership taboo

Securonomics means that there is to be no public takeover of the productive sectors of the economy; or the financial sector; or the big investment funds. Instead, Reeves wants to reduce regulations on the financial sector. Here history rhymes with the last Labour government of Brown and Balls and their 'light-touch' regulation of the City of London that ended up with the banking and mortgage collapse of 2007-8 and the ensuing Great Recession of 2008-9.

1   www.news.sky.com/story/dagenham-fire-couples-wedding-turned-to-dust-after-blaze-erupted-in-london-tower-block-13204197

2   www.scotsman.com/news/politics/scottish-government-told-to-follow-chancellor-rachel-reevess-example-on-housebuilding-4694587

3   www.theguardian.com/commentisfree/article/2024/jul/02/labour-plans-britain-private-finance-blackrock

4   www.theguardian.com/commentisfree/article/2024/jul/02/labour-plans-britain-private-finance-blackrock

Then there are the energy and water utilities. The scandal of these privatized utilities is there for all to see, where shareholders have got billions in dividends, while debt and prices rise. And yet, Labour has no plan to bring these utilities back into public ownership. Instead, it wants 'better regulation'. Apparently, Labour wants less regulation in housing and banking but more regulation in utilities and the postal service![5] But, as Natacha Postel-Vinay of the LSE puts it: 'It's a game of whack-a-mole. You regulate stuff, but the financial system finds ways around the regulation very quickly.'[6]

Labour has pledged to bring railways back into public ownership but only gradually as the private franchises (some ten years long) expire. Labour under Corbyn pledged free broadband for all as a public right. This was called 'communism' by the right-wing press. Labour under PM Starmer only proposes 'a renewed push to fulfil the ambition of full gigabit and national 5G coverage by 2030.'[7]

Short term pain for long term good?

Starmer has called on the British public to accept 'short-term pain for long-term good'. But there have been decades of supposedly short-term pain. After Covid, after double-digit inflation, after austerity, millions of families and whole swaths of our public services are exhausted.

After reviewing Labour's October budget plan, the Joseph Rowntree Foundation (JRF) forecast that average disposable incomes would fall through the current parliamentary term.[8] By October 2029, the average family is set to be £770 per year worse off in real terms compared with today. Real earnings growth would be soaked up by rising housing costs (both mortgages and rents) and continued 'fiscal drag' (tax thresholds failing to rise with inflation). The poorest third of households would see their real disposable incomes fall by 3.3% by October 2029, while the highest income third would see a fall of 1.7%. Absent a plan from government, JRF expects 100,000 more children to be in poverty by October 2029, as well as 300,000 more working age adults.

Right now, the UK economy is stagnating at best. Real GDP per person has been static since 2019! If this continues, then UK economic activity will be 36% lower by 2029 than it would be had it continued to grow in line with its 1997–2008 trend. This would compare with 31% in the Euro Area and 24% in the US.

5   www.independent.co.uk/independentpremium/uk-news/labour-public-ownership-nationalise-reeves-starmer-b2131610.html
6   www.thenextrecession.wordpress.com/2018/10/06/regulation-does-not-work/
7   www.thinkbroadband.com/news/10087-labour-manifesto-pledges-national-5g-coverage
8   www.jrf.org.uk/cost-of-living/the-real-inheritance-uk-living-standards-crisis-at-october-budget

UK real GDP person (2019=100)

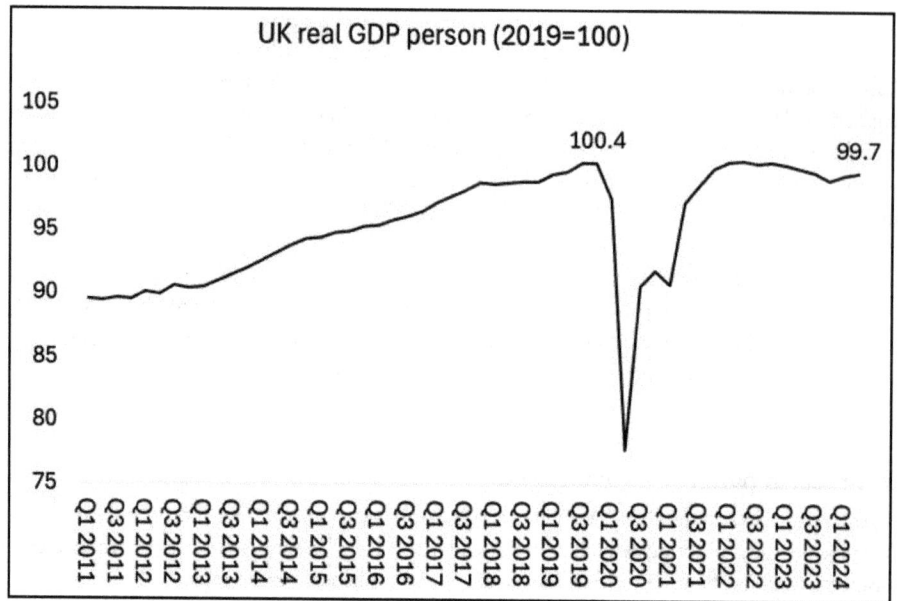

Source: World Inequality Lab

Securonomics is supposedly a strategy for British capital to 'take control' of its economy with the help of a pro-business government, and so to fend for itself in an increasingly stagnant and protectionist world economy. But the UK economy is frail and it has not and will not escape the twists and turns of the global capitalist economy. There is every likelihood that the world economy will enter a new slump before the end of this decade. Slumps emerge every 8-10 years and the last two were the worst in capitalist history. Even without a slump, global growth is slowing and trade is stagnant with little sign of improvement ahead. Labour's plans do not suggest 'security' against the vicissitudes of capitalist accumulation.

Electoral collapse ahead?

The rise of the right is a real danger if Labour fails to mend broken Britain. After each previous slump in the UK, the incumbent government has been ousted (Labour in 2010 after the slump of 2008-9 and the Conservatives eventually in 2024 after the pandemic slump of 2020). In the July 2024 election, the Labour party achieved a 'landslide' victory, while the incumbent Conservatives were decimated. But this 'landslide' was only in seats. Labour's share of the vote was just under 35%, up only 2 percentage points from the last election in 2019, and 5% percentage points lower than Jeremy Corbyn's Labour achieved in 2017. Since the election, Labour's popularity in the opinion polls has plummeted. Labour is now polling between 25-30%, the Conservatives around 25% and the Reform party not far behind at 22-25%.[9] This looks like a one-term Labour government.

---

9   en.wikipedia.org/wiki/Opinion_polling_for_the_next_United_Kingdom_general_election

IN DEFENCE OF THE LABOUR THEORY OF VALUE

PAUL COCKSHOTT

Paul Cockshott is Scottish and has been involved on the left since leaving school. He has qualifications in computing and economics. He worked in the computer industry and as an academic in several Scottish universities and is now retired. He is co-author of several books, most notably Towards a New Socialism and most recently Defending Materialism (2024).

Abstract

The article presents the empirical evidence for the correctness of the classical labour theory of value along with a critique of the scientific credentials of the competing marginalist theory. It shows that past studies using information from official statistics in multiple countries have supported the labour theory of value, which it supports with newly published information on the relationship between labour content and monetary values for Mexican economic sectors.

Keywords:
Value, price, empirical evidence

Introduction

The modern incarnation of the labour theory of value dates from the writings of Adam Smith, who began his career as a moral philosopher, particularly concerned with the analysis of human sympathy,1 but he later turned his attention to political economy and of course, his magnum opus was An Enquiry into the Nature and Causes of the Wealth of Nations (1776). The opening sentence of this work announces a perspective in which labour plays a central role:

> *The annual labour of every nation is the fund which originally supplies it with all the necessaries and conveniences of life which it annually consumes, and which consist always either in the immediate produce of that labour, or in what is purchased with that produce from other nations.*[2]

Smith discusses the interaction between people and nature and the interaction between nations through trade. He discusses concrete labour, which involves producing specific goods, as Marx later called it. However, when he states that a nation's labour indirectly provides it with the produce of other nations, he is referring to labour in the abstract. Smith did not discover that people had to work, but he developed the notion of labour as a source of value, which was unfamiliar to his eighteenth century writers. As Smith remarks,

> *The greater part of people ... understand better what is meant by a quantity of a particular commodity than by a quantity of labour. The one is a plain palpable*

---

1   Adam Smith, The theory of moral sentiments (Harmondsworth: Penguin, 2010).
2   Adam Smith, The Wealth of Nations, Edited by Andrew Skinner (Harmondsworth: Penguin, 1974), 104.

object; the other an abstract notion, which, though it can be made sufficiently intelligible, is not altogether so natural and obvious.[3]

In his book, Adam Smith's abstract notion of labour is not entirely new, as David Hume and John Locke had previously approached the concept[4]. However, Smith further developed this idea, venturing into new territory, and elaborating on what he meant by value. In Smith's Wealth of Nations, he discusses commodity exchange as a result of labour division, leading to money and value. The term 'value' applies to goods and services. We now say that something is 'good value' when referring to a commodity's favourable ratio of useful qualities to price. This aligns with the opposition between 'value in use' and 'value in exchange', which he defines as an opposition inherent in commodities.[5]

> *The word value, it is to be observed, has two different meanings, and sometimes expresses the utility of some particular object, and sometimes the power of purchasing other goods which the possession of that object conveys. The one may be called 'value in use'; the other, 'value in exchange'. The things which have the greatest value in use have frequently little or no value in exchange; and, on the contrary, those which have the greatest value in exchange have frequently little or no value in use. Nothing is more useful than water: but it will purchase scarce anything; scarce anything can be had in exchange for it. A diamond, on the contrary, has scarce any value in use; but a very great quantity of other goods may frequently be had in exchange for it.*[6]

In classical economics, 'value in use' was considered an objective category, with Smith confident in stating that water is highly useful and diamonds have little value in use. However, modern economics has replaced this term with 'utility', which is based on the subjective psychological satisfaction an individual derives from the consumption of the good. This analysis is best applied to highly refined luxury products of advanced cultures, where the satisfaction obtained by the individual is the only factor to consider. Classical 'value in use' is not subjective but is relative to the state of technology, as evidenced by Smith's dismissal of diamonds as having little value in use, which suggests diamond tipped drills were not used for oil exploration in his time. The notion of the central importance of labour to political economy continued up to the middle of the nineteenth century with Ricardo saying,

> *By far the greatest part of those goods which are the objects of desire, are procured by labour; and they may be multiplied, not in one country alone, but in many, almost without any assignable limit, if we are disposed to bestow the labour necessary to obtain them.* [7].

---

3   Smith, 134–5.
4   David Hume had written that 'every thing in the world is purchased by labour' in his Political Discourses of 1752 and John Locke had hinted at a labour theory of value in the chapter on property in his Of Civil Government.
5   The distinction between use value and exchange value is an ancient one in philosophy. Scott Meikle argues convincingly that it derives at least from Aristotle, Scott Meikle, 'The pre-eminence of use: Reevaluating the relation between use and exchange in Aristotle's economic thought,' Journal of the History of Philosophy 47, no. 4 (2009), 523–548.
6   Smith, The Wealth of Nations, 131–2.
7   David Ricardo, Principles of Political Economy and Taxation, Volume 1 of The Works and Correspondence of David Ricardo, edited by Piero Sraffa (Cambridge: Cambridge University Press, 1951), 12.

and the mathematician and economist Babbage writing, 'The cost of any article may be reduced in its ultimate analysis to the quantity of labour by which it was produced,[8] or Marx:

> *Economy of time, to this all economy ultimately reduces itself. ... [E]conomy of time, along with the planned distribution of labour time among the various branches of production, remains the first economic law on the basis of communal production.[9]*

Classical economists emphasized work as the foundation of their analysis, focusing on actual work processes and the reasons behind enhanced production, a focus that later economists often overlook.[10] This classical approach focuses on the actual work processes. One only has to read Marx's comparison of Manufacture and Modern Industry to see how central this concrete analysis of labour processes was.

From the last quarter of the nineteenth century this early focus on labour and value was lost. The labour theory of value was replaced in economics courses with what is called the neo-classical price theory. The notion of value itself got displaced by a focus on instantaneous prices and the fluctuations of supply and demand.

But an underlying reality cannot be completely ignored. Economists might, in their introductions, displace talk of value by just focusing on prices, but as soon as they come to inflation, they have to discuss value again. For what is inflation but a change in the value of money, which implies that value must exist independently of its measurement in money? As soon as you try to compare prices over the long term you have to go back to Smith. If you are told that an average house in 1950 cost £2000, that tells you nothing unless you know how long you would have to work to pay for it. It turns out that a house was worth about ten years wages then and now. An entry-level Ford Focus is now £28,500 which is about one year of average wages. In 1950 the entry level Ford Prefect was £371 which was a year and three months wages. So, in terms of worker's time cars have become cheaper and houses have stayed the same. Of course a modern car is better than a 1950s one, and though a modern house has better heating etc, it will be smaller than a new house seventy years ago *(see Fig. 1)*.

In all these cases we can go back to what Smith called the amount of 'labour commanded' by the goods.

> *EVERY man is rich or poor according to the degree in which he can afford to enjoy the necessaries, conveniences, and amusements of human life. .... The value of any commodity, therefore, to the person who possesses it, and who means not to use or consume it himself, but to exchange it for other commodities, is equal to the quantity of labour which it enables him to purchase or command.[11]*

8   Charles Babbage, The Economy of Machinery and Manufactures (London: C. Knight, 1832), ch. 18, par. 210.
9   Karl Marx, Grundrisse (Harmondsworth: Penguin/New Left Review, 1973), 173.
10   A notable exception is Braverman whose late twentieth-century analysis of labour processes (Harry Braverman, Labor and monopoly capital: The degradation of work in the twentieth century (NYU Press, 1998)) carries on the classical tradition.
11   Smith, The Wealth of Nations, Chapter 5

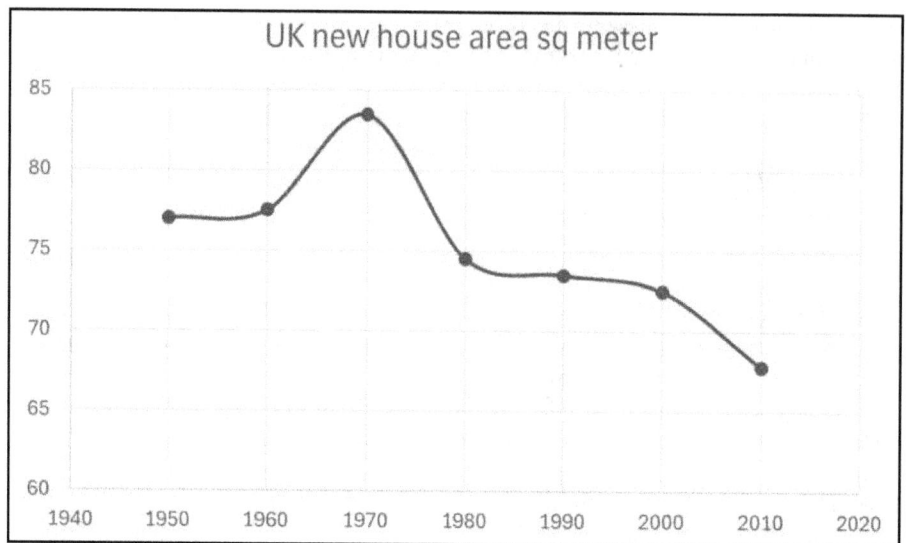

Figure 1: New house sizes have shrunk. Data redrawn from:
Shrinking homes: the average British house 20% smaller than in 1970s
(Which, 14 Apr 2018).

When comparing prices over time some sort of labour value theory is needed if we are to say anything meaningful.

Simultaneous values

It is uncontroversial to use some variant of Smith's labour commanded when comparing prices many years apart.[12] The controversy comes when one applies labour values to contemporary prices. Back in the nineteenth century, Ricardo and Marx pointed out that Smith's definition of labour value was potentially ambiguous.

Smith's definition is pretty clear as it stands but was formulated in eighteenth- century terms. If Smith was thinking of a tailor exchange of shirts, via cash, for the baker's loaves there is no problem. The value of his shirt amounts to the quantity of time it commands from the butchers, bakers and candlestick makers.

In Smith's day, a substantial part of the Scottish economy was still made up of farmers, fishermen, tailors, spinners and weavers who directly sold the product of their own labour. Ricardo and Marx were writing after the spread of the factory system, when cloth, bread etc came to be made by waged workers employed by masters. The meaning of labour commanded became more ambiguous. Bringing it up to date, how exactly do you measure the labour commanded by a Ford Focus selling for £28,500?

Do you just divide it by the average annual wage of £29,600 to get just under a person year *(Option 1)*?

---

12   One must, for some manufactured goods, make quality adjustments, but for staples like electricity, bread, milk this is not an issue.

Or do you add up the hours actually spent, directly and indirectly, to make a random bundle of commodities that sells for £28,500 *(Option 2)*?

Option 2 yields a smaller number than option 1, as capitalism systematically pays workers less than the value of their work's product, resulting in workers working longer to purchase their own product than it took them to create it. According to Marx this discrepancy, which he termed surplus value, was the source of capitalist profit.

Ricardo and Marx held that option 2 was the correct way to calculate values.[13] Marx explained the value of a commodity as follows:

> *If we consider commodities as values, we consider them exclusively under the single aspect of realized, fixed, or, if you like, crystallized social labour. In this respect they can differ only by representing greater or smaller quantities of labour, as, for example, a greater amount of labour may be worked up in a silken handkerchief than in a brick. But how does one measure quantities of labour? By the time the labour lasts, in measuring the labour by the hour, the day, etc. Of course, to apply this measure, all sorts of labour are reduced to average or simple labour as their unit. We arrive, therefore, at this conclusion. A commodity has a value, because it is a crystallization of social labour. The greatness of its value, or its relative value, depends upon the greater or less amount of that social substance contained in it; that is to say, on the relative mass of labour necessary for its production. The relative values of commodities are, therefore, determined by the respective quantities or amounts of labour, worked up, realised, fixed in them. The correlative quantities of commodities which can be produced in the same time of labour are equal. Or the value of one commodity is to the value of another commodity as the quantity of labour fixed in the one is to the quantity of labour fixed in the other.*[14]

Note that for both Smith and Marx value was tied to something outside of commodities, outside of exchange, the real process of work by which our race survives. It is this tie to work, to our species' living being, that allows the theory of value to work across time periods. But Marx's definition of value is much more controversial than simply using Smith's method to compare 1950s prices to those today.

If Marx's definition were accepted capitalist profit would be seen as pure exploitation.

Marshall's alternative theory
Such a conclusion was bound to be unpopular in colleges that were funded by, or dependent on students from, the upper classes. There was a ready market for alternative economic theories that disguised labour time's role in value and profit. Authors like Marshall here, Menger in Austria and Walras in France spotted the opportunity and produced textbooks to fill it. A century and a half of such neo-classical textbooks and whole generations of economists have lived, worked and retired believing that the labour theory of value was hopelessly outdated, the sort of thing believed in the eighteenth or nineteenth century but best forgotten now.

---

13   Option 1 might make sense to an employer wanting to know how much labour they could get done for £28,500, but that is not the same thing as Smith was talking about in the quotation.
14   Karl Marx, Value, price, and profit, vol. 5, sec VI (CH Kerr & Company, 1910).

But was this abandonment of the Labour Theory an actual scientific advance or was it just fashion?

Scientific theories provide explanations and predictions about the material world; while myth, storytelling, neo-classical economics and religion also explain things, they do so with limited predictive power. A scientific theory must make testable predictions: temporal or correlational.[15] Scientific predictions make statements about the world that are not available as prior data, such as the early existence of a missing link, well before Australopithecus afarensis was actually found. These predictions typically involve applying general laws to pre-given data to produce derived data that can be tested.

The derived data need not be in the future or unknown, provided they are not made available as input data. A theory that makes no predictions is never scientific, and one whose predictions have been invalidated forfeits any prior claims to science. If no possible observations would contradict the theory it is vacuous. Neoclassical price theory is vacuous in this sense. Any observed structure of prices can be explained as having arisen from the intersection of unobservable supply and demand curves. Since these invisible curves are imagined to shift and change shape between price observations, no sequence of price observations could ever invalidate the theory.

William of Occam's dictum emphasizes the importance of simplicity in science. Science often chooses simpler theories for better prediction, as it extends knowledge based on the least pre-given information. A theory with added epicycles, special cases, and fudge factors may predict observations well, as they are woven into its very weft, highlighting the importance of simplicity in science. Ptolemy plus epicycles might run Newton a close race, had not simplicity favoured the latter. But compared to the baroque curlicues of neoclassical price theory Ptolemy's theory was positively Calvinist in its austerity. Epicycles are an early form of Fourier analysis of periodic signals.[16]

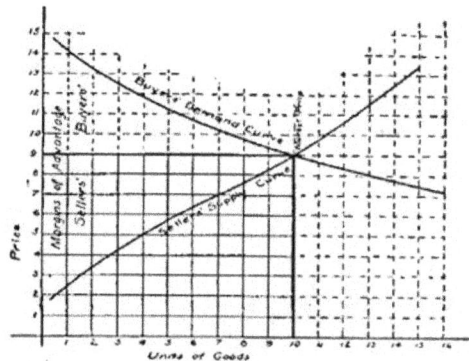

Figure 2: The original supply and demand curves, from Alfred Marshall, Principles of Economics (London: Macmillan, 1890).

---

15   It has been suggested by an anonymous referee that this statement is highly controversial, conservative and wrong. That this could be written illustrates the gulf that still exists between what Snow in 1959 called the two cultures (Charles Percy Snow, 'Two cultures', Science 130, no. 3373 (1959), 419) of science and humanities. Your current author for years taught research methodology to the science faculty post graduate research cohort in one of our ancient universities. I can assure the reviewer that the need for testable predictions is repeatedly emphasised to students starting out as research scientists.

16   Lucio Russo et al., The forgotten revolution: how science was born in 300 BC and why it had to be reborn (Springer, 2004).

Fourier techniques can be used to efficiently compress even random data, efficiently in the sense that a time series with n observations can be fitted by n amplitudes of Fourier components – a very incarnation of Occam's maxim: epicycli non sunt multiplicanda praeter necessitatem.

One may ask whether there is any set of observations that might undermine demand and supply theory. The problem is that for what is termed 'identification' you need at least one measurable variable that enters the hypothetical demand equation but not the hypothetical supply equation, and vice versa. If you couldn't get statistically significant estimates (with 'sensible' signs) of the coefficients on the postulated driver variables that would put the general theory in jeopardy.

Since you cannot simultaneously get statistically significant estimates of all the drivers, because
of the identification problem, then is the whole theory:

- *falsified?*
- *proven unfalsifiable and not even wrong?*

Source: Springer Science+Business Media, 2003

There is a saying that seeing is believing. If as a devout Christian you weekly look at images of the sacred heart of our blessed saviour, it comes to seem real. If for years, undergraduates look daily at images of supply and demand curves, they too come to seem real.

Testing Marx

Unlike Marshall's theory, the labour theory of value is eminently testable. The labour theory of value claims that the money value of output will be determined by the labour required to produce it. As Marx writes:

> *It suffices to say the if supply and demand equilibrate[17] each other, the market prices of commodities will correspond with their natural prices, that is to say with their values, as determined by the respective quantities of labour required for their production. But supply and demand must constantly tend to equilibrate each other, although they do so only by compensating one fluctuation by another, a rise by a fall, and vice versa. If, instead of considering only the daily fluctuations, you analyze the movement of market prices for longer periods, as Mr. Tooke, for example, has done in his History of Prices, you will find that the fluctuations of market prices, their deviations from values, their ups and downs, paralyze and compensate each other; so that apart from the effect of monopolies and some other modifications I must now pass by, all descriptions of commodities are, on average, sold at their respective values or natural prices.*[18]

You can, given modern economic statistics, work out how much labour is directly or indirectly used to produce the output of each industry in a nation. You can then compare the labour content of each industry's output with the total monetary value obtained by selling that output. If the theory is true, then the money values will be highly correlated with the labour content.

Such calculations could not readily be done until

- *Computers were readily available.*
- *Appropriate national statistics, called IO Tables, were being published.*

Year	Deviation
1947	10.5%
1958	9.0%
1962	9.2%
1967	10.2%
1972	7.1%
Average	9.2%

---

17   Note that for Marx and the classicals the term supply means the current flow of production of a commodity and demand the current rate of consumption. This is quite different from supply curves etc.

18   Marx, Value, price, and profit, VI. Value and Labour. At this point in my draft, before I inserted this quote from Marx an anonymous referee commented: 'But there are many factors intervening between the exercise of labour and its quantification and formation of products as prices, so you are not testing value theory at all. Rather a Ricardian embodied labour theory of price which all know to be wrong including Ricardo himself, let alone Marx.'

Indeed, all professional bourgeois economists know that the embodied labour theory of value is wrong. Those who pretend some sympathy with Marx ignore just how boldly Marx states the embodied labour theory in Value Price and Profit. That he was not in fact wrong, we demonstrate in our empirical sections below.

Figure 3: Average percentage deviations between market prices and labour values for the USA for selected years from Anwar M. Shaikh, 'The empirical strength of the labour theory of value,' in Marxian Economics: A Reappraisal, ed. Riccardo Bellofiore, vol. 2 (Macmillan, 1998), 225–251.

Country	year	number of industries	price/labour correlation
Japan	1995	85	98.6%
Sweden	2000	48	96.0%
USA	1987	47	97.1%
Greece	1970	35	94.2%
UK	1984	101	95.5%
Germany	1995	33	96.5%
France	1995	37	97.6%

Figure 4: Comparing the correlation of prices to labour values in different countries reproduced from David Zachariah, 'Labour Value and Equalisation of Profit Rates', Indian Development Review 4, no. 1 (2006), 1–21.

From the late 1980s, the wide use of personal computers, along with the availability of digitised IO Tables allowed economists to start practically testing the labour theory of value. In a whole series of studies[19] they found that the labour theory of value performed outstandingly well.

Examples of published data on the close correspondence of money value to labour content are given in Figs 3 and 4. Typically, the correlations between money values and labour content are found to be over 95%. This is very good for an economic correlation and can be considered confirmatory evidence for the theory. The confirmation is strengthened by the fact that it appears to apply generally in all major capitalist nations studied.

It can help to see the data as a plot rather than as tables. Figure 5 shows comparisons between the actual money value of industrial outputs against the labour required to produce those outputs. The data was calculated using the 1987 Bureau of Economic Affairs Input

---

19   P. Petrovic, 'The deviation of production prices from labour values: some methodological and empirical evidence,' Cambridge Journal of Economics 11 (1987), 197–210; E. M. Ochoa, 'Values, prices, and wage–profit curve' in the US economy," Cambridge Journal of Economics 13 (1989), 413–429; W. P. Cockshott, A. F. Cottrell, and G. Michaelson, 'Testing Marx: some new results from UK data,' Capital and Class 55 (1995), 103–129; Anwar M. Shaikh, 'The empirical strength of the labour theory of value,' in Marxian Economics: A Reappraisal, ed. Riccardo Bellofiore, vol. 2 (Macmillan, 1998), 225–251; David Zachariah, Testing the labor theory of value in Sweden (http://reality.gn.apc. org/econ/DZ{\}article1.pdf, 2004); Nils Fröhlich, 'Labour values, prices of production and the missing equalisation tendency of profit rates: evidence from the German economy,' Cambridge Journal of Economics 37, no. 5 (March 2013), 1107–1126, issn: 0309-166X, https://doi.org/10.1093/cje/bes066, eprint: https://academic.oup.com/cje/articlepdf/37/5/1107/4709769/bes066.pdf, https://doi.org/10.1093/cje/bes066.

Output Table using the methods described by Cockshott, Cottrell, and Michaelson.[20]
It is important to realise that all the studies mentioned total both direct labour and indirect labour inputs for each economic sector. So, for the car industry it adds up the labour used in car factories plus the labour that other industries which supply the car factories - steel, rubber, etc, had to use to deliver supplies to the car industry, right down the supply chain. For the Mexican plot shown in Figure 6 the data were drawn from the Mexican I/0 tables of 1980 (seventy two sectors). They were processed to obtain the total direct and indirect labour contents of the outputs of each industry, with the row 'Remuneracion de asalariados', being used as a surrogate for labour input. This is equivalent to assuming that hourly wage rates and labour intensities were equal across industries.[21] The algorithm used to arrive at the estimates for embodied labour was:

1. Let a_{ij} be the quantity of the j th commodity used in industry i measured in millions of Pesos, w_i be the wages in the ith industry in millions of Pesos, and l_i be the labour input per peso output of the ith industry. Initially assume that all commodities have value $l = 0$.

2. For each industry i compute the total labour input $L_i = w_i + {}^P a_{ij} l_j$

3. For each industry i set $l_i = L_i/M_i$ where M_i is the money total of the industry output.

4. Repeat steps 2 and 3 twenty-five times, resulting in convergence of the estimates.

   This is equivalent to following the supply chains back by 25 levels.

20   P. Cockshott, A. Cottrell, and G. Michaelson, 'Testing Marx: some new results from UK data.' Capital & Class, 19 (1) (1995), 103-130.

21   Note that what we calculate here will be a vector that up to a scalar factor is proportional to labour content. The scalar factor arises from using annual compensation of employees rather than millions of person years per sector as starting data. Mexico does not give statistics on millions of person years. Swedish official statistics used in David Zachariah, 'Labour Value and Equalisation of Profit Rates,' Indian Development Review 4, no. 1 (2006), 1–21 do provide person year figures and his results are practically indistinguishable from ours.

Consequences

Industries with high capital-to-labour ratios have a low profit rate *(for example see Figure 7)*. This effect is as predicted by Marx[22] but contradicts the hitherto influential production price theory.[23] The inverse relationship necessarily follows if prices correlate closely with labour values. The discovery is surprising given that Marxists and their bourgeois critics in Western universities believed the profit rate was the same in all industries. The assumption of equal profit in all industries was accepted by critics of the LTV like Steedman[24] but was taught without empirical evidence, reflecting the idealist apriorism approach in Western Economics.

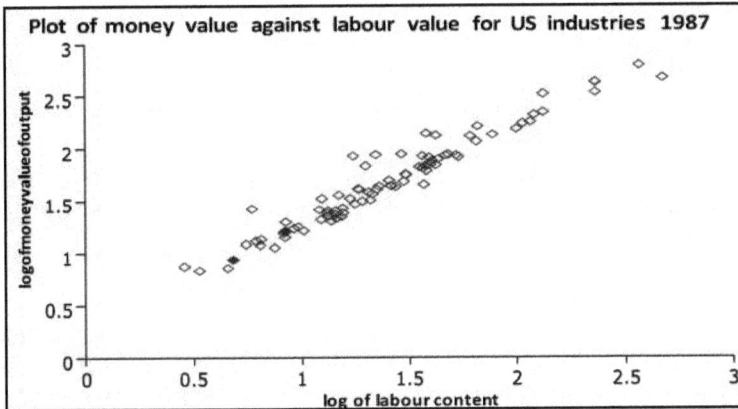

Figure 5: There was an almost linear relationship between monetary value and labour values for the USA in 1987.

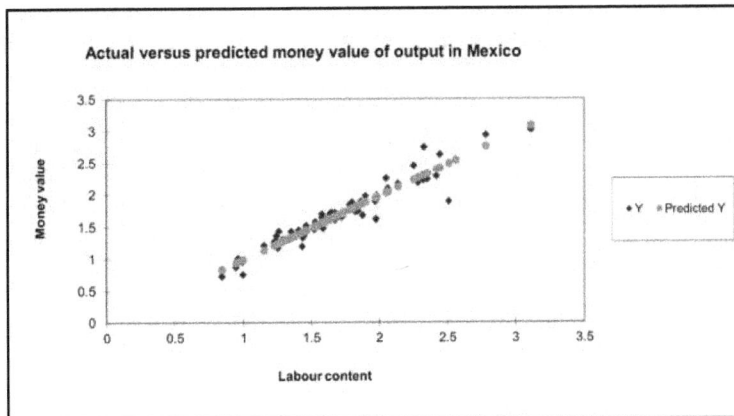

Figure 6: Comparing the actual output values of Mexican industries with those predicted by their labour contents. Axes are in logs of billions of pesos.

---

22   Karl Marx, Capital, vol. 3 (Moscow: Progress Publishers, 1971), Chap 8.
23   Marx, Chap 9.
24   Ian Steedman, Marx after Sraffa (London: Verso, 1981).

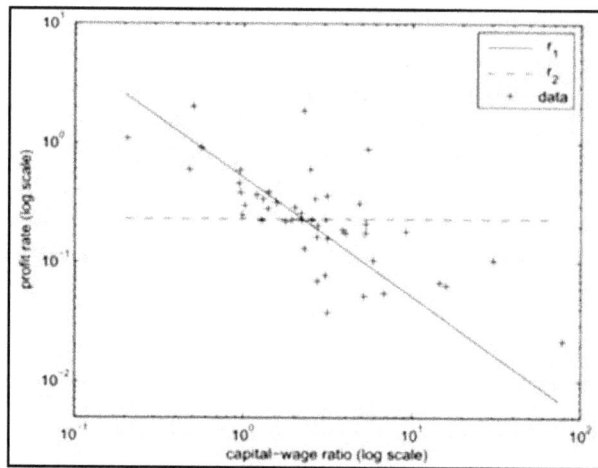

Figure 7: Data for Sweden show that profit rates tend to vary inversely with capital composition (David Zachariah, 'Labour Value and Equalisation of Profit Rates', Indian Development Review 4, no. 1 (2006), 1–21).

Why was this idea of uniform profit rates so persistent? It may be one of Marx's 'illusions of competition', specifically one between stockbrokers. It is expressed through the concept of a general profit rate that is as close to equalization as possible. If a firm's earnings are below this rate, brokers mark down its shares until the return on the market value equals the average profit rate. This makes the average profit rate an ever-present reality for rentiers, brokers, and speculators, but it is an equal rate of return on fictitious capital, that is to say stocks and shares, not real capital.

Objections

Let us now look at some objections that have been raised to these results validating the labour theory of value.

Somewhat surprisingly, one of the most vehement opponents of this line of research was the Marxist economist, Andrew Kliman. One would have expected that any Marxist would be relieved to discover that Marx had been proven right all along. But no, for reasons about which we can only speculate, Kliman declared that any correlation between labour content and money values of output was entirely spurious.[25] The essence of the Kliman objection was that labour used and money output were falsely correlated because there was a third factor, industry size causing both. Big industries employ more people and have a higher value of output, so industry size was the actual causal factor here which had induced a spurious alignment between the plotted variables.

---

25   Andrew J. Kliman, 'The law of value and laws of statistics: sectoral values and prices in the US economy, 1977–97', Cambridge Journal of Economics 26, no. 3 (2002), 299–311, eprint: http://cje.oxfordjournals.org/cgi/reprint/26/3/299.pdf, http://cje.oxfordjournals.org/cgi/content/abstract/26/3/299; Andrew J Kliman, 'Spurious value-price correlations: some additional evidence and arguments,' in Neoliberalism in Crisis, Accumulation, and Rosa Luxemburg's Legacy, vol. 21 (Emerald Group Publishing Limited, 2004), 223–238.

It was soon pointed out26 that there is no unambiguous notion of industry size apart from the number of people it employs. We say an industry is big, if it is a big employer, so far from discovering a third causal factor, Kliman had just renamed the x-axis of the graphs.

A further reason to believe that the correlations are not spurious is that if one uses an input x other than labour as ones value base, for instance steel or oil, directly or indirectly used, we find only weak correlations between x content and money values of output.[27]

Another possible objection28 was that the studies finding strong correlations between labour content and the value of output were cheating because they used total wage expenditure in an industry as a proxy for labour input, rather than total hours worked in the industry. This objection is simply false. Some studies[29] have used actual hours worked either because, in the case of Sweden these are directly recorded in the government statistics, or by using mean hourly wage rates for each industry to work back from money wage totals to hours. Whether the study uses wages as a proxy for labour input, or uses actual clock hours, correlations in the high 90%s are found.

26   Emilio D´ıaz and Rub´en Osuna, 'Understanding spurious correlation: a rejoinder to Kliman,' Journal of Post Keynesian Economics 31, no. 2 (2008), 357–362; W. P. Cockshott and A. Cottrell, 'Robust correlations between prices and labour values: a comment,' Cambridge Journal of Economics 29, no. 2 (2005), 309–316.
27   W. Paul Cockshott and Allin F. Cottrell, 'Labour time versus alternative value bases: a research note,' Cambridge Journal of Economics 21, no. 4 (1997): pp. 545–549.
28   raised for example in Jonathan Nitzan and Shimshon Bichler, Capital as power: A study of order and creorder (London: Routledge, 2009).
29   Cockshott, Cottrell, and Michaelson, 'Testing Marx'

Mechanism

One of the problems with the labour theory of value gaining acceptance was the lack of mathematical account of why it should work. This was changed in the 1980s when a book The Laws of Chaos[30] was published. This applied the forms of mathematical argument originally used in statistical mechanics to show that the law of value is an 'emerging' law from the chaotic and disorganised character of capitalist economies. Statistical mechanics, and then quantum mechanics were a paradigm shift from earlier physics in that they account for the law like behaviour of random processes, whether these be atoms of a gas or photons passing through an imaging system.

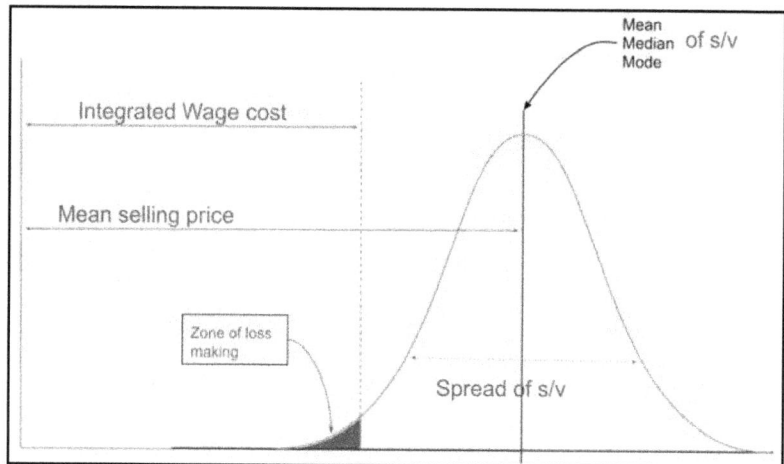

Figure 8: The ratio of profit to wages (s/v) is constrained to be comparatively narrow as a wide distribution for a given mean rate of surplus value would imply too many capitals are making a loss and will close.

Farjoun and Machover argued that capitalism was also a random but law-governed process, involving huge numbers of events: sales and purchases. The prices at which goods sell has, they say, a large random element, but this randomness is constrained. They say that because the final selling price is the result of many independently operating factors, its expected value will have a normal distribution *(Figure 8)*. Anything we measure that is the sum of multiple independent varying factors will have a normal distribution, which is why it crops up so often.

Consider a single sale of an arbitrary commodity. It has a price, and to make the commodity wages had to be paid. If the total wages that were paid, not only by the final producer, but by all the producers of components, add up to more than the selling price, then the firms making the product will be loss making and will quickly fold. Suppose we say that at most 2.5% of sales involve that sort of loss-making right down the supply chain. This constrains the width of the normal distribution of the rate of surplus value in Figure 8. If only 2.5% of sales were in the loss-making range, then we can work out what the standard deviation of s/v must be for any given mean rate of s/v in the economy.

---

30   Emmanuel Farjoun and Moshe Machover, Laws of Chaos, a Probabilistic Approach to Political Economy (London: Verso, 1983).

Suppose the mean s/v was 0.5, then the standard deviation would be at most 0.25. This in turn would imply that the standard deviation of price/labour content in Marx's terms would be 0.25/1.5 = 16.6%.

If we make their more stringent assumption that the distance between aggregate wage costs and the mean selling price is three standard deviations, that is to say only about one purchase in 2000 involves that kind of loss making, then the standard deviation of price to value will be of the order of 11%. For the UK economy Cockshott and Cottrell[31] found the actual standard deviation of price to value to be 10.4%, which was strongly supportive of Farjoun and Machover. It is worth noting that they made the prediction in 1983 several years before any empirical studies were done. Correct and novel predictions made prior to observation are strong arguments in favour of a theory.

Their overall prediction in The Laws of Chaos was that labour values would necessarily emerge from the chaos of capitalist economy. They were correct.

Conclusion

The labour theory of value was the foundation of classical political economy and of the economic theories of Marx. In consequence of its political implications, it has been unfairly rejected by professional bourgeois economists since the late nineteenth century. This led even left-wing economists to be hesitant in advancing it.[32]

In the last forty years a growing body of empirical research has demonstrated that the theory is basically correct. We should boldly uphold the glorious and correct labour theory of value and roundly rebuff the groundless criticisms of it.

Appendix

Look at figure 2, the diagram from which all subsequent neo-classical price theory derives. Consider Marshall's demand curve. It is clearly a second-order polynomial of general form

$$D(Q) = a + bQ + cQ^2.$$

Where does he get this odd formula, with three constants[33] from?

He just makes it up. He plays 'let us suppose'. But he does not write it down explicitly in this form. To do so would reveal it to be completely arbitrary. Marshall's supply curve has two turning points so it must be a 3rd degree polynomial of form

$$S(Q) = e + fQ + gQ2 + hQ^3$$

31   W. Paul Cockshott and Allin Cottrell, 'Does Marx need to transform?', in Marxian
        Economics: A Reappraisal, ed. Riccardo Bellofiore, vol. 2 (Basingstoke: Macmillan, 1998), 70–85.
32   Harvey, D. 2018. "Marx's Refusal of the Labour Theory of Value." Accessed July 2, 2018.
        http://davidharvey.org/2018/03/marxs-refusal-of-the-labour-theory-of-value-by-david-harvey/.
33   He gives actual points on the graph so we can solve the parameters as a = 15,b = –0.805,c = 0.0205.

The actual values are not that important,34 but the important point is that for any actual observation [p,q] of a price and quantity sold, Marshall's explanation introduces seven unknown variables a,b,c,e,f,g,h. Once you remove the visual trick of presenting this as a graph and show the naked algebra it is apparent that as an attempt at a scientific explanation we have an absurdity.

If there were some independent procedure, outside of observed prices, by which the parameters of the supply and demand curves for a commodity in a given year could be determined, then we would at least have a testable hypothesis. We could use this independent data to compute what the supply and demand curves 'should' be and see if their intersections accurately predicted the prices and quantities sold. If the predictions were poor, we could reject the whole Marshallian apparatus.

But there exists no procedure by which, for 100 commodities, we can fix the 700 parameters that Marshall's theory requires. Marshall's theory is not operationally testable.[35]

Editor's note

The labour theory of value has been the subject of controversy amongst Marxist economists. There have been debates between different perspectives on the value of a commodity and on its conversion into monetary terms – and then compared with actual prices, for example. And there have been different perspectives on whether – or not - there is a tendency for the rate of profit to equalise, over time. Paul Cockshott's article presents one point of view on these and related questions, including the question of predictability in the social sciences. Theory and Struggle welcomes contributions to these debates, exploring different perspectives, for the following issue of the journal.

---

34   We can again solve to get e = 1.47,f = 1.08,g = –0.063,h = 0.0029 from his graph.

35   It may be objected that work going on from Slutsky (Eugenio Slutsky, 'Sulla teoria del bilancio del consumatore,' Giornale degli economisti e rivista di statistica, (1915), 1–26) does make the theory operationally testable. But in terms of number of parameters (k) vs number of observations (n) in statistical estimation, it's clear you need n > k to get anywhere. In demand studies the usual set-up is to have several/many observations of each price and associated quantity over time, along with per-time-period. observations of the variables other than own-price that are hypothesised to shift the demand and supply curves, for example consumers' income, the prices of inputs, and the prices of goods that are substitutes or complements for the one in question. The object of the exercise is generally to predict the effect on the price and quantity of a given good that will result from a specified change in one or more of the driver variables – not to predict the vector of prices in a given period, using only data from that period. Since both the simple labour theory of value and that of Sraffa (Piero Sraffa, Production of Commodities by Means of Commodities (Cambridge: Cambridge University Press, 1960)) allow you do exactly the latter they are more empirically testable than demand and supply analysis.

COMBATTING THE PRO-WAR NARRATIVE

ROUND TABLE DISCUSSIONS WITH MEIRIAN JUMP, ANDREW MURRAY, KATE HUDSON AND LIZ PAYNE

Meirian Jump is Director of the Marx Memorial Library and Workers School
Andrew Murray is Deputy President of Stop the War
Kate Hudson is retiring Secretary of the Campaign for Nuclear Disarmament (CND)
Liz Payne represents the British Peace Assembly (BPA)

Abstract

This Round Table discussion explores the ways in which Stop the War campaign, the Campaign for Nuclear Disarmament and the British Peace Assembly have analysed the underlying factors behind the prevalent pro-war narrative. This provides the basis for the development of their strategies to build a broad alliance campaigning against militarism, working for peace and international solidarity.

Keywords:

Anti-militarism, anti-imperialism, peace, Middle East, Ukraine

The Director of the Library, Meirian Jump, opened the discussion.

'This meeting brings together officers from our three peace movements to discuss how to combat the pro-war narrative currently dominant in British politics and indeed globally.

We are doing so in the ecumenical spirit of a former president of this Library, Professor J.D. Bernal, a founder of the World Peace Council who always sought the broadest unity. His papers are housed here at Marx Memorial Library (MML). I will say a little about them shortly.

First to introduce our speakers: Liz Payne represents the British Peace Assembly (BPA), an affiliate of the World Peace Council (WPC) that brings together peace organisations principally from across the global south. I am also delighted to welcome Kate Hudson, General Secretary of the Campaign for Nuclear Disarmament (CND), our main campaigning organisation against nuclear weapons. Andrew Murray, our first speaker, is Deputy President of Stop the War, currently focussing its efforts on campaigning against Israeli aggression in the Middle East.

As a preliminary I'd like to say a little about our Library itself. It was founded in 1933 at a time when fascism and militarism loomed large in Europe, and it was in response to that threat and particularly prompted by the burning of the books in Nazi Germany that MML was established. Our Library contains fifty thousand books and pamphlets in this historic building. The Bernal Peace Library is one of our most significant collections. Bernal was born in 1901 and died in 1971. He was one of the most eminent scientists of his time, a molecular biologist, whose wider research focused on the impact of war on human life. He was a passionate socialist with a vision of the beneficial role of science on society – and a driving force in the world peace movement. His peace library was opened here in 1973, and it has been added to since with smaller collections from regional and local groups. His political papers along with his scientific papers are housed in the University Library at Cambridge.

Our own peace collection was catalogued in 2019 and can be searched online. We have the working papers of the World Peace Council and the British Peace Assembly, related photographs and probably most interesting of all, Bernal's own writings and working notes. It also includes the papers of the peace campaigner Eira Burn who played a prominent role in the Liaison Committee for Women's Peace Groups and Pensioners for Peace. Lesser known are the papers of Theodore Rosebury, the bacteriologist on the threat posed by bacterial warfare. Some of Ivor Montagu's papers relating to peace are also here from his time on the Secretariat of the WPC. Other papers include Artists against the H Bomb.

We also have a wonderful collection of photographs which we are about to catalogue. Another very important peace archive is represented by The Call, the weekly paper of the British Socialist Party, which documents the peace movement during the First World War. We also have the papers of the International Brigade in Spain – including a quote from Charlie Hutchinson, the only black International Brigader we know of from Britain. He went to Spain when he was 18 and he explains why he decided to volunteer – growing up in the National Children's Home he knew that Fascism meant hunger and war.

As well as being used by academic and authors, our collections also have an important political education function. One example was the community-led exhibition for independent museums we co-curated over the past six months. We worked with people locally on what spoke the most to them. Eira, who lives locally, was inspired by this picture of a peace demonstration in the German Democratic Republic (GDR). We also hosted a fortnight ago the local Woodcraft group who made placards also inspired by our peace exhibition.

I think these collections and the work we do around them have an important role, particularly Bernal's papers, for understanding the role of science for the advancement of humanity rather than the destruction of humankind.

I am delighted to welcome Andrew Murray to our panel, to open our discussions'.

Andrew Murray, Vice President of Stop the War

'Before opening the discussion I'd like pay tribute to Kate Hudson who is retiring as General Secretary of CND at the end of the month. Over the last 20 years she has made an outstanding contribution to the peace movement. In particular she has ensured that there is a united anti-war movement in Britain. And we can be sure now, though she is retiring from her official post, she will continue to do so.

In global terms it is clear that today we are in a very dangerous phase of world politics. The danger of world war is real. The right-wing press is leading the discussion in an almost lip-smacking way. It's clear in the Far East where preparations for a war between the United States (US) and its allies and China are quite advanced. At prime minister's question time this week I was struck by the way Rishi Sunak was making one attack on China after the other and the Labour spokesperson agreeing with them all. We now seem to have a bipartisan xenophobia. The danger of conflict is very real.

In Ukraine there is a drive to escalate by extending the capacity of Ukraine to fire weapons directly into Russia. This won't make any difference to the war, but it will bring a direct war between NATO countries and Russia much closer.

And there is also the conflict in the Middle East which is extending from genocide in Gaza to Lebanon, to Yemen, Syria and Iran. In all these conflicts Britain is in the vanguard of the war party. It is as bellicose, perhaps even more so, than the United States. In Ukraine Britain has done all it can to obstruct to obstruct peace and it is providing enormous assistance militarily and politically to Israel. In the Pacific is it involved in the AUKUS Pact and backing this up with aircraft carriers.

At some point there will have to be an examination of why Britain is doing this – why both parties are involved in a bi-partizan way. Britain has retained the mentality of an extremely aggressive imperialist power – both beyond any comparators but also beyond its capability to deliver such aggression unless jointly with the US. Nonetheless, within that alliance, it is itself a force for aggression.

At the same time, and on the other side of the equation, it is striking to me that a quarter of the way through this new century that the two biggest mass movements we have had in this country have been, first, that against the Iraq war in 2002-2003 and then, the movement in support of the Palestinian people over the last twelve months. Both have arisen around international issues relating to war with an anti-imperialist content. I am not saying that there have not been other issues. There clearly have. But those against war, against external aggression, have been particularly noteworthy by their ability to unite many different sections. It also reminds me of what Lenin said about Britain in Left Wing Communism, that he did not know what would break the ice in Britain politically but that it might well be a colonial issue, a colonial struggle rather than an industrial issue. So, I think Lenin might have hit the nail on the head for this particular question and this is what we are seeing today: the huge possibilities of mobilising masses of people against war and the policies of our leaders.

The big question is how we can deepen this and extend it. Palestine is an example. The campaign has been running for a long time. Everyone is familiar with it and the propaganda of the other side has very little impact. It is also a matter of huge importance to the Muslim community that provides a backbone for any campaign. Referring to parliament this week there was very broad pressure – almost united in the Labour Party and the Liberal Democrats – and even many Tories – in challenging the government's passivity of purely rhetorical reservations about Israel's conduct. Opinion is clearly on our side.

It is much more difficult on Ukraine which has not been an easy issue for the peace movement over the last two and half years. And China does not appear as an acute issue at all. But it is more these two areas that are likely to lead to a broader, bigger war than the Middle East, certainly if you are talking about World War III.

So, we have to think how to broaden the movement. One issue we all know is coming soon under some title or other is more austerity, more cuts – more on top of the previous fourteen years of austerity – and at the same time of increasing military expenditure to 2.5 percent or even 3 percent of GDP. This seems the way to broaden the movement and take it into the trade unions: exposing the current arguments that we need militarism to provide jobs when the net effect is to squeeze the entire working class through cuts to social services, health and education while the jobs pay-off is minimal.

There also other ideas that we need to combat in our movement, even on Palestine, that these questions, of war and peace, have nothing to do with us and we should focus on our own bread and butter issues. This is a position that obviously denies internationalism and the interconnection of struggles to issues at home and leaves the movement with a very limited mandate – one that undermines its ability to handle 'home' issues themselves. Interconnections matter.

Another aspect of the struggle we face in securing wider involvement is the need to resist entering into the internal politics of Hamas or Hezbollah on the grounds that they are socially conservative, religious, misogynist or homophobic and so forth. In my opinion we have to stand in solidarity with all who are in their own countries fighting against imperialism and its agencies and not be wondering what we ourselves would be doing in those countries. These are issues they themselves will have to address but for the wider anti-imperialist movement, at the moment, anti-imperialist unity is key.

If there is a major weakness in our movement it is that its base is insufficiently developed locally within communities, on the ground, in workplaces and trade unions, compared with its local strength twenty years ago during the Iraq war. Our national mobilisation is exemplary. Demonstrations have maintained their strength and vibrancy over a long period. But we are not going to win arguments about China not being a threat, or peace being a better alternative to war in Ukraine, unless we engage directly with people locally at a more intimate level beyond the peace movement.

We need to find other ways to do this, not confine ourselves to our own movements. We need to engage in ways that enable us to advance our arguments comprehensively, in many different types of setting, to supplement what we do at national level'.

Kate Hudson, General Secretary CND

'Thanks to the Library for organising this discussion and thanks to Andrew for his kind words. Something Andrew said towards the end of his contribution struck me particularly. That's knowing our history.

When I was thinking about what to say, I was first struck by the rapidity with which we have seen the emergence of a situation of high conflict. However, in reality all these issues have quite long historical roots, issues of war and imperialism. Pretty much everything we are facing in military, foreign and defence policy terms can be traced back to the period of 1989-91. I am sure I don't need to explain what happened then but suffice to say that after the end of the Soviet Union and the socialist bloc, imperialism was triumphant. There was a whole theory about the 'End of History' and that any dialectical process was at an end. Just one global superpower: the United States. One system: Liberal Democracy. And that was that.

This was the narrative at the time. But in actual fact almost immediately there followed the further development of the North Atlantic Treaty Organisation (NATO). While the Warsaw Pact was dissolved, NATO began to expand with members from former state socialist countries. In 1999 the first three new members found themselves at war, ten days later, with their neighbours in the former Yugoslavia. The claimed peace dividend, the supposed 'uni-polar world' of peace and harmony, never happened. Simultaneously, the US President Bill Clinton restarted Reagan's Star Wars project, and the US announced its so-called Joint Vision 2020 that the US should have full spectrum dominance, air, sea, land and then, very quickly, they added space and also information.

This very much shapes what's happening today and it goes back to the Wolfowitz doctrine of 1992 that the US was the sole super power and it was determined to maintain itself in that position. As far as I can see, this is precisely what the US has done for the past thirty five years. Any notion of multi-polarity is seen by the US as a threat. Today there are suggestions that China is such a threat and that this has only arisen relatively recently. But I well remember the Pentagon was doing its war gaming against China in the 1990s.

Then in this century you had Bush and his 'War on Terror' and the Project for a New American Century, a reconfiguration of the Wolfowitz doctrine, the axis of evil and the war on terror leading up to the attacks on Iraq – basically the US wanting to knock out the remaining non-compliant states militarily. And this is what we are still seeing today with the ratcheting up of tension with Iran. US regime change in Iran has been a long running concern for us in CND. I'm pleased to say for our Day of Action this Saturday our slogans are: End Genocide, Hands Off Lebanon and Don't Attack Iran – because this is where the pro-war narrative is strongest and where it most needs to be challenged. There are indeed plenty of people on the Left who think that Iran has nuclear weapons. In fact, they don't. Even the Central Intelligence Agency (CIA) says they don't. The only country in the Middle East which has nuclear weapons is Israel. Andrew mentioned that it's one of the areas where nuclear war could get out of control.

Then we saw Obama's Pivot to Asia. This was not necessarily a military pivot. It was more a matter of strategic influence. But it accompanied Russia's re-emergence from the catastrophe of the end of the Soviet Union and the Yeltsin years and the complete degradation of its economy. Russia has now re-emerged economically with its redevelopment of oil and natural gas.

In these circumstances it was Trump who again shifted the narrative around war. I remember his speech at the United Nations when he talked about hostile autocratic nations, meaning that somehow a danger was posed by former communist or communist-led states, linking Russia and China, to justify a return to a more active development of nuclear weapons after a couple of decades in which nuclear arsenals had actually gone down.

Now they have started to increase again. And Britain is one of the culprits with Boris Johnson's increase in the number of warheads on the Trident missiles – another challenge to the movement in terms of countering the assumption that we somehow need nuclear weapons. It was Trump who then brought in the idea of 'usable' nuclear weapons. Biden said he'd wouldn't proceed with them. But he did. And they are still out there and an enormous challenge for the peace movement.

Additionally, over the past few years we have seen the further expansion of NATO with escalatory nuclear policies as well - bringing nuclear bombs back to Lakenheath, the continuing upgrading of Trident and US nuclear weapons in Europe, an escalatory move especially in light of the Ukraine war. As a result, we have seen Russia bringing its nukes into Belarus in response to more US nukes in western Europe: a serious challenge alongside NATO expansion and a new type of ideological rhetoric. The tendency now in US circles is to refer to the Chinese Communist Party as the 'enemy' rather than China – as if angling for regime change in China. And the terrible war in Ukraine continues. There has been an ongoing debate on the role of NATO in this.

All I can say is that CND has opposed NATO since its formation and today recognises the role of NATO expansion in triggering the Ukraine war. On top of this there is now Gaza and how we counter the US determination to maintain Israel as its key power base in the Middle East - and doing so now that some of its other partners, such as Egypt and Saudi Arabia, are reorienting towards the BRICS alliance (originally formed by Brazil, Russia, India, China and South Africa). The US is therefore now absolutely determined to maintain Israel in a dominant position and refusing to allow Iran to escape from the sanctions that are destroying its economy – with Britain paddling along behind.

I think the reason why Britain maintains this level of involvement is about maintaining the appearance of great power status. You see this in Tony Blair's autobiography in justifying the retention of nuclear weapons: our imperial past. The terrible thing about the Starmer government is, as Andrew said, that it has doubled down on what the Tories were doing – and then some more. This was the point that the Trades Union Congress was at a couple of years ago when the GMB motion was passed that seemed to commit our movement to even higher military spending than the Tories.

In concluding I would say that our areas of work are really clear. Underpinning everything is the need to build the movement as a mass movement and I agree with Andrew on this. It is in the anti-war movement that the ideological challenge is strongest: countering NATO, winning a real understanding of China and countering the myths. There are people on the Left who are progressive on a number of issues but who talk about China as imperialist. We need to identify the real enemies of peace and not focus on a country struggling to bring its population out of poverty and making a massive contribution to economic development in the Global South. The Left took a knock in 1989. We have to regain our confidence in our politics and our philosophy.

In immediate terms we need to mobilise. It is absolutely essential to block the return of US nuclear weapons to Britain, that will see us on the front line.

We have to expose the jobs myth and the deterrence myth. Let's build on the points that Andrew was making about the trade unions and use that industrial power to change policy. Who hasn't wept over the genocide in Gaza and the hundreds of thousands killed in Ukraine? We need ceasefires and then peace settlements. This is at the core of our work. I know everyone here is committed to that'.

Liz Payne, Secretary of the British Peace Assembly (BPA)

'Solidarity greetings from the BPA, and also, as we are an affiliate of the World Peace Council (WPC), from the Council as well.

The pro-war narrative we have been discussing has always been inseparable from imperialism, including British imperialism. While you were both speaking, I was reminded that at the end of the Second World War, at the Potsdam Peace Conference, Churchill spoke with President Truman about British/US military interoperability, as we now call it, and proposed a special relationship between Britain and the US. This was on the first occasion the two leaders ever met. The aim of this interoperability, and all such pro-war alliance-forging, was to enable the US, Britain and their allies to control the resources, labour, markets and strategic supply lines of the world - and also to prevent any rival powers from getting anywhere near them.

The WPC came together precisely to counter the war mongers' narrative and plans. It was formed seventy-five years ago, in the same month as NATO, and has stood against imperialism in all its manifestations ever since. It is the largest peace organisation in the world, with members in more than a hundred countries and with a particularly big voice and influence in the Global South, where some of its affiliates are multi-million strong.

In talking about countering the war narrative, I want to stress how important it is to take our work into the international arena and to bring discussions and analysis from there back into our own peace movement at home. I'll just mention a few of the global members of the WPC - the Brazilian Centre for Solidarity and Peace, the Cuban Peace Institute, the All-India Peace and Solidarity Organisation, the Palestine Committee for Peace, and the South African Peace Initiative. There is also the Sudan Peace and Solidarity Council – from a country in which, today, a terrible 'forgotten war' is being waged by the rival forces of a former dictatorship.

The WPC's slogan is 'No to NATO. Yes to Peace' and we oppose all imperialist wars and occupations of sovereign countries and nations. We've worked together for seventy five years on that. We oppose external interference in the internal affairs of sovereign countries. We want to see the prohibition of all weapons of mass destruction and an ending of every arms race. But most of all we want the cold and hot wars of the world to end and for countries to work together internationally to build a sustainably peaceful future.

John Desmond Bernal, whose collected peace papers are held in this Library, was in fact the World Peace Council's second president. He did a huge amount of work world-wide on what could be done for humanity with war technologies if they were used for peaceful purposes. This remains absolutely crucial for us today, together with the abolition of foreign military bases, universal disarmament and an end to all forms of colonialism and neo-colonialism.

We believe there are no issues that cannot be settled through peaceful negotiation. The Vietnam War was an example. Despite the brutality of that conflict and all the complexities and tensions which many thought would be unresolvable, all sides were ultimately able to sit together and negotiate at the Paris Peace Conference and, despite every obstacle, secure a settlement and lasting peace.

Another reference point might be Lenin's comment during the October Revolution – I think it was in the Decree on Peace on the second day – with regard to Britain, Germany and France.
It was, he said, the responsibility of the workers in each country to challenge the role of their own bellicose ruling classes in the fight for peace across Europe.

Likewise, today it is up to the people of our country to challenge the war narrative and actions of our own government and the forces of wealth and power it represents. We need to expose the terrible impact its actions are having around the world. And we, too, need to take our analysis into the labour movement and out into our communities. It is absolutely essential that everyone understands the roots of war and recognises the possibility of lasting peace and the way to build it.

I also want, before closing, to mention the campaigning of the British Peace Assembly on the closure of all Britain's overseas military bases. First and foremost, there are the Chagos Islands, concerning which a so-called 'settlement' is on the table (though not signed and sealed). This has been set up by Britain in unseemly haste prior to the US presidential election and the general election in Mauritius. The text gives sovereignty of the Chagos back to Mauritius but allows for the leasing back to Britain, the current colonial overlord, of arguably the most strategic and deadly US/UK base in the world, Diego Garcia. This, in effect, gives the US and its UK ally another ninety-nine years to wage both hot and cold war in Africa, in the Middle East, and the Indo-Pacific region. The exiled Diego Garcians were never consulted and there is no possibility of their returning.

There are two British-occupied military bases in Cyprus which have been directly involved in the recent conflicts in the Middle East. They occupy 3% of the island as British sovereign territory. The BPA has been working with WPC affiliate, the Cyprus Peace Council, to lobby our government and to show solidarity with the huge demonstrations against the bases taking place in Cyprus itself. These bases have been directly used for bombing raids and for surveillance activity across the region and for carrying military supplies to Israel to feed its war on Gaza.

In concluding I want to say one final thing about the importance of peace work in the trade union movement. Last week I attended the retired members conference of a major union with over 400 delegates. A host of issues were raised: the denial of winter fuel payments, the decline in services on which older people rely, the need for a national care service and the lack of money to resolve these issues. Yet nothing was said about the huge increase in military spending and how that money could be used to meet the desperate needs of people here. This is a connection it is imperative we make. The World Peace Council, and our own British Peace Assembly, are dedicated, in the spirit of JD Bernal, to doing exactly that'.

CHINA'S EVOLVING SOCIALIST DEMOCRACY AND ITS NEW CONCEPTION OF 'WHOLE PROCESS PEOPLE'S DEMOCRACY'

JENNY CLEGG

Dr Jenny Clegg is a China specialist and former lecturer in Asia Pacific Studies at the University of Central Lancashire. Since retiring she continues to research and write about China. She is member of the editorial boards of World Marxism Review, and the International Manifesto Group, and on the advisory board of the Friends of Socialist China. Her publications include China's Global Strategy: towards a multipolar world (London: Pluto Press, 2009); Storming the Heavens - Peasants and Revolution in China, 1925-1949: a Marxist perspective (Croydon: Manifesto Press, forthcoming).

Abstract

Xi Jinping's introduction in 2021 of Whole Process People's Democracy (WPD) as a new development in conception of socialism with Chinese characteristics draws attention to the centrality of political reform in the People's Republic of China (PRC). This article opens discussion of the WPD concept by offering an approach that is grounded by history, developmental progression and practical application. Sketching out the evolution of socialist democratisation in China through stages, first in settling controversies over the nature of the socialist state given the distinct characteristics of its democratic revolution, followed by the consolidation of the formal structures of government in the era of 'reform and opening up', the article shows WPD as a further stage aimed at embedding China's system of socialist law into society through the strengthening of public participation and representation. Whilst overall this political trajectory is to be set broadly in China's socio-economic transformation from a peasant to a worker-based society, discussion of recent empirical findings covering village elections, urban community organisation and democratic management in workplaces helps to illustrate Party-people interactions at grass roots levels. In these ways, the article offers a range of pointers to bear in mind in following China's pursuit of the ambitious goals of developing into a modern socialist society by 2049.

Keywords:

Socialist democratisation; people's congress system; whole process people's democracy; grassroots participation; role of the CPC

The People's Republic of China (PRC) has seen a remarkable transformation over the last seventy-five years from one of the world's poorest countries, to, by some measures, its largest economy. China's economic advance, especially its shift from a planned to a socialist market economy, has been widely discussed by Marxists in the West. Less considered is the question of how socialist political democracy has developed.

The distinct mark of political practice in China is the extension of democratic centralism to wider society, namely, the mass line - the method of 'from the masses; to the masses' - developed by Mao in the CPC (Communist Party of China) base areas during the anti-Japanese war. Seeking to concentrate and systematise the ideas of the masses into workable policies and practices, the mass line served as the means of handling the contradictions among the four classes supporting the resistance - workers, peasants, petty- and national bourgeoisie - synthesising their different interests to consolidate the United Front.

The mass line lies at the core of the CPC's conception of socialist democracy, linking Party, state and people. Conceived in an environment of close-knit village communities, how is this now made relevant as China modernises?
Setting out the PRC's centennial goal to become a 'strong, democratic, civilised, harmonious, and modern socialist country' by 2049, Xi Jinping highlighted the purpose of a modern socialist democracy:

> *to give full expression to the will of the people, protect their rights and interests, spark their creativity, and provide a system of institutions to ensure that it is they who run the country.*[1]

The concept of 'whole process people's democracy' (WPD) is now being advanced by Xi as a new innovation in the development of the socialism with Chinese characteristics.[2] China's political system, having evolved first from the democratic to the socialist stage, was then to shift from the continuation of class struggle and mass mobilisation under Mao after 1956 to the establishment - after 1978 under Deng - of formal institutions of indirect representation, centred on the system of people's congresses. WPD now reaches out into society, increasing the channels of public participation. Aiming in this way to make governance more effective, it involves an effort to transform Chinese society into one based on law and better suited to the new urbanised and industrialised environment.

Losurdo has contrasted Western Marxists 'in opposition', increasingly focused on 'critical theory' measuring existing practices unfavourably against 'imagined standards of theoretical or moral purity', with Eastern Marxists 'in power', actually engaged in the 'difficult and drawn-out process of building socialism'.[3] In line with the latter, this discussion offers an initial take on how China has gone about building a democratic socialist political system, with distinct characteristics rooted in the realities of a socio-economic transformation from an agricultural, rural-based society to a modern industrialised one.

Opening with a general historical overview, it notes the initial lack of consensus on the nature of the proletarian state given China's particular conditions as a largely peasant-based society, a matter not resolved until the 1982 Constitution of the PRC. Moving on to outline the political dimension of the 'reform and opening up' era, it then takes up the discussion of WPD as a concept, highlighting the aim of shifting social relations onto the basis of socialist law. To provide some grounding, it draws on findings of recent empirical

---

1   Xi Jinping's report at 19th CPC National Congress, November 4, 2017. https://www.chinadaily.com.cn/china/19thcpcnationalcongress/2017-11/04/content_34115212.htm accessed 12 January 2025.

2   Xi Jinping, Speech at the Meeting Celebrating the 100th Anniversary of the Founding of the Communist Party of China, July 15, 2021 http://www.xinhuanet.com/politics/2021-07/15/c_1127658385.htm accessed 23 November 2024.

3   Domenico Losurdo, 2024, Western Marxism: How It Was Born, How It Died, How It Can Be Reborn, Gabriel Rockhill (ed), (New York: Monthly Review Press, 2024), 257-263.

research studies of village elections, new urban institutions, and democratic management in enterprises to offer insights into participative and representative practices at the grassroots. Finally, some general observations are offered on the role of the Party in China's political development as it guides social change toward the realisation of a modern socialism based on 'common prosperity' by 2049.

On the question of the nature of the state

The establishment of the PRC in 1949 was the outcome of a democratic revolution with particular characteristics: led by a proletarian party with only a small working-class base, its anti-feudal anti-imperialist programme had won the support of hundreds of millions of peasants as well as large sections of the national bourgeoisie and intelligentsia. Eight democratic parties representing sections of the latter two groups, accepted the CPC's leadership, contributing to a common programme which declared the PRC a people's democratic dictatorship led by the working class, based on the four-class alliance of workers, peasants, national and petty bourgeoisies.

In 1954, following elections to establish people's congresses at various levels from townships up to the National People's Congress (NPC), the first NPC adopted a formal Constitution ratifying the government system based on the people's congresses. Alongside this, a Chinese People's Political Consultative Committee (CPPCC) involved the eight democratic parties, whilst villages were to be self-administered. Mass organisations of women, youth and trade unions were consolidated to provide the underpinning. Apart from the ten-year Cultural Revolution period, the PRC government has been structured along these lines up to this day.

The 1954 Constitution envisaged a relatively long period of socialist transformation. However, driven forward by the socialist upsurge in the countryside, the 1956 Eighth CPC Congress was to declare a 'total and decisive' victory for socialism with some 90 percent of rural households involved in cooperatives, and the great majority of capitalist industry amalgamated under joint state-private or state-owned operations. As Liu Shaoqi declared in his congress report, 'the people's democratic dictatorship has in essence become a form of the dictatorship of the proletariat'.[4]

This peaceful transition, made possible by proletarian leadership in the democratic stage, was not without contention. The CPC leadership, considering those opposing socialism to be a small minority, with capitalism only weakly developed, accepted the national bourgeoisie as part of the working people and, whilst maintaining the necessity of dictatorship to suppress counter-revolution, envisaged a long-term co-existence with the democratic parties. However, the Congress decision to continue to involve these parties, formed to represent the national bourgeoisie after the socialist transition, was questioned from the Left.[5]

The somewhat extreme measures used to deal with a Rightist backlash in 1957 reflected this hostility to United Front work. That the decisions of the Eighth CPC Congress were

---

4   Liu Shaoqi, Political Report of the CC.CPC to the Eighth National Congress of the CPC, September 15th, 1956 https://www.marxists.org/subject/china/documents/cpc/8th_congress. htm accessed 5 December, 2024.

5   See Liu Shaoqi: 'Some people may ask: Since our people's democratic dictatorship at the present stage is in essence a form of the dictatorship of the proletariat, how is it that other classes, [and] other parties...participate in exercising state power?' see also Mao Zedong On Correct Handling of Contradictions among the People, Selected Works, Vol. V, (Beijing: Foreign Languages Press, 1977), 413-4.

not to be formally legitimised in a new constitution for a further twenty-five years was an indication of the lack of consensus as to the nature of China's socialist state.

The 1958 Great Leap Forward saw villages incorporated into the people's communes at township level, and the Cultural Revolution replaced people's congresses with revolutionary committees of new-formed mass organisations of Red Guards and workers groups, the Peoples Liberation Army (PLA) and the Comunist Party of China (CPC) cadres. A new Constitution in 1975 replaced the 1954 designation of China as a **'people's democratic state'** with the words **'a socialist state of the dictatorship of the proletariat'**.

It was not until 1982 that yet another constitution finally updated the PRC's status to that of **a socialist state under a people's democratic dictatorship** led by the working class based on the alliance of workers and peasants. The preamble explained that 'the people's democratic dictatorship ... is in essence the dictatorship of the proletariat'. In this it followed Liu Shaoqi whose 1956 report noted that Lenin had seen the dictatorship of the proletariat as a 'special form of class alliance' between the proletariat and the majority of the 'numerous non-proletarian strata of working people (the petty bourgeoisie, the small proprietors, the peasantry, the intelligentsia, etc.)'.

'Reform and opening up': the political dimension

At the time that Deng was restored to office in the late 1970s, China's population was still overwhelmingly agricultural. His strategic shift to an agenda of 'reform and opening up' was to realise the next stage of China's industrialisation, requiring a massive rural-to-urban population transition.

As the people's communes were broken up, villages were opened up to market forces. And, to manage the huge population movement to the cities whilst speeding industrialisation around a core of socialist state-owned enterprises (SOEs), the CPC drew upon the assistance of business and professional classes to create employment and upgrade techniques, not least by learning from the West. Whilst steering the direction of change, the Party resumed cooperation with the eight democratic parties as it revived the people's congress system.

The Cultural Revolution had sought to break with the democratic underpinnings of China's proletarian-led revolution, taking class struggle between the bourgeoisie and proletariat as the main contradiction; Deng now reconnected with the distinctive characteristics of Chinese socialism as he prioritised the development of the productive forces. However, whilst unleashing market forces, giving greater scope to the educated classes, rather than relying on mass mobilisations, he sought to deal with the contradictions within socialist society using Party and state power as framed by the four cardinal principles covering the socialist path; the People's Democratic Dictatorship; CPC leadership and Marxism-Leninism-Mao Zedong Thought.

As others have argued, the fact that market reforms in China were introduced step-by-step under the tight control of the Party and the State was the main reason for their success.[6] In this, and following the Tiananmen protests, the CPC learned from Gorbachov's mistake in attempting to carry out economic and political reforms simultaneously, leading to the Soviet Union's collapse. But China's top-down approach should not obscure important developments in the political sphere.

---

6   See for example, Carlos Martinez, The East Is Still Red, (Glasgow: Praxis Press, 2023), Ch. 3, 65-83; Isabella Weber, How China Escaped Shock Therapy: the Market Reform Debate, (London: Routledge, 2021), 268.

A 1982 Resolution on Party History was to clarify the key aspects of socialist democratisation: strengthening the people's congress system; turning the socialist legal system into 'a powerful instrument for protecting peoples' rights'; and gradually realising direct participation in political power at grassroots level, in particular 'democratic management by the working masses in urban and rural enterprises over the affairs of their establishments'.[7]

Since its revival in 1978, the NPC has passed a huge raft of legislation carefully crafting the regulatory environment. Strengthening the people's congress system, nominations are encouraged from communities, workplaces and mass organisations, with the representation of frontline workers, farmers and minorities guaranteed right up to the national level by set quotas. Consultations take place with experts, the mass organisations - trade unions, women's and youth organisations - and the democratic parties which all also assist in gathering opinions and disseminating new laws.[8] Those that particularly concern the immediate interests of the wider public - such as women's and labour rights - are put out in draft form for public debate and comment: the draft fourteenth five-year plan received one million suggestions from the public within two weeks.[9]

Economic reform was to transform relations between Party, state and society as state and collective enterprises began to redefine their relationship with government. The CPC then started to explore more varied forms of participation, introducing competitive village elections in 1998 covering at the time 900 million rural residents. NGOs, including foreign ones, were granted a certain autonomy within legal constraints to not 'undermine the country's unity and security nor harm the interests of the state or the public' began to flourish.[10]

Today, after four decades of reform, the rural population has fallen to around a third (500 million) with the private sector growing exponentially to provide 80 percent of new employment opportunities, for the most part in small, medium-sized and household enterprises.[11] City populations have diversified with a middle income group of some 450 million, well-educated and owning their own homes, co-existing alongside some 300 million rural migrants, many still living in hardship. Meanwhile a new group of several hundred billionaires has emerged.

---

7   CC.CPC, Resolution on Certain Questions in the History of our Party since the Founding of the People's Republic of China, June 27, 1982 https://www.marxists.org/subject/china/documents/cpc/history/01.htm accessed 6 February, 2025. The resolution also clarified that whilst class struggle was no longer seen as the principal contradiction 'owing to certain domestic factors and influences from abroad, class struggle will continue to exist within certain limits for a long time to come and may even grow acute under certain conditions'.

8   Mass organisations both organise along democratic centralist lines and function as part of the wider system of democratic centralism. Subordinate to the overall interests of the socialist state, assisting its work of developing the productive forces and socialist modernisation, they still exercise autonomy so as to effectively represent and protect the rights and interests of their members.

9   China Insight, Whole Process People's Democracy, 3, https://www.bjreview.com/2021pdf/China_Insight_Special_Issue_on_Whole_Process_Peoples_Democracy.pdf accessed 16 December, 2024.

10   Esther E. Song, "Explaining the expansion of the NGO sector in China: through the lens of adaptive corporatist governance", Asia Politics and Society, Wiley Online Library 26 June, 2024 https://onlinelibrary.wiley.com/doi/full/10.1111/aspp.12752 accessed 8 December, 2024.

11   The 2022 Fortune 500 shows 71 percent of Chinese large-scale companies listed were state-owned, Big Data China https://bigdatachina.csis.org/unpacking-linkages-between-the-chinese-state-and-private-firms/#:~:text=Indeed%2C%2071%20percent%20of%20Chinese,state%2Downed%20sector%20in%20China accessed 7 January 2025.

With China's double digit growth rate increasing opportunities and day-by-day improvements in people's livelihoods, public support remained high. But by the late 2000s growth was beginning to slow down - amidst rising expectations. Meanwhile, with entrepreneurs admitted into the CPC in 2001 and a new property law extending protection to private property in 2007, the challenge of reconciling market reforms with socialist values was causing great strain within the Party and a weakening political commitment was evident as the 'get rich' culture spread corruption.

Assuming leadership in 2013, Xi Jinping, responded to these challenges. Whilst affirming the role of the market, he sought to strengthen the Party leadership through launching a far-reaching and highly popular anti-corruption campaign, reviving Marxist study and launching a new drive to set up grassroots Party branches including in private enterprises. In 2021, with power more firmly consolidated, WPD was initiated to advance a rules-based environment more suited to market-oriented modernisation, promoting direct political participation at the grassroots level. Aiming to deliver further on the 1982 socialist democratisation agenda, this reinforced the new shift from economic growth to people-centred development and the longer term goal of 'common prosperity' adopted at the CPC's Nineteenth Congress in 2017.

Whole-process people's democracy: transforming China into a society based on law

As a whole process, WPD covers elections, consultations, decision-making processes, management, and supervision, all as part of an interlocking chain.[12] Seeking public participation at all points, it aims to make government more effective and efficient: socialist democracy is seen to be about 'solving problems that people want solving'.[13]

From the Marxist perspective, the liberal notion of the separation of powers - the executive, legislative and judicial - is an abstraction from the reality of social power relations in which these are all arms of a single state, overseeing a system of exploitative economic relations. In contrast, China's political system treats these branches as parts of a whole system of power to be coordinated together.[14] First, Party leadership formulates views based on science - historical and dialectical materialism - practice, multiparty cooperation and political consultation; these views are then re-examined and substantiated into legislation through the people's congresses; and finally, this legislation forms the basis for the governance system - the rule of law - of the country.[15] Rather than simply focusing on elections then, WPD addresses the whole context of decision-making, implementation and oversight. By international standards, PRC laws are mainly progressive but with China still a developing country, the question is how well legislation is implemented. On the one hand decisions need to be less arbitrary and more scientific, made feasible on the basis of Marxist principles and expert consultations, as well as being responsive to public opinion.

---

12   Xi Jinping, 2021, Speech at a Working Conference of the National People's Congress, excerpt in Quishi Journal http://en.qstheory.cn/2024-05/11/c_985271.htm accessed 5 December 2024.

13   Xinhua, 15 October 2021, "Highlights of Xi Jinping's latest remarks on democracy http://en.npc.gov.cn.cdurl.cn/2021-10/15/c_688745.htm accessed 12 January 2025.

14   Xi Jinping, 'Commemorate the 30th Anniversary of the Promulgation and Implementation of the Current Constitution,' (2012), excerpt in Quishi Journal http://en.qstheory.cn/2024-05/11/c_985271.htm accessed 5 December 2024.

15   See Roland Boer, 'China's socialist democracy' in People's China at 75: the Flag Stays Red, Keith Bennett and Carlos Martinez (eds), (Glasgow, Praxis Press, 2024), 69-70.

On the other hand, weak governance at grassroots levels is to be addressed through more direct participation under the leadership of primary level Party organisations so that 'urban and rural communities can more effectively manage, serve, educate, and oversee themselves'.[16]

Political practice: grassroots participation and representation

Drawing on three pieces of empirical research into participation by election, consultation and supervision in village and urban communities as well as workplaces, this section aims to illuminate how the processes work and how the Party interacts with the public.

Village elections

Open village elections have seen some three million grassroots leaders voted in to three-year terms of office. However greater competition was to prove no guarantee of candidate competence: malpractices occurred with some seeking positions for private gain, vote-buying, factionalising, using kinship networks to build their own 'little kingdoms', even resorting to intimidation and violence.

CPC work teams were sent into villages to rebuild Party branches to restrain misconduct, break the influence of longstanding clan and patronage networks, and help improve local economic opportunities. Township oversight over village elections has been tightened and CPC members encouraged to seek office whilst other candidates have to pass a CPC approval process.

From a Western perspective, Party manipulation of village elections is seen to stifle the voice of the villagers, impeding genuine democracy. However, based on field research, Liu Jingping concluded that these 'consensus elections - in which the Party and villagers come to an agreement on the election candidates - improved practices, and 'sometimes made elected village leaders more accountable and responsive to ordinary villagers than before'.[17]

In one case, a village director - favoured by the township authorities as experienced and politically loyal but 'held in low public regard' owing to some scandal over village economic management - was discouraged by the Party, after a substantial amount of persuasion, from standing again. As one township official said, 'Even if we picked him, the masses would oppose, so we finally decided not to pick him.' According to Liu, this 'consensus election' was praised by both villagers and Party cadres as an example of community solidarity with good selection outcomes. This example shows how the Party influences elections by fostering a pre-electoral consensus with the villagers on whom to select as village leader through repeated discussion and deliberation. Party approval of a list of candidates was generally found to be popular with the grassroots since it signified confidence in their quality where open elections had failed. As to the scale of the problems, in the clean-up operation launched by Xi between 2018 and 2020, out of more than 600,000 villages only 41,700 village officers were removed, only a very small percentage.[18]

---

16   Xi Jinping, Report to the 20th CPC Congress, 16 October 2022 http://my.china-embassy.gov.cn/eng/zgxw/202210/t20221026_10792358.htm accessed 12 January 2025.

17   Liu Jingping, 'Manipulation without Resistance: Consensus Elections in Rural China', The China Quarterly 259, (2024), 696–710.

18   Brian Hillman, 'The End of Village Democracy in China', Journal of Democracy, Vol. 34, No. 3, (2023), 62-76.

Urban grassroots political institutions

Rapid urbanisation, producing diversified city populations, is presenting new challenges for social governance, prompting new initiatives in response.[19] A research study of WPD practices in Shanghai between 2019 and 2021 investigated four participation methods:[20]

(i) Hongqiao Street was one of a number of urban districts selected to serve as basic legislative contact points for the standing committee of the NPC with a view to strengthening the people's congress system by increasing participation in policy-making. The grassroots legislative units gather suggestions for legislation and collect opinions on amendments and draft laws using surveys, street level forums, public hearings, and consultations with experts held in districts, industries, finance, small and medium-sized enterprises as well as government offices.[21] Hongqiao Street was officially reported to have held, in its first year, fifty consultation forums involving 1,000 people with 366 suggestions submitted, of which sixty-six were adopted by the Shanghai Municipal People's Congress. The draft law on the Protection of Women's Rights and Interests was found to have drawn a lot of public interest, receiving the most comments and suggestions backed by a degree of NGO lobbying.

(ii) The '12345 hotline' - these well-used phone lines have been set up in Chinese cities as a mechanism for citizens to seek advice, express complaints and criticise the work of local government. They help to test public attitudes and levels of dissatisfaction, highlighting areas where both regulations and cadres' performance required improvement. Within the eighteen month research period, the number of cases received by the Shanghai government was nearly eleven million, of which 68 percent were resolved, according to official figures.

(iii) Community Consultation Conferences: these serve to tackle particular community issues with a view to seeking problem-solving strategies under the leadership of the CPC. Mobilised through the Residents Committees, they are less formal, aiming to encourage more open discussions. The researchers observed how a neighbourhood parking problem was resolved by consensus reached after full consultation with the residents to ensure the results were universally accepted and as satisfactory as possible.

(iv) 'Participation by mobilisation' work teams: these government-initiated efforts mobilise public participation in projects, such as the renovation of public housing, through groups of community activists. The research investigators observed how a specially established work team handled the matter of lift installations, successfully resolving disputes between residents, living for example on the upper and lower floors.

The research concluded, overall, that these mechanisms of WPD provided improved channels for the public to express their views and exercise their powers, engaging public opinion more fully in the processes of policymaking and government supervision. Participation, however, remained essentially state-mobilised, and the work of the legislative unit in particular lacked both experience and sufficient resources to collect public opinion more broadly. Local government officials still looked to the expectations of their superiors. Nevertheless these mechanisms were facilitating their responses to the public, leading to more effective solutions to specific issues.

---

19   Hu Jieren and Wu Tong, "'Whole Process People's Democracy' in China: Evidence from Shanghai' Chinese Political Science Review, Vol. 9, (2024), 172-199.
20   Hu Jieren and Wu Tong.
21   China Insight, Whole Process People's Democracy, 12.

Workplace democratic management

Democratic management (DM) in the workplace is core to China's political vision: according to the 1982 Constitution, state and collective economic enterprises are required to establish Workers and Staff Representative Congresses (WSRC) to be provided with information on enterprise affairs, as well as establishing employee representatives on directors' and supervisory boards.

Whilst Party control over DM in SOEs has helped to maintain good practice, there has been growing concern that in private and mixed ownership enterprises sectors, DM was little more than a formality, endorsing pre-determined outcomes set by managers, prioritising shareholder interests. In 2012 experimental guidelines were issued for all larger-scale ventures covering, for example, limits on the number of middle and senior managers allowed to stand in WSRC elections.[22] Party branches within the workplace were revived to ensure good practice: by 2021 around half of private enterprises had CPC cells with numbers still expanding. In fact, around 40 percent of private entrepreneurs are Party members.[23]

A recent research study of DM provides some examples.[24] In one joint-venture car factory of 13,000 workers, there were 226 WSCR representatives, 90 percent being frontline workers. The committee met several times a year to deliberate over wages and employment rules, with voting at general meetings by show of hands. On one occasion, rules on sick leave drafted by the employer were voted down. The study found examples of workers voting for representatives based on candidates' speeches; shop-floor hearings on wage and bonus distribution; and an employee hotline to the General Manager which was proving to be an effective way of handling complaints.[25]

In 2024, a new Company Law set out collective rights in enterprises of more than three hundred employees, opening a new era of boosting workplace democracy.[26] Enterprises are required to establish a supervisory board with employees occupying no less than one-third of the positions, or to appoint employee representatives to the board of directors. The law covers an interlinked enterprise structure of Party committee, WSCR, and trade union, the latter with the right to sign collective contracts with the company on matters of pay, working hours, holidays, health and safety, etc., as covered by law.

The law also stipulates that when a company is making decisions on significant matters such as restructuring, dissolution or a bankruptcy application, it should seek opinions and suggestions from the company's trade union and WSRC.

DM practice has adapted then to the variety of forms of ownership, such that whilst legally, employees have the right to oversee management and participate in the decision-making process, this does not, as the research study notes, amount to the ability to decide outcomes: managers manage. However, with the emergence of different interests within enterprises,

22   Wei Huang, 'What Sort of Workplace Democracy can Democratic Management Achieve in China?' Industrial Relations Journal, (2022) November issue.

23   Christopher Marquis and Qiao Kunyuan, Mao and Markets: the Communist roots of Chinese enterprise, (New Haven: Yale University Press, 2022), 225-231.

24   Wei Huang, 'What Sort of Workplace Democracy can Democratic Management Achieve in China?' (2022).

25   Wei Huang, 14.

26   CC.CPC, Further Deepening Reform Comprehensively to Advance Chinese Modernization, July 21, 2024, https://www.mfa.gov.cn/eng/xw/zyxw/202407/t20240721_11457437.html accessed 21 December, 2024. This new development may have been prompted by the wildcat strikes which spread across southern China involving thousands of workers in the latter part of the 2010s.

as management has become more complex and demanding, the Party plays a key role in the workplace, synthesising and coordinating multiple and often divergent views into workable decisions, ensuring the employees' voice is heard and that legislation and government policies are adhered to.[27]

Conclusion

As China now enters the final stages of transformation into a modern, industrialised, socialist society, it looks towards the goal of common prosperity, eliminating rural-urban inequality, also reflected in the different strata of rural migrants and middle-income households in the cities.

As it guides reform, the Party has called upon businesspeople and professionals to facilitate the transition from a peasant to a working-class based society. Managing the contradictions unleashed by market forces involves a delicate balance between utilising the expertise of this new strata whilst preventing more powerful groups from capturing the state's political institutions.[28] Public ownership provides the mainstay, interlinked into the larger private enterprises through cross-sharing holding systems, whilst Marxism serves as the guide, keeping focused on the long-term interests of the working class. In these ways, with popular support, the path to capitalist restoration is blocked.

Overall, whilst extreme poverty has been eliminated and the livelihoods of the Chinese people continue to improve steadily, there nevertheless remain problems of hardship, inequality, exploitative work practices and abuses of power. As has been seen, Party interventions at grassroots level have sought to dismantle efforts by powerful families to control village administrations as well as to enforce legal practices within enterprises and prevent urban disputes from getting out of hand. Widening participation at grassroots level, the Party uses mass-line patterns of repeated discussion and deliberation to mediate differences and disputes. In this way the different interests involved in the socialist market economy are synthesised into practicable solutions within the framework of the law.

With working people now the most numerous class, Xi looks to strengthen people's democracy in practice through WPD to oversee the final stages of rural-urban integration and socialist modernisation. Whilst drawing on past methods, WPD marks a political development in the conception of socialism with Chinese characteristics as it sets out to re-build social relations around the implementation of the law.

Adapting Deng's system of indirect representation, WPD aims to secure inclusivity across diversified social groups in government as well as in enterprise management by opening spaces for direct grassroots participation, so as to ensure the interests of workers and farmers are protected, with their voices contributing to shaping the overall direction of decision-making.

The Chinese state will continue to be tested amid the social strains of its ambitious goals, not least given the prospects of an increasingly hostile international environment. This demands robust mechanisms to manage social tensions, and to maintain motivation and a strong sense of confidence in the socialist political system. Will the socialist legal system prove sufficient?

---

27   Whether DM in private enterprises is to serve as a transitional measure towards future public takeover is a matter for the much longer term.

28   So long as these new elites contribute to building socialism, they are regarded politically as part of the people. For a discussion on how the state handles China's billionaires, see Kyle Ferrana, *Why the World Needs China*, (Atlanta, USA: Clarity Press, Inc, 2024), 179-197.

Success would see China's diverse population integrated into a more unified and mature working class by 2049, a base for further advancement of socialist democracy. China's primary stage of socialism will no doubt remain for some time to come. For now it remains for WPD to diffuse and disseminate good practice throughout diverse grassroots conditions. There is still some way to go though.

This general discussion has suggested that China's distinctive political approach is to be understood within its long-term development trajectory. Limits of space have precluded more in-depth discussion of the contradictions in Chinese society whilst consideration of the impact of external pressures from the US-led New Cold War, together with the impacts of socialist democratisation in national minority regions, amongst other issues and angles, would have added useful dimensions.

It remains incumbent on Western Marxists to penetrate the fog of anti-China prejudice that saturates academia and the media alike to gain better appreciation of China's socialist practices and strategic perspectives.

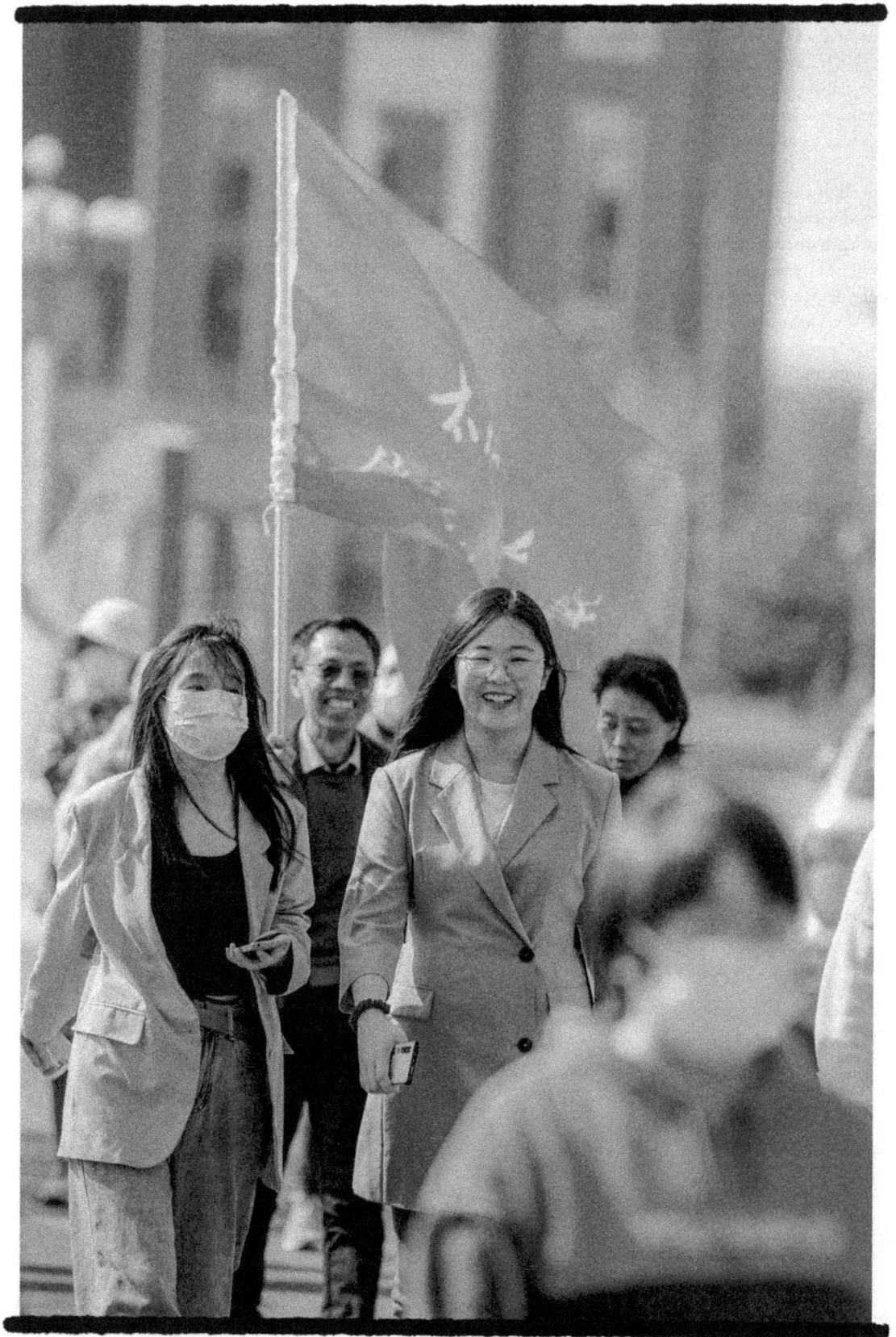

THE ORGREAVE TRUTH AND JUSTICE CAMPAIGN: MARKING THE 40TH ANNIVERSARY OF THE MINERS' STRIKE

KATE FLANNERY

Kate Flannery was a trade union activist and member of Sheffield Women Against Pit Closures throughout the 84-85 miners' strike, organising collections, food distribution and fundraising; and helping to get supporters to meetings, pickets and demonstrations. Her parents, Martin Flannery and Blanche Flannery, were also unwavering activists and supporters of the strike. This article presents the speech that Kate gave at Wortley Hall, on 18 August 2024, as part of the South Yorkshire Festival. She was speaking on behalf of the Orgreave Truth and Justice Campaign, marking the 40th Anniversary of the state sanctioned police violence against striking miners.

Abstract

The Orgreave Truth and Justice Campaign has been pressing for an inquiry into the state orchestrated violence that was perpetrated by the police, attacking striking miners in 1984/5. This article explains the background to these events. An inquiry is essential to achieve justice for the miners who were seriously assaulted and abused by the police and for the 95 miners who were wrongly accused of unlawful assembly and riot by the police, who behaved with impunity and perjured themselves in court. To also help to try to restore public trust in government and policing, the Orgreave Truth and Justice Campaign (OTJC) wants: the public to know the truth; to reset standards in public life including those of the media; to reinforce the operational independence of the police; to reset democratic diligence in public office; and a public acknowledgment and public apology.

Keywords

Orgreave Truth and Justice Campaign, 1984-85 Miners Strike, Women Against Pit Closures, Women's Support Groups, Police violence

Reflections on the Orgreave 40th Anniversary

The election of the Thatcher Tory Government in Britain in 1979 was a bitter blow to us all. The Tory friendship with fascist and right-wing regimes and their devotion to neoliberalism, monetarism and increasing the role of the private market, required them to shift politics sharply to the right, just as had happened after the fascist military coup in Chile in 1973, a coup that they had supported and from which they were learning.

They were making clandestine plans to develop a more militarised police force to stifle dissent and smash the British Trade Union movement, to introduce a mass privatisation programme and to legislate against workers and human rights. They had never forgiven the National Union of Mineworkers (NUM) for Saltley Gate and successful miners' strike in the early 1970's.

Against that background, we knew what we were up against when the National Coal Board, supported by the Tories, revealed its plans for mass pit closures. The 1984-85 miners' strike against pit closures was necessary to defend jobs and communities. It was a wonderful display of strength and resistance to fight against a class that was hell bent on destroying our class and undermining organised labour at any cost. It was a momentous time of political organising, solidarity and support. A time of struggle, hardship and uncertainty that galvanised all of us who understood what was at stake and what we needed to do to support workers who were striking not just for their own futures but for all our futures. We had never seen solidarity quite like this.

I had the privilege of being a trade union activist and member of Sheffield Women Against Pit Closures throughout the strike, organising collections, food distribution and fundraising as well as helping to get supporters to pickets and demonstrations. My mum, Blanche (Flannery), was President of Sheffield Trades Council throughout the strike. Monthly meetings were attended by well over 100 delegates representing Sheffield's Trade Union movement. The Trades Council, led by Blanche, convened weekly miners' support group meetings throughout the strike and beyond. Along with other dedicated and amazing comrades, they ensured daily collections in Sheffield City Centre. They organised many demonstrations, pickets and meetings and hosted events in Sheffield, working with the NUM, Women Against Pit Closures and many miners' support groups. Sustaining the miners' strike became part of our daily lives.

The steel city of Sheffield, which relied on coal, had a magnificent labour and Trade Union movement. People whose lives had revolved around working in the difficult and dangerous conditions of steel production had also devoted their lives to making this world a better place. The Tories had tried to destroy the Sheffield steel industry in the 1970s but the magnificent resistance from the engineering unions and steel strikers had continued to make us, in Sheffield, very proud. The state and police violence displayed on many of those steel strike picket lines and on picket lines throughout many strikes throughout Britain made it clear what our movement was up against, and why it was essential to keep on fighting.

The Orgreave Truth and Justice Campaign started 12 years ago, after the September 2012 report of the Hillsborough Independent Panel, set up by activists committed to campaigning for an inquiry into events related to the police riot at Orgreave on 18th June 1984. The focus on Orgreave is important because this is the key to understanding what happened during the rest of the year-long strike. An analysis of the events relating to this day can provide answers as to how and why violent policing across mining villages and communities was allowed to happen throughout the strike. Orgreave constitutes one of the most serious abuses of police and state power in our trade union history – abuses which have never been acknowledged by the Conservatives or the state. Instead, they have lied and covered up what happened.

A well organised National Union of Mineworkers had been organising regular pickets at Orgreave to prevent coke being transported to Scunthorpe steel works. There had been a lot of police violence used against the pickets. So, the NUM called for a mass picket on 18 June 1984 at the Orgreave coking plant. Thousands of miners arrived at Orgreave from all over Britain, only to be met by thousands of police deployed from many different forces. The police ran amok, charging their horses at people peacefully gathering, and attacking miners with truncheons and dogs. It is a miracle that no one was killed.

We need an inquiry to achieve justice for the miners who were seriously assaulted and abused by the police and for the 95 miners who were wrongly accused of unlawful assembly and riot by police who behaved with impunity and perjured themselves in court. It is in the interest of any democracy to examine why government and police lies and cover-ups have been allowed to continue for so long, as well as to expose the role that the media and judiciary have played in colluding. Many miners have died since the strike and many others are elderly and ill. It is in all our interests for justice not to be denied and delayed any longer.

We already know that many elements of the 1980s Tory government were involved in the strike while professing 'non-involvement'. We know that Thatcher had asked her government, as early as 1981, to plan how they could withstand a coal strike; that the Conservative Government actively put public resources into the implementation of this strategy; and that during the strike there was state sponsored organisation against the miners and their livelihoods. From the Government's own archives, we read documents that confirm that Parliament and the public were knowingly lied to. Government involvement in the strike and the policing of it has never been publicly acknowledged. The extent of this involvement requires an inquiry.

The implementation of this Tory government plan also served to destroy the coal industry which, in 1984, directly employed over 180,000 people. Miners had 'powered' Britain, having provided the main energy source to most British industries for centuries, including through two World Wars. Workers who wanted to save their industry, to provide British coal to industry and the wider population, through gainful employment for themselves and the generations that followed, were punished by the government with a militarised police force pitted against them.

Orgreave marked a turning point in the strike and in the policing of public protest. The extensive government interference in operational policing and industrial relations, that was seen in 1984, continues to this day. Questions remain about the origins of the brutal police tactics used and the operational manual in which they were being secretly instructed by the Association of Chief Police Officers and the Home Office, in 1983. Questions also remain about the application of these tactics at Orgreave, tactics that are still being used against protests today.

With no accountability of policing at Orgreave, the message was sent to the police that they could employ violence with impunity. This established a culture that enabled the police cover-up in 1989 at Hillsborough. That police lied to the public and got away with it is a contravention of the standards to which officers should be held. The Orgreave Truth and Justice Campaign (OTJC) want answers to these questions about the plans for the police's systemic violent and lying behaviour. We need to know how police officers on the ground were briefed and how that briefing came about. We need to know why the police were not held to account by the Director of Public Prosecutions or by their own employer.

There is no doubt that events around Orgreave are of great public interest and concern and this is reason enough to hold an inquiry. The events at Orgreave show a government that actively worked against its own population, the population that it had been elected to serve, handing the police paramilitary powers and destroying an industry in the process.

The Government's failure to look after those who wanted longevity of work in the coal industry - or to create new jobs in energy production to replace the jobs lost - resulted in an immediate increase in coal imports from other countries employing cheap and non-unionised labour. This resulted in the destabilisation of Britain's energy security, for the longer term. This flies in the face of responsible government. The result was devastating to industrial Britain at every level: to individuals, to communities, and to the wider society.

The determination to avoid an inquiry and the lack of police and government accountability has continued to reinforce a culture in which public servants can get away with horrific behaviour. Today, as many of us know, police at protests still violently attack people in such a manner that, were they not wearing the police uniform, they would likely be arrested, charged and brought before a court. However, we now have a Labour Government who have clearly stated in their manifesto that there will be an inquiry into what happened at Orgreave.

The Orgreave Truth and Justice Campaign (OTJC) wants an inquiry so that the public know the truth; so that we can reset standards in public life including those of the media; to reinforce the operational independence of the police and to reset democratic diligence in public office. We also want public acknowledgment and public apology for the wrongs done. We believe this can help to restore public trust in government and the police.

It's vital to our campaign is that many miners quickly secure such a public acknowledgement of why and what the State did to the miners and their communities. This is an urgent need given the age and health of those who were involved. An inquiry with full disclosure can help to right the wrongs of the past and influence the future behaviour of the state and public officials. As such, an early and suitably empowered inquiry into government and police action in relation to events at Orgreave, 18 June 1984 is essential. Our latest OTJC report has been circulated to the Home Office and all major political parties and we have requested a meeting with the new Home Secretary to discuss the format of an inquiry.

Finally, I want to pay particular tribute to the role the women played in sustaining the miners' strike and the role they continue to play in our movement today. Women Against Pit Closures (WAPC) and women's support groups were formed all over Britain. The women came from a variety of cultures and backgrounds. In addition to the many miners' wives, partners, daughters and families, there were local government workers, home workers, engineers, students, trade union activists, peace and anti-racist campaigners among others – all united in the desire to see a successful conclusion to the strike, a future for communities and the preservation of the coal industry. The women fundraised, fed communities, went on pickets, marched, organised events, meetings and rallies and spoke at many meetings in support of the strike. This was unprecedented and life changing for many of us. Many of us women were already activists. Women continue to play an essential role in organising the Orgreave Truth and Justice Campaign.

Women have often been at the forefront of political struggle, playing key organising roles. And they have had to endure abuse and sexism, (and not just the abuse and sexism that has been meted out by the state, but sadly sometimes from within our own movement too). From the Matchwomen to the Chainmakers, Suffragettes to Women's Liberation protests, Grunwick to Greenham Common, Women Against Pit Closures to Reclaim These Streets, we have seen extreme acts of psychological and physical abuse by the state and by the police. The Women Against Pit Closure anthem is as true today as it was 40 years ago—WE ARE WOMEN, WE ARE STRONG.

TRADE UNION STRATEGIES IN POST-TORY BRITAIN

CHAIR: GAWAIN LITTLE, *GENERAL FEDERATION OF TRADE UNIONS (GFTU)*

PANELLISTS: FRAN HEATHCOTE, *PUBLIC AND COMMERCIAL SERVICES (PCS),* **DAVID GODÉ,** *CONFÉDÉRATION GÉNÉRALE DU TRAVAIL (CGT RAILS),* **SARAH WOOLLEY,** *BAKERS AND ALLIED WORKERS UNION (BFAWU),* **ALEX GORDON,** *NATIONAL UNION OF RAIL, MARITIME AND TRANSPORT TRADE UNION (RMT)*

On 5 December 2024 Gawain Little, general secretary of the GFTU, chaired a discussion of the new challenges facing Britain's trade union movement. Fran Heathcote (general secretary PCS), Alex Gordon (RMT President), Sarah Woolley (general secretary BFAWU) and David Godé of France's CGT combined a review of the immediate challenges of maintaining and enhancing members' pay, terms, conditions and legal rights and freedoms under the current government with the more strategic issues of how collectively to create a movement in communities and workplaces that can combat the arguments of the far right and redevelop wider class solidarity.

Gawain Little, general secretary of the General Federation of Trade Unions, introduced the meeting by outlining the challenges likely to be faced in developing trade union strategies for today's post-Tory Britain.

'Today we face a critical juncture. The removal of a Tory government after fourteen years in power and the election of a Labour government should present huge opportunities for working people and for the trade union movement. And yet, after forty-five years of neo-liberal politics and economics under both Tory and Labour governments, there remain major questions about our ability to realise those opportunities for change.

We have an economy that has seen very serious underinvestment in its productive sector, been massively de-industrialized leaving it crisis-prone and particularly weak on the supply side - as we saw during the cost-of-living crisis. Public services have been decimated and in local government the very democratic fabric of our society has been stripped away. A huge transfer of wealth to the richest in our society has taken place.

Undoing the damage would itself be a challenge – even if we were all on the same page as to what the remedies are. There are big questions about the pressures on the current Labour government and the compromises it is willing to make. Here trade union strategy will be critical. It is whether the movement simply adopts the status quo, or the politics of partnership as Keir Starmer would call it or develop a more combative stance that might shift the government's position.

This is the challenge we have asked our speakers to address. We are very pleased to have with us Fran Heathcote, general secretary of the PCS union, representing one of the biggest contingents of the public sector workforce, Sarah Woolley, general secretary of the Bakers and Allied Food Workers Union, representing the retail and consumer sector and Alex Gordon, president of the RMT which over recent years has been one of the most effective of all unions in taking on both the government and the private train operators. In addition, we are very pleased to welcome from France's trade union movement David Godé, a representative of its biggest confederation, the CGT, responsible for rail transport.'

Fran Heathcote, General Secretary, Public and Civil Service Union

'In the PCS we are on a bit of a high at the moment. We have just won a ten-year battle at the Supreme Court over the Tory government's attempt to break the union by ending the check-off of union subs direct from salary. Originally the dream child of Francis Maude, the attack has now definitively failed. But it was a very near thing. The government had already implemented it in three of our biggest departments when we took them to court. Initially, at the first stage, we did not win. As a result, we had just three months to sign everyone back into membership. It was a real testament to our reps and activists that we achieved this. But the government did not learn and went on roll it out through all departments.

What we have now secured after ten years is a judgement in our favour from the High Court, unanimously from all five judges. It's the government that will now have to pay up something like £10 million to the union – although sadly it will be a Labour government and not the Tories.

However, Gawain is right. There are real challenges for us in the coming period and it is on that which I want to focus.

For the first time in far more than a decade millions of public sector workers are getting above inflation pay increases, in the rail industry, the junior doctors and elsewhere. New employment rights are promised, and this is a fairly comprehensive list. It includes extended rights to parental leave and bereavement leave, the outlaw, or at least curtailment, of fire and rehire, the repeal of strike ballot thresholds and minimum service levels, potentially to bring in electronic balloting everywhere. On top of this there is the biggest wave of 'insourcing' in a generation and, as part of it, rail franchises are being brought back under public ownership.

Now some of this is only partial. And much is as yet unrealised. But it's a better agenda than anything we have had on the table for sixteen years. We are not in the heady days of tripartite working, but the government is engaging with trade unions again, a real sea- change. In the civil service it's the first time we have had real engagement in sixteen years, and we think we can now deliver some gains out of the Employment Rights Bill for our members even before the legislation passes through parliament. We will always be ballot-ready and are not complacent. But at least we are back at the bargaining table and, importantly, the government has dropped former plans to cut 72,000 civil service jobs.

But at the same time there is concern over the 2 per cent efficiency targets. If savings can be made from better procurement, less outsourcing and containment of the use of overpriced consultants, then there will be absolutely no argument. But if it is like the proposal by the last government and it is expected to come from our members' pay, jobs and pensions, we will organise and fight back as we did before. At the TUC last September every union backed the call for pay restoration. The cost-of-living crisis was not some blip under Liz Truss. It started a decade before and continues to this day. In the Department of Work and Pensions (DWP), my previous department, one in five of our members are having to claim Universal Credit or a similar benefit to make ends meet. The stories we hear are absolutely horrific, especially when you remember that these are direct government employees.

As a result, there are backlogs in the courts, in the Home Office and many other departments. Pay restoration in the civil service, local government or the National Health Service is essential if we are to retain and recruit the workers that we need to get this country back on its feet. Across government we have members working on outsourced contracts. Some are now employed by companies such as G4S, ISS and OCS. Yes, it's now a commercial sector but its employees would have been civil servants if their jobs had not been sold off. The majority of these contracts were won by the company that made the lowest bid – on the basis of the minimum wage without paying sick pay, without even having to recognise a trade union, The only way they can make a profit is by driving down pay.

Many of these workers are now in dispute. Workers such as security guards, cleaners, caterers are paid the minimum wage to clean and look after the offices of some of the richest people in the country, yet their terms and conditions are absolutely shocking.

So, the 'biggest wave of insourcing' cannot come soon enough – and we have yet to see much implementation of that particular pledge. Our job is to push this Labour government to deliver and to go beyond their existing commitments so that people can see actual improvements.

There is a real risk that a well-organised and well-funded far right is waiting in the wings. Labour won the general election with a landslide – but not a popular landslide, just under thirty-four per cent of the votes, less than Corbyn got in 2019. The Conservative vote imploded but the vote for Reform increased significantly. And this summer (2024) we saw an online axis of evil mobilising an increasing number of people on the basis of hate, division and misinformation. A new social media is replacing Murdoch - serving out misinformation on smart phones. Yet Elon Musk and Andrew Tate can only flourish when there is despair and disillusion with politics and unions.

There are some hopeful signs that Labour is doing better than the Conservatives on a range of fronts. The Rwanda scheme has been scrapped. More resources are going into processing claims – although on immigration too often the rhetoric mirrors that of Farage and Braverman. For youth the Youth Guaranteed Scheme announced recently comes with some additional funding and with work coaches.

More troubling is Labour's approach to disability benefits and the reform of the work capability benefit, however. Despite 'not backing' Tory plans they have also said they will deliver £3 billion of cuts to those who are already facing higher levels of destitution. This is causing huge levels of anxiety.

We, as a trade union movement, have to unite working people and oppose those who are seeking to divide us. A trade union movement that celebrates, not suppresses, our unity as a class must stand firmly against fascism and the far right and take seriously our responsibilities to educate and to represent. In that way we can turn around the perilous situation that currently faces our country and our class'.

David Godé, representing the rail section of France's biggest trade union federation, the Confederation Generale du Travail (CGT), formed in 1895.

'Where are we in France? Karl Marx in The 18th Brumaire of Louis Napoleon noted that "if history repeats itself the first time it is tragedy; the second farce". This seems to be where we are in France today. After the general election in July (2024) we have found it impossible to compose a majority government. The New Popular Front is the biggest group in the Assembly with 193 seats – combining socialists, communists and ecologists – and formed to bar the way to the far right. However, the President, Emanuel Macron, our Napoleon III, has used his influence to block any possible coalition between the Popular Front and the centre – giving control of the government to his own protegees, politicians of either the Centre or the Right. The result has been legislative chaos and the danger of increasing support for the far right.

The response of the CGT as France's biggest trade union federation, has been to campaign in a mass way, across communities, on key issues facing working people, not just alliances among trade union federations but among all sections of working people.

The most unifying campaign is the defence of the retirement age which Macron has sought to increase by two years. It's an issue that affects everyone. And in the National Assembly it crosses all parties. Thousands of amendments have been submitted to the legislation. The CGT works outside the Assembly in workplaces and communities mobilising pressure on deputies, creating petitions and holding meetings explaining the consequences and doing so as the basis for general strike action. More strategically this campaign puts organised labour at the centre of the action and demonstrates the need for unity across all sections – cutting the feet from under the far right.

The second area of struggle is the fight against privatisation. Macron's government seeks to privatise freight transport and the docks and also, finally, the whole railway system. This fight involves the workers themselves but also communities that rely on public transport– particularly working-class communities. The CGT sees its role as involving these communities and exposing the consequences of such privatisation elsewhere. It is combined with campaigns against sackings and plant closures, as currently at Michelin.

The third area is to defend the rights of "those without papers", and France's immigrant communities more generally, those with dual nationality, against the agenda of the National Front to deny them pensions, medical assistance and employment – and to show that division here will injure the overall ability of working people to confront Macron and his succession of puppet administrations. The demand for his resignation now – not in 2027 – is gaining ground.

But the big danger is not Macron. It is that his political follies will open the door to the extreme right. Our task is to build a real mass movement of working-class unity to stop this'.

Sarah Woolley, General Secretary of the Bakers and Allied Food Workers Union and President of the General Federation of Trade Unions.

Sarah Woolley began by apologising for not being able to attend in person, having just walked in from Rathbone's, where she had been discussing the site closure affecting 400 people. She thanked all those who have signed the petition, written to the Chief Executive Officer, and encouraged their MP to sign the Early Day Motion in the Commons. With a big thank you to Henry Fowler and his team at the General Federation of Trade Unions for their unwavering support.

'We have welcomed the prospect of a government that is more sympathetic to the needs of workers' she continued, 'but we have to acknowledge that the hard work has only just begun – as already outlined by Fran.

I want to talk about the problems that have plagued our members – issues that have plagued working people generally for over a decade: stagnant wages, insecure contracts, chronic underfunding of the public services on which too many of our members depend while struggling to make ends meet. In the food production sector, for example, we see the impact of low pay and precarious work on the mental well-being of our members. Our union will not shy away from holding a Labour government to account. Their pledges to introduce fair pay agreements, ban zero hours contracts, strengthen workplace rights must be delivered and delivered quickly.

But even with these reforms our work does not end. We must demand that pay, terms and conditions are not only restored to pre-austerity levels but enhanced in ways that give workers real security and dignity. Nobody should be using food banks in 2024 in one of the richest countries in the world.

The time has come to push for bold structural changes such as sectoral collective bargaining where unions negotiate pay across whole industries. This would be transformative for low paid and fragmented sectors like food, manufacturing, hospitality and retail. Labour's commitment around this gives us an opening. But it's up to us as a movement, as a class, to ensure that these promises are transformed into action. Under the new Labour government, we have got a chance to reverse the draconian anti-union legislation introduced over past decades. But again, this requires pressure from the entire movement. We need a legal framework that actively supports and empowers trade unions. A vital part is abolishing the 2016 Trade Union Act, and its balloting requirements, to enable unions to organise freely. This government needs to work with us, not against us, to create a level playing field for workers and ensure that these gains are protected from future governments by ensuring legislation is not easily dismantled.

But while these immediate challenges are important, we also face a deeper and more strategic one. How do we rebuild solidarity and combat the toxic narratives that have divided our communities for too long? They are ingrained in generations now. Even under a Labour government, the forces of the far right and their divisive arguments - not only in Britain - will not disappear of their own. The far right will continue to exploit economic insecurity and cultural anxiety, blaming migrants, refugees and marginalised groups for the problems caused by systemic inequality and corporate greed.

It's not a new problem but one which requires a renewed focus from our movement. As a trade union movement, we cannot afford to exist solely as a workplace organisation. We've got to be the beating heart of a broader social movement, which means engaging people where they live, not just where they work, building coalitions with community groups, anti-racist campaigns, housing activists and environmental movements and being clear and unapologetic about our values.

Every worker, regardless of race, nationality, gender or sexual orientation, deserves fair pay, decent conditions and the right to live free from discrimination and fear. A Labour government provides an opportunity to invest in the political education of workers –

a critical step in rebuilding class consciousness and solidarity. Marx Memorial Library and the GFTU are doing fantastic work. Too many people have been told that trade unions are relics of the past, that their interests are at odds with those of their neighbours. We've broken through some of that but nowhere near enough. We've got to show that unions are not only relevant but essential to achieving a better life for all.

This involves providing practical training and resources but also creating spaces where workers can come together to share their experiences, learn from one another and develop a collective understanding of the challenges they face – reframing debates about migration, inequality, the economy in terms that highlight our shared interests rather than division.

We may now have a government that claims to be on our side. However, history teaches us that progress will not be handed to us on a silver platter. It must be demanded and fought for. Labour governments in the past have made significant advances for working people. But sometimes they have bitterly disappointed us when they start to appease powerful elites. It is no different now.

Labour's commitment to economic growth must never come at the expense of workers' rights or economic sustainability. Promises of reform must not be diluted by corporate lobbyists or media barons. Labour's rhetoric of fairness must be matched by action that tangibly improves the lives of working people. Our role is clear. We must be both partners and critics. We will work with Labour to deliver its promises but not hesitate to call them out if they if they fall short. We have got to continue to build power from the ground up and ensure that the voices of ordinary workers are heard loud and clear in the corridors of power. It will be our members and their collective power, the working class as a whole, that will drive the changes we need'.

Alex Gordon, president of the rail union, the National Union of Rail, Maritime and Transport Workers (RMT), replacing the General Secretary, Mick Lynch, who had to be in Lancaster to mark the relaunch of a branch of the union.

'I want to start with the reality of our workplace relations as they are today – with how much it depends on institutional bullying, particularly in outsourced companies. I remember meeting PCS members in the British Library at Kings Cross during the 2020-23 strike wave. One woman who had been working there nineteen years was paid the minimum wage, not the London living wage, but the minimum wage, as a skilled librarian working in the National Library. She said that "the only way I can do this job is because my husband has got a proper job which pays a proper salary". PCS are now standing up for such workers.

I'd next like to refer to the quote in Labour's Manifesto calling for the biggest wave of in-sourcing in a generation, not a very ambitious claim as we have never before had such a "wave". But it is an important target for the trade union movement, and I'll come back to it.

I also want to express solidarity with the National Education Union (NEU) taking strike action today across thirty-two non-Academy sixth form colleges across England and Wales calling on the government to ensure that they receive pay that is consistent with the rest of the teaching profession. Further strike days have been called. Solidarity also with all those workplaces taking action for an immediate ceasefire in Gaza and for peace in Palestine and Lebanon.

Our subject today is a post-Tory Britain, and I don't think we can talk about "post-Tory" Britain without recognising that, much to people's surprise, the trade unions contributed so much and - perhaps more so than any other actors – had already shaped the policy contours of the incoming Labour government. In the final months of Covid, from December 2020, UK employers, including some of the biggest, were embarking on a scorched earth policy towards collective bargaining. In December 2020 British Airways Cargo Division decided to fire and rehire their entire staff with worse pay and conditions. Their union Unite responded very quickly, and within the nineteen days required within our very restrictive strike laws, had secured a strike ballot. British Airways backed off because of its reliance on the minute-by-minute delivery of cargo.

British Gas workers in Centrica were not so lucky a month later. Their union, the General, Municipal, Boilermakers and Allied Trade Union (GMB), was not able to get a ballot within the nineteen days. The firm pressed ahead and many of these highly trained technicians left the industry. Then in March 2022 P&O fired 896 staff by email, some even on their ships at the time, and faced them with new contracts with conditions of employment that were massively inferior. Almost all were replaced by much lower paid staff with minimal conditions of employment.

This was 2022. Boris Johnson was prime minister. The Tories were confident of their ability to defeat a weakened movement. But the trade union movement turned it round. We did so by mobilising public anger in a context of rampant inflation and monopoly-based price gouging by energy cartels, landlords and banks, all of whom took advantage of very weak government regulation. There were strikes in the health service by outsourced cleaners organised by GMB and Unite – cleaners who had been called heroes during Covid and were now simply asking to be given permanent employment and better wages.

But it was RMT's strikes for train cleaners that lit the blue touch paper and then spread across telecoms, the postal sector, schools, civil service, the health sector, bus workers, doctors. In face of rampant inflation there were more strike days lost than since the early 1990s. And the Tories then dumped Boris Johnson. Not because he told lies about parties in Downing Street but because he had lost the popular touch.

The Tories then repealed the 1974 legislation protecting agency workers and enabling them to be used to break strikes. And they introduced the Minimum Service Levels Act, the most draconian act since the Combination Acts covering, among other areas of employment, nuclear waste management, border and immigration controls, education, fire and rescue services and health.

Labour's election victory on 4 July 2024 was an emphatic rejection of the Tories – but it was a very weak vote, a mile wide but an inch deep. with a very weak programme despite some highlights like rail nationalisation, a bill which received Royal Assent thirty-one years after its privatisation. It was promised by the previous Labour government but knocked back by John Prescott, a member of my union, among others. This injustice has finally been put right even though it's weaker than we would want. Further legislation next year will create Great British Railways, integrating the different parts of the fragmented privatised system. A very speedy legislative response. Employment Rights is going to take a lot longer and will be a much more contested process.

Finally, to sum up then: what are likely to be the key issues?

Training within the movement and within employment will be one of them. Social partnership will be another. We don't want to be embroiled in phoney partnership schemes. We saw that in the 1980s and 1990s with the European Union's "Social Partnership" which legislated for social dialogue and works councils. Now the Prime Minister is offering regular meetings – though probably without the beer and sandwiches.

There are also three areas in particular on which I think we should concentrate.

The first area is that of peace. There is a real threat of nuclear conflict – with nuclear weapons being used. It is therefore important that the 2024 TUC in Brighton carried a unanimous resolution on Palestine and a ban on arms sales. And they carried a motion on the wider escalation of war in the Middle East. But we need to build on this to make trade unions part of the social movement for peace and to engage with all those young people, mainly not in unions, who have mobilised and on the streets for peace in Palestine and further afield.

The second area is to win an understanding of the importance of pushing forward on the issue of in-sourcing. Though hardly started, this has great potential. It will strengthen the capacity and effectiveness of the public sector – and at the same time bring people back into unionised workplaces and strengthen the trade union movement.

The third area is that of the right to strike. Significant areas of anti-strike and anti-trade union legislation are scheduled for repeal. But these still only take us back to the period of the last Labour government. There is, as John Hendy has repeatedly reminded us, still no legal right to strike in Britain. There never has been. Political strikes, general strikes, solidarity strikes, remain illegal – and technically so do any strikes when not conducted in specific conditions as laid down by statute and hence protected from civil law liability.

These are all key issues for the trade union and labour movement for the coming period'.

IF YOU ONLY HAVE A HAMMER, EVERYTHING AROUND YOU WILL LOOK LIKE A NAIL.[1] *THE ISRAELI PEACE MOVEMENT SINCE OCTOBER 7TH 2023: POSITIONS, CHALLENGES, AND PROSPECTS FOR THE FUTURE*

DANA MILLS

Dana Mills joined Peace Now Youth when she was thirteen, in 1993. After receiving her doctorate from Oxford and writing four books, she returned to Israel-Palestine, where she works in civil society, among other positions, as Director of Peace Now. She is currently the Resource Development Manager of +972 Magazine, an independent collective of Palestinian and Israeli journalists.

Abstract

This article looks at the Israeli peace movement in its historical context while surveying its challenges and possibilities after the October 7th Hamas attacks and in the light of the ongoing situation in Gaza. The article focuses on women's activism and conscientious objectors as two sources of activism which would be able to offer an alternative to militarism. Lastly, the article surveys the discourse on solutions before and after October 7th.

Keywords

Peace activism, women's activism, conscientious objection, two-state solution, political imaginary.

On a crisp autumn day in October 2022, a bus full of Israeli peace activists travelled from Tel Aviv to the Occupied West Bank. We were heading there to help in the olive harvest. State sponsored settler violence had been escalating steadily and made it nearly impossible for the Palestinian communities to harvest. The presence of Jewish activists had a twofold objective; first, as a gesture of solidarity, giving helping hands for the manual labour of the harvest. More significantly, the settlers were more hesitant to attack Palestinian landowners when Jewish activists were in the near proximity. Debates around Jewish supremacy seem profoundly unnecessary when you

---

1   Quote from the late Vivian Silver, founding member of Women Wage Peace, who was murdered on October 7th. , Israeli Canadian Peace Activist Killed in amas Attack, Democracy Now, 20 November 2023, https://www.democracynow.org/2023/11/20/vivian_silver, accessed 17 November 2024.

are aware that your very bodily presence is a human shield against violence, that other people, who belong to your religion, will stop their violence towards people and nature because you are there.

Not far from our destination, we suddenly noticed an Israeli army jeep. Two soldiers signaled to us to stop. They notified us that the area was 'a closed army territory'. This means no one besides the Israeli military is allowed forward. Not Palestinians, not activists. The Israeli Military does not need to give a reason for such a motion. 'Security reasons' suffice. And a whole community's life changes.

We did not give up. We went around by alternative routes and made it to the olive harvest. We stayed a shorter while than we had planned; it was Friday, and prayers were called for the harvesters. As we were ushered back on our bus to Tel Aviv I reflected on the absurdity and violence of it all. The military presence, the settlers, jeering at us as we harvested, the joint lunch which felt like a possibility yet to be realised, working together, Israelis and Palestinians, focusing on taking fruit from the land, committing to the joint actions involved.

A year later, in October 2023, I found myself reflecting on that day. Even within the context of both the settlers and the Israeli military's violence that we had experienced then, that memory of harvesting together, felt like a long-departed dream. Under the fog of war of Israel's bombardment of Gaza there was even a starker escalation of settler violence. As much of the military had been re-deployed to Gaza, only the most zealous soldiers remained in the Occupied West Bank, forming violent militias together with the settlers 1 often using formal military uniforms while patrolling Palestinian villages, violating property, pillaging resources, and enacting violence on communities.

At the time of writing this article (December 2024), over 45,000 women and men have been killed in Israeli attacks on Gaza. The International Court of Justice (ICJ) is currently discussing South Africa's petition against the Israel government under the Genocide Prevention Convention. And seventeen communities have been evicted from the West Bank by state sponsored settler violence. Under these conditions, the role and presence of an Israeli peace movement seems nearly impossible. Yet, perhaps paradoxically, more necessary than ever.

This article will discuss the role and challenges of the Israeli peace movement since 7 October 2023. It will start by mapping the peace movement both in its historical and contemporary contexts. It will then proceed to focus on two key elements that have been continually present within the peace movement as well as crucially after October 7th; the women's peace movement and conscientious objectors. Then the article will conclude by looking at the situation regarding the discourse around solutions at this moment in time. And the article will map some suggestions for possible directions forward. It will also consider what might move the Israeli public towards a peaceful end to the occupation and apartheid regime, beyond a much necessary ceasefire in Gaza.

Much of the article will focus on the Jewish peace movement, though some of it will examine some attempts for peace work together with Palestinian organisations or activists. Especially after October 7th, there has been a crackdown on dissent and anti- war advocacy among Palestinian citizens of Israel. This means that advocating a vocal position against the war and for peace has become an even more dangerous position to hold. Thus, the scarce,

---

1   Hamdan Ballal al-Huraini, Settler-soldier militias threaten Susiya with death and displacement, +972 Magazine, 31 October 2023, https://www.972mag.com/susiya-settler-soldier-militia-displacement/ accessed on 12 November 2024.

yet important, attempts for joint work will be noted here, despite them being largely under the radar and far less public than Jewish initiatives.

The Israeli peace movement: historical context

Influential lawyer and advocate Daniel Seidemann notes that the Israeli peace movement was founded as a response to the 1967 war, and specifically, to the Greater Israel movement, which sought to bring Jewish presence to the newly Occupied Territories, first through the settlement movement and then through formal annexation plans. The dialectic of the peace movement vis-à-vis the Greater Israel movement remains to this day. Seidemann also marks a formal moment in the formation of the peace movement in the foundation of Peace Now.[2]

In March 1978, in the wake of the 1973 war, 348 officers sent Prime Minister Menachem Begin a letter[3] which urged him to change the direction of his policy towards the arc of peace. This letter is the reference point for the foundation of Peace Now. Peace Now gained more strength during the Lebanon War of 1982, against which it had organised what was then the largest mass demonstration for peace and against war. This was known as the 'four hundred thousand' demonstration referring to its estimated size. Peace Now has remained a marker in the field of the Israeli-Palestinian peace movement map, with its focus changing to the West Bank, and specifically to the settlement enterprise there. This has involved embarking on an ambitious project to map and archive all settler activity in the West Bank, through its 'settlement watch' project which is a trusted resource for the mapping of settlement activity.

Since its first decade as a mass movement, Peace Now has retained its central position in Israeli peace activism. Against the backdrop of several wars: 1973, 1982 and then the first Intifada, it had seen a different challenge and opportunity in the 1990s when the Oslo accords were signed, and then, in the wake of the murder of Prime Minister Yitzhak Rabin. In addition to the political movement, a youth movement sought to bring Israeli and Palestinian youth together in 'people to people' dialogues, in which young people from both sides of the border (as it had been framed then) were brought to shared spaces in order to get to know each other and form relationships.

Peace Now has been a focal point for the Israeli peace movement since its foundation. Many other organizations have been founded since, Combatants for Peace (which is comprised of former combatants on both sides of the border), the Parents Circle (which is comprised of bereaved Israeli and Palestinian families), the Geneva Initiative (a lobby group pressurising for the two-state solution), to name but a few. All these organizations, and many other smaller organizations, focus mainly on the West Bank as key for any political resolution for ending the conflict. Gaza has been, by and large, absent from discourse around peace in Israeli society, and hidden from the Israeli psyche in the eighteen years in which it had been under blockade. The peace movement has, in the main, also ignored Palestinian citizens of Israel, who were not seen as part of the Palestinian quest for sovereignty or indeed parties in peace negotiation. The Nakba[4] (the violence which accompanied the creation of the state of Israel) was hardly discussed in Jewish circles, let alone recognised by peace activists. 1967 was a watershed moment in the founding of the Israeli peace movement and had remained so.

---

2   Daniel Seidemann, The Israeli Peace Movement: Origins, Impact, and Prospects, Harvard International Review, 7, 3 (December 1984), 22-23.

3   The officers' letter, available on Americans for Peace Now https://peacenow.org/entry. php?id=2230, accessed on 15 November 2024.

4   For a discussion of changes in discussion of the Nakba in Zionist and mainstream discourse, see Ben Reiff, the Israeli left has broken the Nakba taboo. Will the right of return be next? +972 Magazine, 23 June 2022, https://www.972mag.com/israeli-left-nakba-taboo-return/ accessed on 20 November 2024.

In the last part of this article, I examine some changes in the composition of the peace movement in recent times. In the next section, I investigate one key element of the peace movement that has undergone a seismic shift since October 7th: the women's movement.

Women and the Israeli peace movement before and after October 7th 2023

The 7 October 2023 was a traumatic moment for Israeli Jews. For many Palestinians, it showed the discrepancy in power relations. Israel enacts many 'October 7th' attacks on Palestinians, the state itself taking people into administrative custody with no due process, settlers and army going on killing sprees and enacting rampages of violence on Palestinians with no explanation and no accountability to law enforcement authorities. The death toll in Gaza is around 45,000 at the time of writing (December 2024), around 11,000 children and 6,000 women amongst them. The suffering inflicted by the Israeli government on Gaza is unimaginable and feels endless.

After Hamas militants killed over 1,200 people and abducted over 200 to Gaza, Israeli Jewish society was in shock. The Israeli Military defense had failed to come even after there had been explicit cries for help (notably, from female soldiers acting as 'observants' who had understood what was unfolding before senior military staff did so and warned central intelligence in real time about the events). Another element which is not often discussed - yet has been used in fascist discourse discussing the events of October 7th - was the high percentage of those targeted by the Hamas attack who had been central figures in the Israeli peace movement. The cousin of the previous chair of B'tselem, Israel's leading human rights organization, was kidnapped to Gaza. Ziv Stahl, Director of Yesh Din, another Non-Governmental Organisation (NGO) which deals with monitoring settler violence in the West Bank, lost her sister-in-law in the Hamas led attack and spent the attack in a bomb shelter in her childhood home[5]. Many other rank and file activists from an organization called 'the road to recovery', which transports sick patients, especially children, from the Gaza border to Israeli hospitals, found themselves implicated in the attacks. This made right wing activists' discourse on the naive, well-meaning lefties who still believed in peace, despite being in constant danger, take hold swiftly. Fascism was spreading like wildfire in the harmattan wind.

One of the most famous symbols of the casualties of October 7th, and indeed of the Israeli peace movement, was Vivian Silver. Silver had been a leading light in the peace movement for decades. Missing after October 7th, it had been assumed that Silver had been kidnapped to Gaza. On 13 November it was confirmed that she had been killed in the attack and her remains were identified in Kibbutz Be'eri.[6]

Vivian was a founding member and central activist in 'Women Wage Peace', an organization founded in the aftermath of the 2014 war in Gaza, which sought to bring Israeli and Palestinian women together (as well as other women from Druze and Bedouin communities). The rationale of Women Wage Peace, and indeed of the women's peace movement, stems from the United Nations (UN) resolution UNSCR 1325 which affirms that peace and security efforts are more sustainable when women are equal partners in the prevention of violent conflict, the delivery of relief and recovery efforts and in the forging of lasting peace.

There have been different approaches to the necessity of women's roles in peacebuilding processes. Some accentuate their maternal roles and thus responsibility to the troops.

5   Orly Noy, Listen to Israeli survivors, they don't want revenge, +972 Magazine, 25 October 2023, https://www.972mag.com/israeli-survivors-hamas-massacre-revenge/, accessed 20 November 2024.

6   Samah Salaime, a tribute to Vivian, +972 Magazine, 14 November 2023, https://www.972mag.com/vivian-silver-tribute-peace-activist/, accessed 30 November 2024.

Others emphasise not their vulnerability but their agency in peacebuilding processes, through the concept of 'inclusive security', as well as their ability to bridge seemingly unbridgeable divides.[7] But women's movements have been central in the Israeli peace movement since its earliest days. The roots of this movement in Israel comes from 'women in black', founded against the backdrop of the first Intifada (uprising), and 'women in green', founded in 1993, against the backdrop of the Oslo accords.[8] Whereas women in black protested the wrongs of occupation and apartheid, women in green protested the concessions the Israeli government was prepared to make to Arafat. This divergence shows the aporia in the assumption that women will naturally gravitate towards peace and nonviolence. Women in black focused on protest within Israeli society, but other women's peace movements sought to create cross-border dialogues as well as to organise joint events such as a large peace conference in 1991.[9] Many of those movements were founded after historical moments, such as Women Wage Peace which was founded in 2014, after the first Israeli assault on Gaza following its siege on the Strip.

Women Wage Peace has been a constant force in the Israeli peace movement but gained centrality and prominence following Silver's murder. From the right, it was attacked for its naive and misread perception of reality; Silver opted to live close to the Gaza Strip as she realised the centrality of Gaza for Palestine and wanted to make coexistence her central ethos and praxis. After her death, those sceptical of the possibilities of peace claimed in effect that she had aided her murderers. On the other hand, those who push for peace within Israeli society held on to her message which had become key in the movement. Her unwavering faith in peace, rather than just ending wars, has been carried on by her son, Yonatan Zeigen.

The question of women in the peace movement continues to be central post October 7th and after a year of a genocidal war in Gaza. Women's protests to return the hostages, especially, have been largely unsuccessful in impacting public opinion, however. Several of the hostages' mothers have become public personalities; Einav Zangauker was named one of BBC's 'people of the year' for 2024. The question of women's activism in peace movements unravels both the problematics within the peace movement itself, its limitations within Israeli society (including, specifically, its marginal position in shaping public opinion), but also the problematic within women's activism more broadly. In a militarised heteronormative society, in which women are seen as primarily military wives and mothers, the scope of activism and influence is tied to delimited views of womanhood. At the same time, the significant influence that singular women have had on the movement since October 7th; from Silver to Zankgauker, shows that the prospect for change and mobilisation in Israeli society is slim without these women's movements and activists.

Conscientious objectors after October 7th

A central yet complex element of the Israeli peace movement is the role played by conscientious objectors. Israel has compulsory draft with exceptions only due to religious faith – the ultra-orthodox are exempt, or those with mental health issues. Palestinian citizens of Israel are also exempt from the draft. Many basic elements of Israeli society hinge on military service. First year university students receive a large discount in their fees if they serve in the military (or comparable form of national service, offered to religious women

7   Swanee Hunt and Christina Posa, women waging peace: inclusive security (2011). Foreign Policy, 124 (124), 38.
8   Hunt and Posa, 43.
9   Gila Svirsky, organizing for peace in Israel: why Israeli and Palestinian women want a peace movement of their own, The Women's Review of Books, 21, 12 (September 2004), 25-26.

usually). Israel is a highly militaristic society, with conscientious objectors forming a stern, small and consistent challenge to the centrality of the military in Israeli society.

Noted historian Idith Zertal published an extensive study of the Israeli refusal movement.[10] Drawing on Hannah Arendt's writing during the Eichmann trial, she analyses different movements in different historical periods as foundational in posing a robust ideological alternative to a country that has been fighting one war after another and presenting them all as necessary. Crucially, Zertal illuminates the long-lasting effects of a militarised society on the ability to think critically and challenge mainstream perceptions of security and consequently, peace. One of the reasons that there is a focus here on conscientious objectors is that they remain one of the only groups in Israeli society which present an overarching critique of the militarisation and henceforth an alternative vision for communal life not based around glorification of war and violence.

There are different scopes and varieties of conscientious objection and/or refusal in Israeli society. We can find instances of refusal to obey specific orders within military service itself -- for example, the noted Kafr Qasim massacre in which the Israeli military police killed forty-nine Palestinian civilians after a curfew was placed and some of them had not known of it. The massacre is taught in military historiography as 'an unlawful order' which, it is widely agreed, the soldiers should have refused. Then, there is selective refusal within military service itself, such as refusal to serve in the Occupied West Bank. There is also refusal to return to reserve duty on ideological grounds, which tends to create a substantial impact, especially if those refusing have access to social capital and are able to mobilise this act of refusal further as an act of dissent. All these acts of refusal are part and parcel of the Israeli history of peace activism.[11]

Perhaps the most interesting and most challenging cases of conscientious objection are young people who refuse to join the military altogether. Firstly, at the age of eighteen, refusing the draft requires both a clear ideological stance as well as a willingness to serve time in a military prison. In addition to the formal punishment, Israeli society imposes sanctions on those who refuse to join the military. Whereas the refusal movement is diverse, oftentimes those who choose to use their objection as a public act come from strong support networks, from families with a background in peace activism who support and defend them, and well networked communities in which their act of refusal would not undermine their job prospects. (Many jobs in Israel require military service as a precondition for an application.) There have been some conscientious objectors who have become symbols and leaders in the Israeli left following their act of refusal. Thus, refusing the draft is an act of personal dissent, an act of ostracism for some, and an act of taking leadership for others. It is worthwhile to pause and reflect on the act of refusal in Israel before moving to those who chose to refuse the draft in the context of the current violence.

Israel is a country which was founded on the ruins of collective trauma, and on the Zionist ethos of 'never again' - transforming acts of collective violence enacted towards Jews to acts of violence enacted by Jews. There are seldom any moments in which this foundational ethos is challenged in any substantial way. There are few institutions that have a stronger unifying force in Israeli Jewish society than the military. It is viewed as the great equaliser, a place for bonding from all walks of Jewish life, in which class and ethnicity do not mean

---

10   Idit Zertal, Refusal (Hakibbutz Hameuchad Publishing House Ltd., 2018).
11   Randy Friedman, 'The challenge of selective conscientious objection in Israel', Theoria: A Journal of Social and Political Theory, 109. (2006), The Politics of War (April 2006), 79-99.

anything. (This, of course is widely disputed; elites from Jewish society form elites in the military, whereas working class and Mizrahi Jews form the manual labour class in the military.) There are few who dare to ask what the price is, as a whole, for this unifying ethos; the complete exclusion of Palestinians from this so-called 'melting pot', and the erasure of collective trauma enacted by the Israeli military, namely the ongoing Nakba. Thus, those eighteen-year-olds who refuse to join the military challenge the Israeli military ethos – and consequently the structural impossibility of forming an effort for a just peace – in a foundational and structural way.

October 7th: a traumatic moment

October 7th was a traumatic moment for Israeli Jewish society, which was mobilised by the Israeli government and mainstream media to reenact collective trauma on Jews over and over again. Tales of hiding in closets and safe rooms during Hamas's attacks were retold as proof that the pogroms of yesteryear had not disappeared from our hinterlands (and instead of any reportage or coverage of the strife enacted in the name of the Israeli citizenship in Gaza, which had been absent from mainstream media reportage). Moreover, little discussion was granted to the conditions that were the context for Hamas's attack; eighteen years of siege on the Gaza Strip, a grave humanitarian crisis and almost annual attacks on the Strip by the Israeli military. One of the widest military reserve duties in Israeli history was called immediately, recruiting some 300,000 reserve soldiers to active duty. Meanwhile, many training courses were cut short and cadets repositioned swiftly to combat. Israeli Jewish society rallied round the military, mourning the inevitable losses in life (including on October 7th itself, when women surveillance soldiers who had warned about the attack in real time and were greeted with disbelief; some are still held hostage in Gaza). Israeli society, which in its 'everyday' is highly militarised and militaristic, became, in a way, entirely drafted to combat.

In this climate, the act of refusing the draft has significant weight. The first conscientious objector since October 7th was Tal Mitnik, an American-Israeli who refused and was imprisoned in December 2023.[12] After him Sophia Orr[13] refused the draft. Last, in the first half of the war, Ben Arad[14] refused to join the military, citing Tal Mitnik's refusal as significant for him. There have been, to date, eight conscientious refusers (including one woman, Orr) who have served time in military prisons for refusing to join the Israeli attack on Gaza. These conscientious objectors all reported death threats and other violent responses, especially in the military prison in which they have been incarcerated for refusing to serve. A network of past conscientious objectors provides support and legal aid, but they serve their sentencing alone. They have attracted media interest (both supportive and critical), right-wing protests as well as protests of support, and significantly more international interest than conscientious objectors who have refused in other periods.

In addition to these conscientious objectors, more and more reserve duty soldiers refuse to return to service, some on ideological grounds, including open letters in the press citing the Israeli government's neglect of the hostages and futile assault in Gaza as the reasons for

---

12   Oren Ziv, 'I refuse to take part in a revenge war': Israel jails teen for opposing army draft, 972 Magazine, 28 December 2023, https://www.972mag.com/tal-mitnick-conscientious-objector-israeli-army/, accessed 3 December 2024.

13   Oren Ziv, 'People say I'm naive, antisemitic, a traitor': Israeli teen jailed for draft refusal, +972 Magazine, 26 February 2024, https://www.972mag.com/sofia-orr-conscientious-objector-israeli-army/, accessed 10 November 2024.

14   Oren Ziv, Israeli teen jailed for refusing draft: 'I'm willing to pay a price for my principles', +972 Magazine, 5 April 2024, https://www.972mag.com/ben-arad-conscientious-objector-israeli-army/, accessed 1 December 2024.

their refusal. Then, there is 'grey refusal', reserve duty officers who do not return to service without a public announcement of their refusal. Some do not return to active service for financial reasons, with the state's continuous demands on their time costing them in terms of their time with their families as well as in terms of their loss of income. Overall, the gradual weakening of the military force is perhaps the only response to the centrality of the military ethos in Israel.

Refusals to join militarism (in all its forms), as well as conscientious objection, are still small in Israel. The most forceful power that draws many to the military is the ethos of togetherness, responsibility to the peer group formed in active service and sustained through reserve duty. Still, those who penetrate this web of militarism form a small yet crucial part of the peace movement. By the refusal to join the military ethos and practice so central to Israeli Jewish life, they provide an alternative vision of solidarity, and a possibility to imagine a future not based on perpetual war. The cumulative effects of the various forms of refusal since October 7th present a tear in the shared militarised fabric of Israeli society. In fact, it may be argued that to imagine a truly just peace, the role of those who have refused association with the military in any shape or form will be crucial; they hold the possibility for an alternative imaginary, a way out of the ideational deadlock in Israeli society in which peace plays little to no role.

Solutions not sides: the peace movement and discourse around solutions post October 2023

Perhaps one of the most dramatic changes in the Israeli peace movement, and indeed one of its greatest challenges, is to combine a pragmatic solution to end the apartheid regime and ongoing occupation (the longest in the twentieth century) with activism for peace.

From the 1990s, the Oslo Accord era and the years that had followed it, peace activism in Israel was centered around the two-state solution. Peace Now, especially, positioned itself as advocating 'peace based on the two-state solutions'. Other organizations, such as the Geneva Initiative became lobby groups for the two-state solution.

Two processes have occurred since the 1990s and up to our current times, processes which are perhaps interleaved. First, the centrality of the two-state solution in public discourse has waned. The classic two-state solution (henceforth 2ss) centres its effort on the foundation of an independent Palestinian state residing side by side with an Israeli-Jewish state, based on the 1967 borders and withdrawal from settlements in the West Bank. The 2ss is no longer the unequivocal response to all war, violence, and occupation, however. Even before October 2023, a poll from January 2023 showed an all-time low in support for the 2ss.[15] Indeed, the acceleration of de-facto annexation via settlement building in the West Bank has meant that many, on both sides of the border, see the 2ss solution as non-viable and undesirable. Since October 7th, the 2ss solution has sunk even lower in popularity, shifting from broad disinterest before the attack on Gaza to a stern opposition, after it had occurred.[16]

Second, the equivocation of the peace movement and the defence of a two-state solution, now no longer in the mainstream of public opinion, occurred at the same time as a push for

---

15   Israeli-Palestinian Poll Shows Support for Two-state Solution at All-time Low, available at the Peace Index, 25 January 2023 https://en-social-sciences.tau.ac.il/news/news/peace-inex-haaretz-jan-23, accessed 15 November 2024.

16   One poll states the incredible 65% resistance to the 2ss. Jewish News Syndicate, 65% of Israeli Jews oppose two- state solution post October 7, 24 July 2024, https://www.jns.org/65-of-israeli-jews-oppose-two-state-solution-post-oct-7/, accessed 2 November 2024.

the 'NGO-isation' and neo-liberalisation of the peace movement. Peace Now, for instance, now has a salaried team, most of whose budget comes from donations from overseas, rather than remaining a mass grassroots movement, as it had been in the 1980s. The fact that much of the peace movement arose from elites no longer key in Israeli society, elites who had ignored other tensions within Israeli society itself (such as racism towards Mizrahi Jews and the oppression of Palestinian citizens of Israel -- two issues that were entirely absent from its agenda) meant that many in Israeli society came to see the historical peace movement as obsolete and no longer responsive to their concerns. But an alternative has failed to emerge.

The classic 2ss, which is by and large Zionist (i.e. supporting the need for a Jewish state), does not recognise that the Nakba has been centrally important from the origins of the Israeli state. 1948 was the watershed moment rather than the dramatic occupation of 1967. Ethnic cleansing has been on ongoing process, rather than simply being unleashed by the events of 1967. The classic 2ss does not recognize the right of return nor the oppression of Palestinian citizens of Israel, often termed as 'Arabs', colloquially, and their national identity and indeed affinity with Palestinians in the West Bank and Gaza, often their immediate family members, whitewashed. Perhaps one of the biggest crises of these movements has been in May 2021, when attacks from Gaza occurred in tandem with unrest in the so-called 'mixed cities' within Israel itself as defined within its 1948 borders, often presented as beacons of cohabitation and yet in which Palestinian identity is constantly erased, and communal life has been under attack from Jewish populations there. So, 2ss has come to be seen as having little to offer; it was not discussing Gaza, nor was it taking into account the ongoing oppression of Palestinians within Israel's 1948 borders.

The response to this crisis of the peace movement, that had occurred long before the Hamas October 7th attacks has been twofold. On the one hand, organisations that challenged the centrality of 2ss were founded. Specifically, One Land for All, which advocates for a federation (without requiring settlements' evictions, while recognizing the Nakba, the right of return and discussing Gaza as part of any solution). The organisation has garnered significant interest, especially since October 7th, and its directors and public personae have become a public voice for the peace movement, showing the push away from the classic 2ss.

On the other hand, over the past few years, and especially since the events of May 2021, the success of Standing Together, a popular movement modelled on the British movement Momentum, has grown. The movement is centered around joint actions of Palestinians and Jews within 1948 Israel, while advocating for the two-state solution but mobilising actions from below. It is proudly populist, countering the NGO-isation and neoliberalism of other segments of the peace movement, and boasts a socialist agenda as a central ethos and praxis. Standing Together has grown in its influence both locally and internationally. It is especially vital in areas in which Palestinians and Jews live closely by and seek locations for collective action together which are still sorely absent from civil society. Since October 7th Standing Together has also been among the only voices connecting Palestinians within Israel's 1948 borders to the attempt to stop the violence in Gaza. Specifically, one of its most successful campaigns has been a mutual aid campaign to stop starvation in Gaza.

At the same time, within certain circles, mainly non-Zionist or anti-Zionist, there is a growing interest in a one-state solution, in which equal citizenship for all between the river and the sea would replace the current apartheid regime which is seeping into a Jewish one-state solution: ethnic cleansing in the West Bank and Gaza, Jewish supremacy as an underlying principle and continual denial of rights from all Palestinians based on a tiered system of citizenship.

It would be most accurate to state, perhaps, that most Jewish Israelis see the egalitarian one-state solution as utopia at best, undesirable at worst. However, there are many Israelis, voters of the Zionist left and centre parties, who wish to preserve Jewish supremacy and utilise the 2ss to advocate separation between Palestinians and Jews rather than coexistence. The other discussed solutions, namely confederation and 2ss, are mostly non-issues in Israeli public discourse. Even left-wing parties have pushed those matters away from their election campaigns and they are rarely disputed in the press or in popular discourse. Indeed, the word 'peace' is absent from our hinterlands, perhaps when we need it the most. The waning of discussions of solutions has occurred in tandem with the loss of faith that peace is even possible and can be achieved through diplomatic discussions and political agency. Many Israelis can only imagine the end of the occupation either through international pressure or, more likely, cannot imagine it at all, and believe that they are destined to live in never-ending war.

Wanted: a new political imaginary

For two years in a row, the olive harvest, which was once a celebration of connection to land and community, often punctuated by singing songs and dancing dabkeh, the Palestinian national dance, has become a lonely and dangerous endeavour.[17] Communal songs are replaced by the sounds of shrapnel, bombs and Israeli fighter planes. In the West Bank, too, the olive harvest has been underway in the shadow of escalating settler attacks. There is something deeply symbolic when this practice, that had been once a space for communities to come together, and at times, to host Israeli peace activists, has become so precarious and dangerous. Our bus stopping at the entrance to where the harvesting took place in October 2022 feels like a vaguely optimistic memory.

This article has focused on the changes in mainstream peace activism since October 7th, with a specific spotlight on those areas of peace activism which are seen as key for any public mobilisation against militarism and war. There are, of course, many more examples of resistance to the Israeli assault on Gaza and violence in the West Bank; from 'protective presence', Israeli and international activists who go to areas in danger of ethnic cleansing in an attempt to stop military forces and settlers from erasing Palestinian presence off the ground, especially, in the South Hebron Hills. There are examples of Israeli activists who join Palestinian resistance (one noted example is Jonathan Pollak, who has been jailed multiple times for his activism in solidarity and together with Palestinians). But these remain small organising efforts, not least because they put the Israelis who choose to take this path in danger; the danger that accompanies the lives of Palestinians under occupation, day in, day out.

The mainstream, older peace movement, is mostly Zionist, representative of the elites no longer influencing Israeli society. The rise of religious Zionism which attempts to weaken the influence of the Supreme Court (commonly known as 'the judicial overhaul'), signified a conscious attempt to overthrow those elites in favor of an overtly religious Jewish supremacist elite. The attack on the old elites also included attacks on civil society, including attacks on the peace movement; draconic laws circumscribing funding received from foreign countries and organisations (which comprise the bulk of civil society, organized around NGOs); public campaigns against leaders who are termed as 'traitors' for showing even the smallest solidarity with Palestinians or belief that those are equal to them; and demonising the word 'peace' in and of itself.

---

17   Taghreed Ali and Ibtisam Mahdi, For Gaza's olive farmers, the war has left little to salvage, +972 Magazine, 19 November 2024, https://www.972mag.com/gaza-olive-farmers-harvest-war/, accessed on 3 December 2024.

The official (and unofficial) attacks on the peace movement; the waning of faith in any kind of political resolution and indeed, the waning in belief that the occupation and apartheid must indeed end; and the unignorable fact of complicity towards the war crimes in Gaza within the Israeli Jewish public seem like plausible causes for despair. It is hard to write about a new imaginary, a new vista for peace, so sorely needed at this moment in time.

'If you only have a hammer, everything around you will look like a nail,' said the late Vivian Silver. It feels like the Israeli peace movement has been working mostly with hammers and thus unavoidably becoming bruised with many nails. However, as long as some people, even a few, raise their voices against war and violence; as long as young people refuse to join militarized society; as long as women challenge the hegemonic militarised mainstream discourse and provide an alternative vision, we might find something other than a hammer to mend the broken Israeli peace movement, and indeed, our hearts. Peace activism that sees peace as inevitable rather than utopian, that does not start from the assumption we are forever to live on our swords, that seeks to expand the collaboration with Palestinians from all parts of the land between the river and the sea, that sees the importance of coexistence as well as co-resistance against apartheid is the way forward, away from hammers.

MARXISM, IMPERIALISM AND NATIONAL LIBERATION BASED ON THE TRANSCRIPT OF A LECTURE AT MARX MEMORIAL LIBRARY AND WORKERS' SCHOOL ON 23 NOVEMBER 2024

OFER CASSIF

Ofer Cassif is a member of the political bureau of the Israeli Communist Party (MAKI) and a member of the Knesset, the Israeli Parliament, as a representative of the Hadash alliance (Democratic Front for Peace and Equality) of which MAKI is a part. He has been barred from the Knesset for six months for, in essence, opposing the current line of the Israeli Government.

Abstract

Ofer Cassif, a Communist member of the Israeli parliament, assesses the shift of the Israeli state towards fascism in the wake of genocide in Gaza, considers the remaining bases of resistance to it and stresses the importance of international solidarity. He uses the writings of Marx and Lenin to interrogate and understand the relative merits of a 'one state' and 'two state' solution as applied to Israel and Palestine.

Keywords

Israel. Imperialism. Marx and Lenin and the two state solution.

Editor's note

This lecture was given in November 2024. Since then there have been and continue to be many changes in the situation in the Middle East. But the basic arguments that Ofer Cassif set out in this lecture remain relevant. He began with the background to his own suspension from the Israeli parliament, the Knesset.

This, he said, 'was obviously a political issue, not a personal one. So, I would like to start with this in order to give you a wider picture of the political situation both in the occupied Palestinian territories but primarily within Israel proper. I do so because I think we are on the verge of a serious transformation of Israeli society and the Israeli State apparatus into a full-fledged fascist dictatorship.

We have already passed many cornerstones that might define Israel as a fascist state but we are still not at the end of that road. Metaphorically, we are already deep in the bottom of the abyss but in the bottom of the abyss there is a lot of mud. We have begun to sink in the mud but still our nose is above it. However, we are very close to feeling the mud within our nose. I will try to explain, as briefly as possible, what the situation is in Israel currently.

Genocide in Gaza

Let me begin with the obvious. Israel has not been waging a war against Hamas but a genocide, a war against humanity in Gaza. At the same time, our party, Maki, is also clearly and explicitly against the massacre committed by Hamas. I want to be very clear about this. What Hamas did on 7 October 2023 was a vicious, sadistic war crime, a crime against humanity.

In the area where the massacre took place in the south of Israel there are many kibbutz and still some activists against the occupation who oppose the oppression of the Palestinian people and the siege that was already taking place in Gaza on the eve of the massacre. Some of them were, and are, associated with Hadash and the Communist Party. Some indeed are comrades. A dear friend of mine, who was associated with Hadash, was murdered with her husband literally minutes after she texted me from the security room in her kibbutz. This crime should never be tolerated. What Hamas did was an anti-human and definitely anti-Communist crime, as we, in the Communist Party and Hadash, have said many times since October 7th 2023.

Israel, however, has been guilty of crimes against Palestinians since the Nakba of 1948 along with all the crimes that have been committed since the occupation of 1967. By the same token, the crimes that Israel has been committing since October 7th cannot be justified by the massacre of October 7th. There is no justification for either sets of crimes.

The crime of genocide is very clearly being committed. You must be blind, especially morally blind, to ignore the real facts of the situation in Gaza, an assault that has been going on for more than a year. This genocide, the atrocities, the crimes against humanity are war crimes and have nothing to do with the security of Israel or the Israelis. They have nothing to do, even, with the release of the Israeli hostages who have been dying in agony in the hands of Hamas in Gaza. We should remember that the hostages are victims too.

The genocide which we have been witnessing in these terrible months is not only to be described in terms of the death toll – although this is unimaginable. We are talking now [in November 2024] about more than 50,000 victims. The numbers are eventually going to be higher, much higher apparently. There are some speculations that we are going to see about 185,000 deaths overall. There are many bodies under the rubble and many others not identified. Hopefully not. But 50,000 is the minimum that we know about at the moment.

But it is not only about the death toll. The Gaza Strip hardly exists now. We are talking about thousands and thousands, probably hundreds of thousands of Palestinians who have been seriously wounded and thousands who lost limbs, not to mention the trauma, the psychological impact. The vast majority of the victims, more than 70 percent, are innocent civilians that have had nothing to do with October 7th, and who have nothing to do with Hamas. Some of them were actually peace activists.

I have a good friend, Dr. Izzeldin Yash, for example, who lost three daughters about sixteen years ago in yet another Israeli assault on Gaza. A direct missile hit his house. He has told me just recently that in the current genocide, no less than thirty members of his extended family were killed. Yet he's a man of peace. After his daughters were killed, he published a book titled 'I Shall Not Hate: A Gaza Doctor's Journey on the Road to Peace and Human Dignity'. And he continues with this stance of his as a man of peace. He is not the only one either. There are thousands.

You will know that the Israeli Government and many members of the Coalition, and of the Opposition, not to mention the Israeli public at large, have been arguing that there are no innocents in Gaza. That reminds me of another era and another place in which the attitude was exactly the same in regard to my people, the Jewish people. You can imagine what I mean by that. Of course there are innocents in Gaza. The vast majority are innocents, as in each and every other normal society on earth. But a process of demonising the Palestinians is taking place - in order to justify the carnage, the destruction and torture that Palestinians have been going through.

It is not only about the death toll. Nor is it about the numbers of people who have been and are being traumatised. Entire neighbourhoods and villages have been wiped out. Hospitals were directly targeted and demolished as well as religious institutions, mosques, and churches and, of course, people's houses. And there has been starvation. People have been starving in Gaza for months, including children and babies. There's a phenomenon of death among newborn babies because they have no food. Their mothers cannot feed them with milk; they cannot produce milk because they themselves do not have adequate nutrition to do so. How can anyone refer to this situation as anything other than a genocide? That's what's going on in Gaza.

But you cannot even say that in Israel. That's the main reason why I've been suspended from the Knesset - because I insisted on telling the truth and, as well, to representing with my comrades the public who voted for us and for me as part of the list - in order specifically to pursue these values.

Meanwhile, under the screen of that genocide, ethnic cleansing is also going on in the West Bank. More than twenty communities, especially of farmers and shepherds, have perished because of settlers' violence. Settlers have been invading Palestinian communities under the auspices of the occupation forces and sometimes their active participation. More than twenty communities could not stand it anymore and had to flee.

The situation within Israel itself and Israel's imperialist supporters

First, I should like to say a few words about the ongoing situation within Israel and then something about the involvement of the imperialist powers, especially of the United States. It is important to understand the sources of support that have enabled the Israeli government to pursue these crimes.

Israel, it should be emphasised, was never a real democracy. You cannot cling to a definition of a state as a democracy that defines it as belonging to one specific ethnic or national group and do so despite the fact there is a minority belonging to another group. Modern democracy is based on the idea of equality and equal rights. But the state of Israel is defined by, and has been acting upon, the idea of Jewish political supremacy. There are privileges and rights to which only Jews are entitled. And what is going on now under the guise of fighting terrorism since October 7th is to turn Israel into, as I said before, a fascist dictatorship.

First of all, there is systematic political persecution of anyone who dares to raise a voice against the genocide, against the occupation, and even just against the government – including demonstrators against the genocide. And demonstrators who do take to the streets to struggle for justice and the release of the hostages have been beaten by the police. The police force is now acting as if it was, or perhaps it is, a private militia of the Government and of the Minister of National Security rather than an organisation that is supposed to serve the people. People have been arrested for posts and tweets that expressed sorrow or sympathy for the people of Gaza. People have lost their jobs, their places in universities. There are so many examples.

I would like to make some reference to imperialist involvements and their impact on the right of Palestinians to national self-determination, starting with a quotation from something that Lenin wrote - and he wrote a lot about national self-determination and imperialism. One of his most important statements was his insistence that 'the essence of imperialism is the distinction between the oppressed and the oppressive nations. This distinction is essential in order to pursue the revolutionary struggle against imperialism.'

Today, in terms of national oppression, there are, along with the ongoing genocide in Gaza and ethnic cleansing in the West Bank, massacres and homicides in Lebanon. Forty villages have been entirely wiped off the earth in Southern Lebanon. None of this could not have happened without the assistance of US imperialism and its proxies in Europe. It is not only that the US has supported the government of Israel throughout the last year. It has also been providing the arms and serving the interests of the weapons industry in the United States.

This is exactly what Lenin noted more than a hundred years ago. There are fundamental contradictions between the interests of imperialism and peoples' rights to national self-determination. So, we can see here that the struggle of the Palestinian people - against the genocide, against the occupation, and against the oppression of the Palestinian minority within the state of Israel proper - is also part of the wider struggle against imperialism. We cannot distinguish between the two. If we want to struggle against imperialism and oppression by the imperialist powers, we must endorse the Palestinian struggle for liberation.

That does not mean that we must endorse each and every means of that struggle. Definitely not. As I said before, we are totally against the massacre committed by Hamas. There are things we cannot tolerate. Bu if we want to be against imperialism, we must support that aim of Palestinian liberation.

Ways forward: the two-state solution

I would like to make two points about this. The first is that we still support the two-state solution. I want to explain why.

It is because no other scenario is realistic at the moment. There is no immediate way forward to a one-state solution. In principle, ideologically speaking, I do not have any difference with the goal of a one-state. But we in Hadash and the Communist Party do believe that under the present circumstances, even before October 7th, let alone after, there is no immediate way forward to a one-state solution.

To explain further. Many years ago, even before I was first elected to the Knesset, I had a meeting with Bassam al-Salhi, Secretary General of the Palestinian People's Party (PPP), previously the Palestinian Communist Party. A few weeks later I had a meeting with Nayef Hawatmeh, the Secretary General of the Democratic Front for the Liberation of Palestine. The Palestinian People's Party has always supported the aim of the two-state solution while the Democratic Front has supported the one-state solution ever since it was established in the late sixties.

In the meeting with Bassam al-Salhi of the People's Party we discussed the aim of a one-state solution versus a two-state solution. He said that they had always embraced the two-state solution but that if, after a two-state solution had been achieved, both parties could indeed agree and a one-state solution could be developed based upon mutual consent, it would have their support. In a subsequent meeting with Nayef Hawatmeh, he said that although they supported the one-state solution, they did also understand that the two-state phase must come first.

So those two opposite poles, both within the left side of the political spectrum, each understood the importance of aiming for the two-state solution, even if this was just a stage towards a one-state solution in the future. But, for now, we cannot give up on the two-state solution.

Lenin's writings have been very relevant in stressing the right of nations not only to self-determination but also the right to secede.[1] Leaving an existing statehood, that of an oppressor nation, might be the best solution because it would lead to the liberation of an oppressed people. In turn it would also facilitate moves in the direction of socialist and anti-imperialist struggles. It would do so, first, because it would reduce hostility between the proletariats of both peoples – a hostility that makes it much easier for the bourgeoisies of each side to mobilise such hostility for their own ends. Secondly, once there is secession and peace achieved, it would create the circumstances in which the proletariats of both sides can concentrate on the class struggle against their respective exploiters.

So, in my view, that is another reason why the liberation of the Palestinian people to form an independent Palestinian state, covering all the territories that Israel occupied in 1967, is the right solution under the present circumstances. And, as I have already explained, this is indeed another part of the struggle against imperialism as well.

Marx himself reflected on these questions. In his first analysis of the Irish Question, he considered that there must be a common class struggle of the proletarians in both Ireland and England against their exploiters, against both the English and Irish bourgeoisies. But he changed his mind subsequently and took the view that the Irish people must first be liberated from British imperialism. They must form their own independent state so as to reduce that hostility between the two national proletariats and this would pave the way for the proletarians of both nations to deal with their own bourgeoisies.[2]

So, to conclude with this specific point, we cannot separate the Palestinian struggle for liberation and national self-determination in the form of statehood from the wider struggle against imperialism and particularly American imperialism.

Final reflections

There is just one other question that is important for me to raise.

Many people have said that there is no opposition in Israel and in doing so they include the Israeli Parliament. However, this is incorrect. There is opposition. It is both in the streets and also within the Parliament – although the only consistent, truthful opposition is by Hadash, the coalition of the Communist Party and its allies largely within the Palestinian community in Israel. Hadash was the only grouping in the Knesset that opposed the attack on Gaza from day one, even before it was clear how massive and fundamental that attack would be.

Even before the attack had fully begun, both in the Parliament and outside, on social networks and other places, we denounced the coming assault on Gaza. We said that this

---

1   Lenin, 'The Right of Nations to Self-Determination' (February-May 1914), Collected Works, Vol. 20, Progress, Moscow, 1972.

2   Marx to Engels 10 December 1869, Marx Engels, Collected Works, Vol. 43 (Moscow), pp.396-399.

would result in the deaths of the hostages. Unfortunately it has done so. We said that it would also lead to a genocidal massacre in Gaza.

Up till now we have been the only opposition in Parliament. I'll give you a few examples. A defining issue was the decision by International Criminal Court (ICC) to issue arrest warrants against Gallant and Netanyahu. The vast majority of opposition parties immediately opposed it. This was not only Yesh Atid which is the biggest faction at the moment and Benjamin Gant's party, which has always been a kind of a camouflage for Netanyahu and a collaborator with him. It also included the chair of the ex-Meretz party and the Labour Party, the new party called the Democrats, which is a combination of Labour and ex-Meretz, previously called the Leftist Zionist party. The chair this party publicly posted an accusation against the ICC. We were the only ones who published support for the ICC decision.

In the Parliament there was an attempt to impeach me because I signed a petition in support of South African appeal to ICJ (International Court of Justice). I was accused of supporting violence and terrorism against Israel because I signed a petition against violence. George Orwell would not have believed that something like that could happen.

And I was almost impeached. They needed ninety members to carry the vote in favour. They had eighty-six. If you make a very simple calculation you can see that sixty-four votes were from the governing coalition and twenty-two were from the opposition. A third of Attid's group voted for the impeachment as did half of Gantz's party. The rest of them, those who did not want to vote for the impeachment, nonetheless said that I should not be a member of the Knesset and celebrated my suspension. They claimed the only reason they did not vote in favour of my impeachment was because it was not being done within the correct legal procedure. That's the opposition for you.

But there is opposition on the streets. We in Hadash have succeeded in organising more than sixty anti-occupation, anti-genocide, human rights organisations, mostly civil rights and civil society movements, that has for many months now has been very active in demonstrations against the genocide. Sometimes these have been in collaboration with some of the families of the hostages who oppose the genocide, families who lost their dear ones on October 7th and people whose relatives were killed by Hamas, some very close to us politically. There have therefore been huge demonstrations: not enough, not big enough, but still big demonstrations every Saturday against the Government, against the genocide and for releasing the hostages.

There have also been meetings, including meetings to give evidence regarding the ordeal that people have been going through, Palestinians and Israelis alike. People who lost their dear ones come together to speak about their loss, to build bridges between the nations, between peoples, to stop those crimes and atrocities.

But of course, and I finish with this, we do need international support. Without such support from the international community, we are doomed because the political persecution which, as I said, is on the rise, is going to target us very soon. And I mean target physically. We have already been beaten by the police during demonstrations and people have been arrested for nothing. And there have been attempts to bar Hadash and all Arab parties from participating in elections. That would mean that the extreme fascist right could rule for good.

So, we do need your assistance. We need to stop the genocide, and we need to liberate the Palestinians. This is also, Hadash argues, in the interests of the liberation of Israelis themselves. What I've been saying here is not against the interest of the Israelis. The situation between the Palestinians and the Israelis is not the situation of a zero-sum game, in which, if one wins, the other necessarily loses. Exactly the opposite. The situation is either a win-win or a lose-lose situation. Either both peoples win by achieving peace - a just one, which, of course, by definition, means ending the occupation. Or there will be a lose-lose situation by which both peoples are going to perish.

So we do need your help. We do need your support in different ways, including pressure on your own government. We must stand up and say stop the genocide, stop the crimes and end the occupation. Both peoples deserve better'.

WHAT CAN PALESTINIANS EXPECT FROM TRUMP?

AQEL TAQAS

Aqel Taqas is Coordinator for International Relations for the Palestinian Peoples Party and a member of the secretariat of the World Peace Council. He is also a doctor who lives and works on the West Bank. The Palestinian Peoples Party was formerly the Palestinian Communist Party. Until recently it held the Labour portfolio in the Palestinian Authority government.

Abstract

This article anchors its analysis in a history of imperialist dominance across the Middle East since the First World War, the region's territorial division based on the 1916 treaty between Britain and France and, after the 1948 Nakba, the Israeli state's growing alliance with the United States and their joint role in maintaining imperialist control across the Middle East. It warns against the wider consequences of Israel's assault on Gaza and Lebanon, stresses the enormity of the civilian casualties and the urgency of securing peace on the basis of the 1967 UN resolutions and the establishment of two states, of Palestine and Israel, based on pre-1967 borders.

Keywords

Palestine, Imperialism, the Two State Solution

What can Palestinians expect from Trump? When asked this question before Trump took office on 20 January 2025, we replied that there was no reason to be optimistic. Trump will not differ in his second term from Trump in his first. Then it was characterized by hostility to the aspirations of the Palestinian people to self-determination and to any establishment of their own independent state alongside Israel. Then Trump recognized Jerusalem as the capital of Israel and moved his country's embassy to it, closed the Palestine Liberation Organization office in Washington and cut funding to UNRWA. He would go further in his second term. It would be the same policy of hostility to the Palestinian people but more aggressive.

Trump did not delay in confirming these expectations. The first order he signed was to cancel some of the formal sanctions taken by his predecessor against some of the most extremist settlers. He then invited Benjamin Netanyahu, accused of war crimes and wanted by an order from the International Criminal Court, to be the first foreign leader to be received in the White House. The direction of his policy was clear.

However, before we delve into the details of Donald Trump's new positions, we must go back a little further. We need to trace the origins of the on-going conflict in the Middle East back more than a hundred years to the end of World War I. At that time Palestine was part of the collapsing Ottoman Empire – with the dominant colonial powers Britain and France.

Well before the end of this war these powers discussed a sharing of the spoils. They reached a secret agreement, known as the Sykes-Picot Agreement – an agreement quickly exposed by the Bolsheviks as they came across the documents in the aftermath of the 1917 October revolution.

This was to control the peoples of the East and to colonise them, sharing their wealth and strategic location. Palestine, Jordan, Iraq, some Gulf countries, Egypt and Sudan were to be subject to British control. Syria, Lebanon and part of North Africa were to be under French control. In the wake of this agreement, on November 2, 1917, the British Foreign Minister Lord Balfour launched a promise to the Zionist movement to work to establish a homeland for the Jews in Palestine. Thus began the tragedy of the Palestinian people. It is one that continues to this day and one that is becoming increasingly bloody and violent.

Imperialism and the division of Palestine

The actual implementation of the Balfour Declaration saw active collaboration between the British Mandate Authority and the Zionist movement. Waves of Jewish immigration to Palestine began. So did the process of controlling the lands of the country's indigenous population. More importantly, the process of arming Zionist gangs by the British army started. These gangs began practicing all forms of terrorism against Palestinians in an attempt to force them to leave their lands, cities and villages. These gangs committed dozens of transgressions between the beginning of the British mandate and the partition decision in 1947 and the establishment of the State of Israel in 1948.

It is worth noting here that at the end of the First World War the Jews owned less than 3% of the land. Thirty years later they were given more than 55% based on the partition resolution by which Israel was established and gained legitimacy. Although initially all attempts to control the land did not succeed in securing more than 6% of the area of historic Palestine, the establishment of the State of Israel and the first Israeli war saw the Israeli government seize half the area on which the Palestinian state was supposed to be established and subjected the remaining area, namely Gaza and the Arab Bank, to the control of Egypt and Jordan, and did so without any geographical continuity between the two regions. The main goal of the imperialist powers allied with the Zionist movement was to prevent the establishment of a Palestinian state and to displace as many Palestinians as possible from their lands to facilitate the realisation of the Zionist movement's dream: that is, to claim that Palestine is a land without a people for a people without a land.

Continuing with the same policy which the Zionist movement had used before the establishment of its state, the new state committed numerous massacres against the Palestinian people in the border villages. Perhaps the most prominent was the Qibya massacre led by Ariel Sharon in October 1953. This was followed by the Khan Younis massacre in 1956 and the Qalqilya and the Kafr Qasim massacres both in 1956. This behaviour characterised the actions of terrorists and this has been tacitly supported by the imperialist powers ever since Israel's establishment – providing political and military cover and in 1956 directly participating in the tripartite aggression against Egypt. The 'Suez' invasion of Egypt, the occupation of Gaza and massacres of the Palestinian people before withdrawal under threat from the Soviet Union.

After the failure of this Tripartite Aggression against Egypt in 1956, the Israeli government launched a new large-scale aggression in June 1967. This targeted three neighboring Arab countries, namely Egypt, Syria and Jordan, and occupied large parts of their territories. The most damaging result of this war was the occupation of the West Bank which completed the occupation of all the historic lands of Palestine.

The outcome saw the annexation of Jerusalem as the eternal and unified capital of Israel and the imposition of military rule on the rest of the West Bank. This caused a new wave of displacement of Palestinians from their lands, the majority of whom were already refugees expelled in 1948, and saw settlers attempt to burn the Al-Aqsa Mosque in 1968. After this the Israeli government began to attack Jordanian and Lebanese territories to pursue Palestinian resistance cells that were established in response to the occupation. This aggression against Jordan continued until 1970 when the Palestinian resistance forces left Jordan after a conflict with the Jordanian regime.

We remember the reaction, represented by the Black September organization, which then became active in response to their removal from Jordan. The Jordanian-Israeli border witnessed a relative calm that continued despite the outbreak of a new war in 1973. Taken at the initiative of Egypt and Syria it took the government of Israel by surprise. At this point the Israeli state almost lost the initiative and would have suffered a major defeat if the United States had not intervened to save it.

However, this did not prevent the Israeli government from continuing to pursue the Palestinian resistance forces. These were now led by Fatah, the largest and largely secular Palestinian organisation that was founded in 1965 and adopted the leadership of the Palestine Liberation Organization (PLO) in 1968 – founded in 1964 under the auspices of the Arab League led by Nasser's Egypt.

The adoption of the 'two-state' approach by Palestinians

In 1974, the PLO, under the leadership of Yasser Arafat, presented the first Palestinian initiative for a solution involving a willingness to establish a state alongside Israel This was through what was called at that time the ten-point program. Yasser Arafat went to the UN General Assembly telling the world that he came with an olive branch. He called on the Assembly to make it possible for him to keep that branch in his hand.

The Israeli government had a different opinion. It rejected the initiative and continued the policy of attacking the PLO in Lebanon – to which country it had moved after expulsion from Jordan in September 1970. This culminated in the Israeli government's full-scale invasion of Lebanon in 1982, besieging its capital Beirut for more than 80 days, without any action from the international community. The Israeli government enjoyed the full support of the Western powers controlling international institutions in order to force resistance forces out of Lebanon. These now moved to a number of Arab countries that agreed to receive them including Tunisia, Yemen, Algeria and Sudan. The Israeli state continued to target the leaders of the Palestinian national movement assassinating them in Tunisia and Syria and some European capitals.

Anwar Sadat, after he assumed the leadership of Egypt, adopted a completely different policy from that of his predecessor, Gamal Abdel Nasser. Sadat declared that Egypt was ready to make peace with Israel because he believed that the key cards were all in the hands of the United States and that he was not ready to fight America. He went to the Israeli Knesset and subsequently signed the Camp David Treaty in 1978. This effectively removed Egypt as a state that would confront the Israeli state at the same that Syria remained committed to the armistice as agreed after the 1973 war. This meant that the Palestinian national movement was now isolated - especially since Lebanon was engaged in a long civil war that lasted for more than 15 years.

However, at the same time there was a new development in Lebanon with the establishment of the Lebanese National Resistance Movement with active participation from the Lebanese Communist Party to halt the Israeli occupation of Lebanese lands. These aggressions have continued for decades – the most recent instance lasting from October 2023 until the time of writing.

In 1987 the first popular uprising took place in Palestine. In the same year Hamas was established. This forced the Israeli government to start negotiations with the PLO and to reach the Oslo accords of 1993. These accords were scheduled to be completed by 1999 with the final settlement of all remaining issues such as Jerusalem, the return of refugees, the borders and questions of security.

The Israeli government, however, used this time to allow more settlements to be built and to construct the Wall across the West Bank. It took no steps towards a solution. Again, in doing so it had the full support of the US and other governments in the West. The Israeli Knesset took the opportunity to vote through the so-called nationality law which gives the right of self-determination in historic Palestine only to Jews. This year it passed another law to stop any establishment of a Palestinian state and indicated the intent to ban the work of the United Nations Relief and Works Agency (UNRWA).

After the 1994 Oslo agreement a Palestinian authority was established. It is, however, practically without any authority. Even Areas A, under the Oslo Agreement, are open for regular invasions by the Israeli army of occupation and later by settlers.

2002 saw a second uprising. The violent retaliation by the Israeli army resulted in the destruction of infrastructure built by donations from across the world. No action was taken against the Israeli government for these acts.

In 2004 Yasser Arafat, the historic leader of the Palestinian movement, passed away and in 2005 Mahmoud Abbas was elected as president of the Palestinian Authority. He has taken the position that only negotiations can achieve results and solutions. The 2006 elections to the Legislative Council, made conditional by Western Powers for continued support for the Palestinian Authority, saw Hamas winning a majority.

The West refused to accept the results and boycotted the government. In 2007 Hamas took control of Gaza and the siege began. The Israeli state unleashed wars on Gaza in 2008-09, 2011 and 2014. 2021 saw a major attack on Gaza with huge destruction and casualties among the innocent population within one of the most populated regions of the world: around 2.2 million people within 365 square kilometres.

Then, in 2023, as Egypt was attempting to achieve a long-term cease-fire, Hamas was preparing a sudden attack on the Israeli army and some settlements around Gaza with the objective of taking hostages that could be exchanged for thousands of Palestinian prisoners in Israeli jails.

The Israeli response was a huge attack on Gaza. More than 60,000 Palestinians have been killed and more than 110,000 injured, at the time of writing, hundreds of thousands of homes have been destroyed – as have hospitals, schools, mosques, churches and the UN installations. This was a real genocide in front of the TV cameras and without any reaction from the so-called international community especially the western leaders who, from the first moment, supported the Israeli government and failed to issue effective calls for a halt.
The Israeli government had the full support of the United States which supplied it with weapons needed to destroy Gaza and to force people to leave. It put pressure from the first day on Egypt to open borders and continued to block humanitarian aid, cutting food, water, electricity, fuel and medical supplies. It was and still is a real genocide and ethnic cleansing – and the whole world has been watching it directly from their TVs.

Regardless of the stance on the events of October 7, which were condemned by most countries in the world, as well as some Arabs and Palestinians, we must understand history. Today Israel and the West are trying to portray the situation in Palestine as if it started on 7 October 2023 and that the problem is Hamas and not the occupation of Palestine itself. This is the narrative that the capitalist propaganda machine is working to promote to the world. It is not the necessity of ending the occupation after decades of killings. These killings continue.

Going back to Lebanon, the National Front for Resistance was established in 1982 in the same year as Hezbollah, an Islamic organization, when the resistance began its operations against the Israeli occupation of southern Lebanon. After 18 years this resulted in forcing the Israeli army to withdraw from the south and helped create an alliance between Hezbollah, Hamas and the rest of the armed factions. They fight the same enemy. Together they seek to liberate the occupied land in Palestine and Lebanon and have enjoyed the support of Syria, Iran, Yemen and some armed forces in Iraq. Their entrance into the battle to support the Gaza Strip from the eighth of October led Israeli forces to carry out attacks on all Lebanese territory, not only the south, where it succeeded in assassinating many of the leaders and cadres of Hezbollah, headed by Hassan Nasrallah, Secretary-General of the party. The attack then spread across all parts of Lebanon. When a ceasefire was achieved in Gaza all attacks from Lebanon, Yemen and Iraq stopped and it was agreed that the Israeli forces would leave Lebanese territory within 60 days. A five-member committee was headed by United States. After the 60 days, the Israeli government asked for and gained three weeks more from the US, ending on 18 February 2025. Once again, the Israeli government did not comply and demanded, 'for security reasons', continuing control of five strategic points in the south. This complicates matters further and threatens the outbreak of conflict again.

The challenge of Donald Trump

It can be said, (at the time of writing) that the truce is so far holding as agreed and prisoners and hostages are being exchanged. But the main problem facing the region is the position of the American President Donald Trump, who has returned to the old plan. This is to move the population out of Gaza. The Israeli government and the United States have not abandoned this objective over the past decades because of the strategic importance of the Gaza Strip together with the abundance of its natural resources, especially gas. Trump seeks to add the crime of ethnic cleansing to the crimes of genocide in Gaza This is in addition to the insistence of Netanyahu and his extreme right-wing government on returning to war after the liberation of all the hostages and thus carrying out the long-term aim of displacement - an aim which can only be implemented with the support of the United States and agreement of the surrounding Arab countries. They destroyed Gaza in order to make it unviable in order to justify the ethnic cleansing scheme and prevent any rescue for its people. Yet, as they attempted this nightmarish scheme, they saw millions of Gazans crawling to the destroyed north of Gaza from the destroyed south, rejecting the idea of displacement and adhering to their determination for survival there.

Nonetheless, we see positive signs. These Israeli plans were rejected by the vast majority of the countries of the world, especially the Arab countries targeted by this plan, namely Egypt and Jordan. It is also known that Lebanon has a clear position on settlement for internal Lebanese reasons. The weak point remains Syria under its new rulers. They did not oppose these plans because of the close links with the external forces that supported their arrival to power. In addition, the new Syrian rulers provided a precedent for occupation by giving Syrian citizenship to thousands of non-Syrian fighters who fought with Al-Julani and now share the control of the country.

If we look at the regional situation in the Middle East it is very dangerous. There is, first, what happened in Syria and what the country may face from internal conflicts after the new government took control and the increasing Turkish role there, the Israeli occupation of new Syrian territories, the results of the war on Lebanon and the US-backed Israeli threats to Iran. All those are risks to the Palestinian cause. In addition to Trump's madness, it can be said that the region is facing dramatic developments, including the Israel government's return to the war of annihilation against the Gaza Strip and the return of the war in Lebanon if the Israeli government continues to refuse to withdraw from the south according to the ceasefire agreement. There is also the possibility of the Israeli government going it alone, or with US participation, to strike Iran with the consequences that may ensue.

We believe that the international community, especially the active countries in it, must fulfill their obligations to implement international resolutions, especially those related to Palestine, which require a solution on the basis of the withdrawal of Israel from the Arab territories it occupied in 1967, especially the Palestinian territories, enabling the Palestinian people to determine their interests on their land and establish their independent Palestinian state on the borders of 4 June, 1967, with East Jerusalem as its capital, and the return of refugees in accordance with Resolution 194.

Virtually the whole world wants peace in Palestine and the Middle East and wants to respect international laws and conventions. Only the governments of the United States and Israel flout them. There is therefore an opportunity to build a global coalition to isolate the United States as well as the government of Israel.

The international movement of solidarity, for peace and justice, which demonstrated its active and important role during the genocide can continue to play the same role in forcing governments to change their position of supporting the government of Israel and the policies of US in order to achieve peace and stability in the region and hence in the whole world. Because in addition to the situation in the Middle East, the Ukrainian war with the participation of superpowers is also threatening world peace.

Only in this way can the madness of the Trump-Netanyahu alliance be stopped.

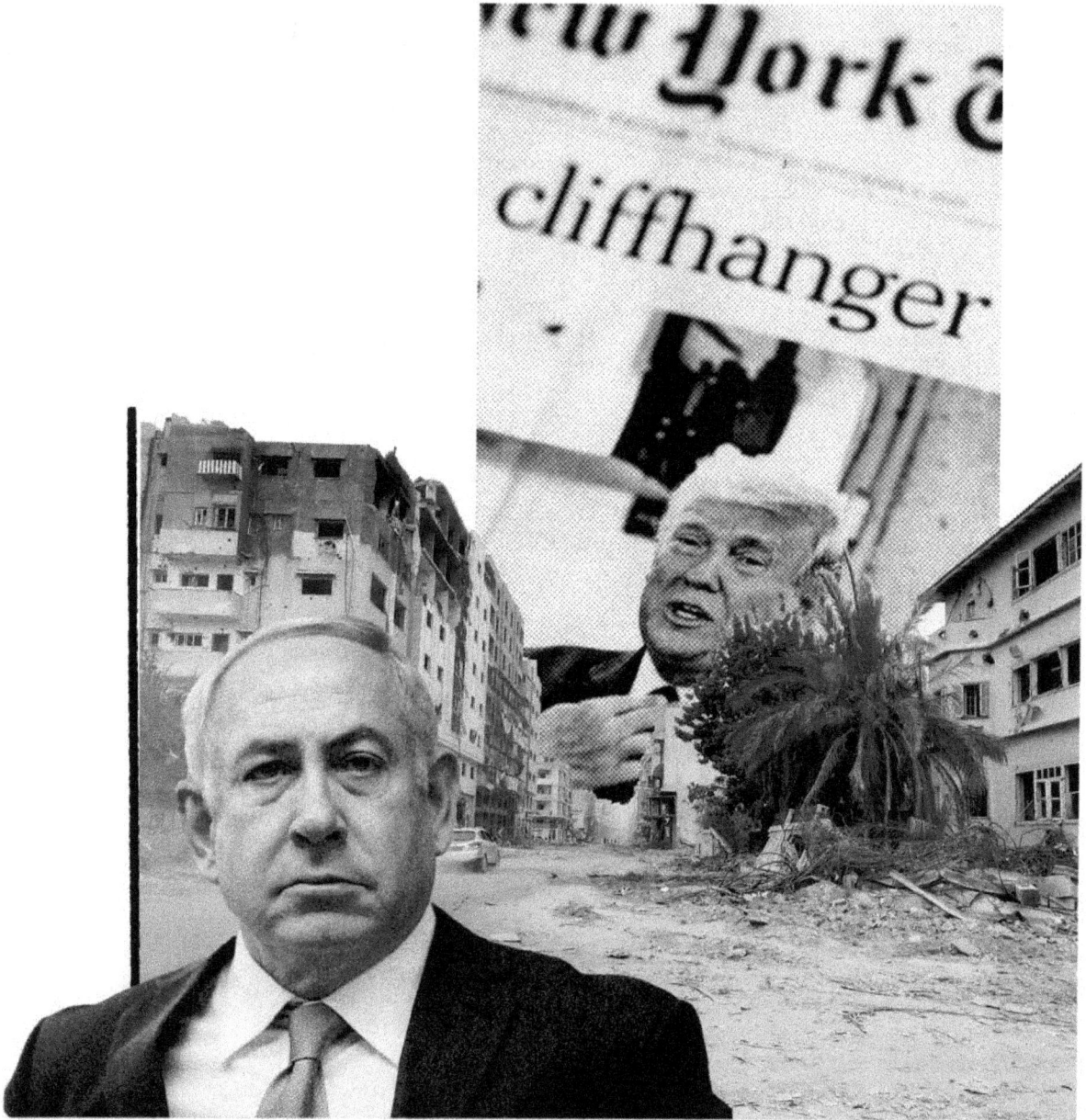

RADICAL CLERKENWELL REINTERPRETED AT THE MARX MEMORIAL LIBRARY & WORKERS SCHOOL (MML)

MEIRIAN JUMP

Director of MML

The summer of 2024 saw the MML embark on an innovative project, bringing local residents in to engage with our archives to co-curate an exhibition on radical history. A dozen of them – the majority recruited through our partners at the Peel Community Centre – selected items from our historic collections focusing on a number of themes including squatting, the black press and the Aid Spain movement.

Usually, the archives housed in MML's three-storey building are available to researchers in our reading room only by appointment or through coordinated group visits. Visitors rarely have the chance to 'browse' our archives on socialist history. This can add to a perception of archive collections – despite their genesis in the working-class movement – as being academic and inaccessible. We know from recent audience research that people on our doorstep simply don't know who we are and what we do.

At the 2023 focus groups on the Finsbury Estate neighboring the MML participants thought the MML seemed to be 'a secret society' and commented 'I'm not sure what it does'. However, when, at this same group session, they were shown images from the archives including photos from the Battle of Cable Street, for example, they responded with great enthusiasm; this is so interesting. I love it!'

This knowledge spurred us on to invite local people who were new to the MML into the archives for this, our first co-curation project. We simply told them 'we want to hear from you'!

The project 'People and Protest: Radical Clerkenwell Reinterpreted' was funded by the Association for Independent Museums 'New Stories, New Audiences' stream which asks small museums to work with new partners to speak to a more diverse audience. This is also supported by the National Heritage Lottery Fund. The local focus fits with MML's audience development strategy; to reach out specifically to local communities and school groups. It is also timely, set against the backdrop of the redevelopment of Clerkenwell Green, meshing with our joint 'Reds on the Green' programme with Islington Council; a series of free monthly introductory sessions on key individuals and episodes in local radical history. At the first project workshop in June 2024 we brought reproductions from the archives out to the Peel Centre, gave an introduction to the radical history of the area – from the

Peasant's Revolt in 1341 to the May Day rally that still gathers on the Green today. We asked participants which subject areas spoke to them today. The response was striking; almost everyone in the group thought that housing should be addressed in the exhibition with reflections on the current crisis and the rising cost of living. There was also interest in the women's movement and the role of the radical press in the area.

Another take-away was the sense of hopelessness that emerged. The discussion spiraled down with comments like 'nothing much has changed' and 'we can't do much about it anyway'. As project coordinators and facilitators we were keen to challenge this; it is something we returned to in the second and last workshops. These involved inviting them to visit the MML and enabling them to have 'hands on' time with the archives. We also posed a series key questions; how have people tried to change the world, why, with what success and what challenges did they meet? Finally, and most importantly, we asked them 'what does this mean to you today?'

Individual items were selected by participants. Dee picked an issue of the West Indian Gazette commenting 'Us as Caribbeans have to keep our archives; it is up to us to tell our children. The oppression – is it really about colour or is it on people – it sounds the same to me – one is called a workhouse and one is called a plantation'.

John was drawn to a scrapbook created by housing activist Annie Mills and to a piece that featured the occupation of the Ritz by the unemployed in the 1930s. He reflected 'it is a great expression of class structure. We've got working-class people at the Ritz. The idea is that they are not supposed to be there – it's not for them – 'know your place' – I love [challenging] that idea'.

Ray had his own recollections of squatting in Islington, while Eira contributed a photograph of her on a peace demonstration as a young child. This evocative image mirrors the photographs of mothers and children on demonstrations that are held in our own archives. We worked with our exhibition designers and grappled with the best way to incorporate reproductions from the archives with some context alongside the voices from the community. Another challenge was the question of how we could display this within the limits of MML's current building; our Main Hall which also incorporates archive stores and a meeting and education space. The displays would have to be striking and discrete, mobile and hardwearing.

Simon Leach Designs created eye-catching 'banner' style designs which we hung on the cabinets housing our Spanish Collection. They include caption texts and context from the MML, alongside dynamic portraits of people, taken by Len Weiss photographer, showing people engaging with the archives in their own words.

The display which now – in 2025 – is on tour to other venues including the Peel Centre and the Holloway Neighbourhood Group has had very positive feedback. Visitors have particularly praised the connections that have been made between history and the present day, and the way in which voices from the community have been incorporated. The exhibition has also inspired u to set up new Vinyl stickers on MML's windows to enhance our visibility to passersby and to challenge the perception of our library as 'closed'.

This has been an important learning experience for the Marx Memorial Library. The questions posed at the second and third workshops - on how people band together to make a difference and what impact it has and why - worked very well as a prompt for broad discussions, requiring no prior knowledge of the historical episodes that were documented in the archives. Furthermore, we saw that when people were given permission to engage deeply with the archives and the stories of people's agency through history, they did so in a meaningful way. This process prompted the unearthing of memories, and the development of more fundamental discussions about the challenges faced by the Labour and Progressive Movement today. It was often moving and confessional. With time, initial feelings of hopelessness were shaken off; and other perspectives emerged.

Gerry reflected 'all the marches we went on – its coming back now – the doctors, Palestine, the nurses and teachers...during Covid I went on a march for the doctors and nurses and it was so good...that was wonderful'.

Initial impressions of MML were also challenging; when asked what they thought of MML at the beginning of this process participants used words including 'lefty legacy', and 'closed', 'inaccessible', and 'academic'. When asked for their thoughts now (after engaging in the process) they described MML as 'an empire of knowledge' and 'alive and still relevant'. This impact on the individuals who were involved is born out through their lasting relationships with us. Four are still in touch; two as regular volunteers assisting in collections work and two as ambassadors who attend our twice-annual socials with staff trustees and volunteers.

The success of this project is shaping our vision for exhibitions and interpretations in a redeveloped Marx House. Alongside a permanent display, we envisage having a community exhibition space with annual rotating displays stemming from partnerships with the local community and with heritage, student and creative groups.

Photography © **Karl Weiss**

MARX GRAVESIDE ORATION 2025

HER EXCELLENCY MRS ISMARA M. VARGAS WALTER
Cuban Ambassador

Comrades, Friends, and Honored Guests,

It is a profound privilege and honor to stand here today at this hallowed ground, Highgate Cemetery, this sacred place of memory and struggle, where Karl Marx, the titan of revolutionary thought, rests, but continues to inspire the struggles of the working class and oppressed peoples across the world.

I extend my gratitude to the Marx Memorial Library and the Communist Party of Britain for this invitation, and I share this platform with pride alongside Dr. Ashok Dhwale, a steadfast champion of India's farmers and workers.

We gather today not only to honor Karl Marx's legacy but to reaffirm our commitment to the ideas that ignited the Cuban Revolution and continue to guide our struggle for justice, sovereignty, and socialism. Marx once wrote, "The philosophers have only interpreted the world in various ways; the point is to change it." These words became a compass for Cuba. When Fidel Castro, Raúl Castro, Che Guevara, and their comrades launched the assault on the Moncada Barracks in 1953, a defining spark of our Revolution, they did so not merely to overthrow a dictator but to dismantle the capitalist and imperialist structures that enslaved Cuba.

The triumph of the Cuban Revolution in 1959 was not just the fall of a tyrant; it was the birth of a socialist project inspired by Marxism, by the belief that the workers and peasants must be the true owners of their destiny. It was a victory against not just Batista, but against an entire system designed to keep Cuba subjugated as a neo-colony of the United States. It was an affirmation that revolution is not only necessary but possible, even in the face of overwhelming odds. The Cuban Revolution was born from Marxist analysis. We understood that our island, exploited by U.S. imperialism, could only achieve liberation by uprooting the class divisions and foreign domination Marx so rigorously dissected. The Granma expedition, the Sierra Maestra guerrilla struggle, and the triumph of January 1, 1959, were not just military victories; they were the culmination of a Marxist-Leninist struggle tailored to our material conditions.

Marxism is not a relic in Cuba; it is a living practice. The U.S. blockade, now living its seventh decade, was designed to strangle our economy and demoralize our people. Despite the relentless attacks against our right to self-determination, Cuba stands firm, proving that socialism is not only viable but necessary in the face of capitalist crises, growing inequality, and environmental destruction. The blockade is not just an economic measure; it is an act of war, an attempt to crush a people who refuse to kneel before the empire.

Our youth learn Marxism not as dogma but as a tool for critical thinking. In classrooms, workplaces, and community debates, we ask: How do we reconcile globalized technology with socialist values? How do we combat climate change within a U.S.-dominated capitalist world order? The answers lie in Marx's emphasis on collective action and scientific planning. Cuba's advances in biotechnology, universal healthcare, and education, achieved under a true siege, are testaments to this approach. When Cuba sends doctors, not bombs; when we develop vaccines, not monopolies; when we educate, not exploit, this is Marxism in action.

Marxism is not a dogma; it is a tool for liberation. The challenge we face today is how to make its lessons accessible and relevant to new generations, both in Cuba and worldwide. We must continue to innovate in how we teach and apply Marxist principles, ensuring that they speak to the challenges of our time: digital capitalism, climate change, and the need for a multipolar world. The digital age has brought new forms of exploitation, platform capitalism, algorithmic oppression, and the commodification of human attention. But it has also created new avenues for resistance, for organizing, for mobilising, for spreading revolutionary consciousness. Our task is to harness these tools for the people, not for profit.

In our modern era, the struggles have evolved. We now face the crises of rampant digital surveillance, ecological degradation, and uncontrolled artificial intelligence development, challenges that the founders of Marxism could scarcely have imagined.

Marxism, for Cuba, has always been internationalist. Che Guevara reminded us that "the true revolutionary is guided by great feelings of love," not just for one's own people, but for all humanity. It was this love that sent Cuban doctors to fight Ebola in Africa, that saw us defend Angola against apartheid South Africa, that compels us today to stand in solidarity with Palestine.

The capitalist system, in its latest stage of neoliberalism, continues to push millions into poverty while a handful amass unimaginable wealth. Wars are waged for profit, and entire nations are subjected to unilateral measures and economic warfare to break their resistance. Imperialism has adapted, but it has not changed its essence. It still seeks to divide, to plunder, to dominate. And we must stand united against it.

Cuba's Marxist Revolution stands with Palestine, demanding an end to genocide. Cuba's Marxist Revolution stands with Venezuela and Nicaragua against U.S. criminal unilateral coercive measures. Cuba's Marxist Revolution stands with all nations resisting imperialism because Marx taught us that capitalism's exploitation is global, and so too must be our solidarity.

Marxism teaches us that the working class has no borders, that the struggles of the Cuban people, the Indian peasantry, the striking workers around the globe, and the youth rising against imperialism all share a common goal. The unity of our struggles is the key to building a future beyond capitalism.

From Havana to Gaza, young people are rediscovering Marxism not as a 19th-century doctrine but as a roadmap for survival and resistance. And they are proving that the fight is not over, that the revolution is not a relic, but a necessity.

To them, we say: Study Marx not to memorize quotes, but to grasp the method. Organize not just in parties, but in unions, schools, and digital spaces. Fight not only for better wages, but for a better world where "the free development of each is the condition for the free development of all."

Let us return to Marx's grave with renewed resolve. As José Martí, Cuba's national hero, declared: "One just principle from the depths of a cave is more powerful than an army."

Today, Marx's principles are not in a cave but in the hearts of millions. Let us carry them forward, until dignity, solidarity, and socialism prevail.

The future belongs not only to those who believe in the beauty of their dreams but also to those who dare to strive for it.

Thank you.

GRAVESIDE ORATION

DR ASHOK DHAWALE

Member, Polit Bureau, Communist Party of India (Marxist) – CPI(M)
National President, All India Kisan Sabha (All India Farmers' Union) - AIKS

Distinguished Chairperson of this august gathering and Secretary of the Marx Memorial Library (MML) Professor Mary Davis, Her Excellency the Ambassador of Cuba to the UK Ismara Vargas Walter, General Secretary of the Communist Party of Britain (CPB) Robert Griffiths, Chairperson of the MML Alex Gordon, Treasurer of the MML Harsev Bains, distinguished representatives from the Embassies of China, Vietnam, Laos, Venezuela, Sri Lanka, and my dear comrades and friends,

At the outset, I profusely thank the leadership of the CPB and the MML for giving me this great honour and privilege of delivering the 2025 Marx Oration to mark the death anniversary of the greatest revolutionary thinker who ever lived, Karl Marx. On behalf of the one million members of the Communist Party of India (Marxist), and the 15 million members of the All India Kisan Sabha, I convey my warmest revolutionary greetings to you all.

On 17 March 1883, 142 years ago, the great Frederick Engels was here, close to this very spot, paying homage at the fresh grave of his closest comrade and friend. Engels said, 'Marx was before all else a revolutionist...His name will endure through the ages, and so also will his work.'

How prophetic Engels was! The name and work of Marx has not only endured, but has greatly enhanced, through the ages. Marx wrote in his youth, 'The philosophers have only interpreted the world in various ways; the point, however, is to change it.' His scientific, critical, and revolutionary method of the analysis of society has indeed changed the world, and there is no doubt that it will change it even more.

His discovery of the science of dialectical and historical materialism, the theory of surplus value which uncovers the reality of exploitation, and his stress on the necessity of a political class struggle to achieve revolution, liberation, and socialism, have been borne out by the actual experience of gigantic struggles. The historic saga of various socialist revolutions and their spectacular achievements, and of the iconic and victorious struggle of the Soviet Union against world fascism, will always live on through the ages.

The state of the world today proves the relevance of Marx' analysis. Let us take just three brief quotes of Marx and see how perfectly they apply today.

In Capital, Volume 1 (1867), Marx writes, 'If money, according to Augier, "comes into the world with a congenital blood-stain on one cheek," capital comes dripping from head to foot, from every pore, with blood and dirt.' Here, Marx adds a footnote quoting T J Dunning, 'With adequate profit, capital is very bold. A certain 10 per cent will ensure its employment anywhere; a certain 20 per cent will produce eagerness; 50 per cent, positive audacity; 100 per cent will make it ready to trample on all human laws; 300 per cent, and there is not a crime at which it will scruple, nor a risk that it will not run, even to the chance of its owner being hanged. If turbulence and strife will bring a profit, it will freely encourage both.'

In Capital, Volume 1, again, Marx writes, 'Accumulation of wealth at one pole is, therefore, at the same time, accumulation of misery, agony of toil, slavery, ignorance, brutality, mental degradation at the opposite pole, i.e. on the side of the class that produces its own product in the form of capital.'

In the Communist Manifesto (1848), Marx and Engels write, 'The need of a constantly expanding market for its products chases the bourgeoisie over the whole surface of the globe. It must nestle everywhere, settle everywhere, establish connections everywhere.' Marx and Engels in this prescient passage, hint at the globalization to come – a full 177 years ago!

With the development of capitalism, Lenin enriched this concept of Marx in his seminal work, Imperialism, the Highest Stage of Capitalism (1917).

What do we see in the world today, which underlines the relevance of Marx?

Gross and obscene inequalities abound. The world's richest 1 per cent own more wealth than the bottom 95 per cent of humanity. Since 2020, the richest 1 per cent have grabbed nearly 67 per cent of all new wealth – nearly twice as much as the bottom 99 per cent. Billionaire fortunes are rising by $2.7 billion a day, even as inflation outpaces the wages of 1.7 billion workers.

On the other hand, in 2023, 46 per cent of the world's population, or over 3 billion people, are living under the global poverty line of $ 6.85 (2017 purchasing power parity) per day. Of these, 700 million people live in extreme poverty, surviving on less than $ 2.15 per day. 10.7 per cent of the world population (864.1 million) is affected by severe food insecurity, and of these 60 per cent who go hungry are women and girls.

The global unemployment rate today is 5 per cent, and the global youth unemployment rate is 13 per cent. Newer technologies and artificial intelligence are aggravating unemployment and exploitation and leading to still greater super-profits for the large monopolies and corporate houses. In 2024, 54 countries were in a debt crisis, and net resource transfers from developing to developed countries have averaged $ 700 billion per year.

There is not a shadow of doubt that all the above stark facts are a direct result of the policies of neo-liberalism and imperialist globalization, which have intensified in the last four decades. These policies met with a rude shock in 2008 with the global financial crisis which began in the USA, spread to Europe and all over the world, and forced many capitalist world leaders to turn to none other than the 'best hated and most calumniated' Marx to get a credible explanation for these events! What a poetic irony that was!

The rising social unrest as a result of these extreme global inequalities between the Global North and the Global South, economic and social inequalities within each nation, and the attacks of the ruling classes on the working people through 'austerity measures', is being broadly channelized in two directions, depending upon the concrete situation in each country.

One is the rightward shift in many countries, which sometimes takes the form of far-right and neo-fascist attacks on racial, religious, and other minorities, including immigrants.

Ironically, this same policy of Hitler then is being faithfully copied by Netanyahu now, and also by some others. In many countries, the political-ideological bankruptcy of social democratic parties and their unprincipled compromises have helped the far-right to advance.

The opposite trend is the leftward shift in some countries of Latin America, Asia, and Europe, where left forces could win over sections of the people.

Donald Trump of the USA is the latest and classic example of the far-right, neo-fascist, authoritarian offensive. There is a method in his madness. It is a systematic last-ditch attempt to arrest the inexorable decline of the USA. This attempt is bound to fail. Under Trump, the likes of Elon Musk and other large corporate cronies are now directly calling the shots in the US government. This will make it even more plutocratic, neo-liberal, anti-people, and anti-democratic. Neo-liberalism thus creates the conditions for neo-fascism.

Trump's ridiculous claims on Greenland, Canada, Panama Canal, and Gaza, and the tariff and trade wars that he has unleashed, are being strongly resisted all over the world. His severe attacks on, and cutting off funds to, the United Nations and its affiliated organizations, and his disastrous steps to undermine the crucial global issue of climate justice are also being opposed tooth and nail by many forces. His stand on the Ukraine war has now ranged Western Europe against him. But on the inhuman Imperialist-backed Zionist genocide by Israel against the courageous Palestinian people of Gaza, leading to the deaths of nearly 50,000 people, with 60 per cent of them being women and children, the entire imperialist camp is fully united.

On this occasion, we salute the socialist countries like Cuba, China, Vietnam, Laos, DPRK, and the left-led countries of Latin America and Sri Lanka, who are working hard to ensure the rapid and just socio-economic progress of their people, and many are also boldly opposing Imperialism and Zionism.

In other countries too, struggles and resistance are increasing. In my country India, we saw in 2020-21 a truly iconic and united nationwide struggle by millions of farmers who blocked the national highways leading to the nation's capital Delhi for a full one year and fifteen days. They were fighting against the three pro-corporate, anti-farmer Farm Laws imposed by the central government at the height of the Covid pandemic. Over 700 farmers were martyred in this struggle, which eventually forced the government to repeal the three Farm Laws, leading to a historic victory. Now the same government is trying to implement the draconian four Labour Codes, which are equally pro-corporate and anti-worker. A massive united nationwide general strike by the working class, supported by a rural strike of the peasantry, in which several million workers and peasants will participate, is being planned for next month against this serious assault.

The World Social Forum (WSF) has an attractive slogan signifying hope: Another World is Possible! At the graveside of the towering revolutionary Karl Marx on his death anniversary, we need to modify it a bit to: A Socialist World is Possible! Socialism for the 21st Century is the only Alternative!

Marx and Engels concluded the Communist Manifesto with these resounding words, 'The proletarians have nothing to lose but their chains. They have a world to win.'

Comrades and friends: Let us work unitedly to prove Marx right yet again! Let us bend all our efforts to win over the minds and the hearts of our people! Let us fight with all our energy, strength, power, intelligence, and imagination, to win this world!

Thank you very much.

Down with Imperialism!

Down with Capitalism!

Down with Feudalism!

Long Live Democracy!

Long Live Socialism!

Long Live Marxism!

ENGELS MEMORIAL LECTURE. ENGELS AS POPULAR EDUCATOR: MAKING MARX ACCESSIBLE

MARJORIE MAYO

Marjorie Mayo is editor of Theory and Struggle and a trustee of Marx Memorial Library. She has taught and researched in community education and development.

Abstract

This lecture explores Engels as political educator as well as theorist and political activist. The focus is on his contributions to making Dialectical Materialism and Historical Materialism widely accessible – concluding with his particular relevance for popular political education today.

Keywords

Engels, Popular Political Education, Dialectical Materialism, Historical Materialism

Introduction

Popular education is not the aspect of Engels' contributions to Marxist theory and practice that most immediately springs to mind, perhaps. He is probably better known and valued in so many other ways, as Marx's co-author of the Communist Manifesto and other works, as well as being the editor who deciphered Marx's handwriting, preparing the second and third volumes of Capital for publication. Although he was extremely modest about his contributions, famously describing himself as having been happy to play 'second fiddle' to Marx's so excellent 'first violin'[1], he was of course, an activist and author in his own right. His publications remain highly relevant even in the light of changing circumstances[2] and with the benefit of additional knowledge.

In contrast, this discussion focuses on Engels as a 'great teacher of the proletariat', as Lenin described him[3], as well as a great activist. This activist background enabled him to reach his audiences and readers particularly effectively, taking account of their varying situations, their issues and their concerns, linking Marxist theory with progressive political practice. These aspects have continuing relevance for political education, including popular political education, in the contemporary context, as it will be suggested in more detail, subsequently. Although Gramsci has been widely identified as a significant, if not the most significant theoretical source for popular/ political education in recent times, this lecture set out to argue that Engels has so much relevance too - making Marx accessible for wider audiences and developing a dialectical materialist basis for understanding the role of language and the promotion of class consciousness in different contexts.

---

1   F. Engels, 'Speech at the Graveside of Karl Marx' in Marx Engels Selected Works, (London: Lawrence and Wishart, 1968), 429-43.

2   L. Clarke, M. Edwards, and P. Watt, 'Engels and the Housing Question 150 years on: A roundtable discussion' Theory and Struggle (2023) Number 124. 66-71.

3   V. I. Lenin, Marx, Engels, Selected Works (Lawrence and Wishart, 1968). 22

The first section focuses on the roots of popular political education in Britain and elsewhere today. This sets the context for the discussion of Engels' own contributions in these respects, drawing on Socialism: Utopian and Scientific[4] and 'The Part Played by Labour in the Transition from Ape to Man' for illustrations[5].

The third section then moves on to explore some of the ways in which Engels' writings have been trail blazing, leading to the development of Marxist understandings of language, cultures and changing consciousness, understandings which have significant implications for popular/political education today. Firstly, however, we begin with a brief discussion of popular/political education and its increasing significance in recent times.

Popular political education in context

Popular/political education has a long and contested history, predating the contributions of Engels himself. The purposes of 'really useful knowledge' were set out in The Poor Man's Guardian, for example, a popular people's paper that came to be edited for a time by Bronterre O'Brian (known as the Chartists' schoolmaster'). In contrast to the 'useful knowledge' that was being promoted to increase workers' productivity, 'really useful knowledge' was to explore how to enable men to judge correctly of the real causes of misery and distress so prevalent. How to 'get out of our present troubles? How to break the chains that bind us?'[6]

These quotations highlight the importance of critical understanding as the basis for developing effective strategies for social transformation – approaches that have been summarised as 'popular political education'. The Brazilian adult educator, Paulo Freire, has been widely quoted in popular educational contexts, along with influences from Gramsci, influences that Freire himself also came to acknowledge.[7] Both Freire and Gramsci have been quoted and misquoted in support of widely differing political agendas, however. Gramsci's writings on the ideological and cultural dimensions of class struggles have been misinterpreted by Eurocommunist writers for example, domesticating Marxism in the process - re-evaluating the ideological and cultural dimensions of social change processes – at the expense of the basic tenets of historical materialism.

Gramsci himself was extremely clear about his own position here. There most certainly was a battle of ideas to be waged, he emphasised, challenging the 'common sense' notions that reinforced the status quo. Cultural and ideological struggles had to be understood in relation to the economic base, however. This was central to his approach both in theory and in political practice. Economic relations were indeed the mainspring of history, although not in a vulgar economistic way. Gramsci referred back to Engels here to differentiate economism from historical materialism, whilst continuing to emphasise the importance of the superstructure.[8]

4   F. Engels 'Socialism: Utopian and Scientific' in Marx Engels Selected Works (London: Lawrence and Wishart, 1968) 375-428.

5   F. Engels, 'The Part Played by Labour in the Transition from Ape to Man' in Marx Engels Selected Works, (London: Lawrence and Wishart, 1968), 354-364.

6   K. Hughes 'Really useful knowledge' in eds. M. Mayo and J. Thompson, Adult education, Critical Intelligence and Social Change' (Leicester: NIACE, 1995), 97-110.

7   P. Freire, Pedagogy of the Oppressed (Harmondsworth: Penguin Books, 1977); M. de Figueiredo-Cowen and D. Gastaldo (eds), Paulo Freire at the Institute, London: Institute of Education, 1995).

8   A. Gramsci, The modern prince and other writings (New York: International Publishers, 1968).

As Engels wrote in a much-quoted passage from a letter to Joseph Bloch in 1890, 'According to the materialist conception of history, the ultimately determining element in history is the production and reproduction of real life. More than this neither Marx nor I ever asserted', going on to refer to the various elements of the superstructure that impact upon the course of historical struggles, in addition, and 'in many cases preponderate in determining their form'.[9] More of Engels' writings on ideology and consciousness, subsequently.

Firstly, it is worth focussing on the similarities between Engels' and Gramsci's approaches to political education more specifically. Both were directly engaged in this - Engels through his involvement with the German Workers Educational Association in London and as an intellectual leader of the growing social democratic movements and the new unions, for example, and Gramsci through his involvement with the Factory Councils in Turin. These differing experiences both involved linking theory and practice, engaging with working class movements as well as providing leading cadres with the ability to apply Marxist concepts in their changing circumstances. The masses - as well as the leadership - needed to grasp what was at stake, a process which required long persistent work on the part of the party, as both Gramsci and Engels himself emphasised. This was about learning through engaging in processes of critical dialogue, promoting the capacity for critical thinking rooted in Marxist theoretical understandings.

Engels had already come to similar conclusions about the importance of dialogue. His initial idea for what became the Communist Manifesto was to produce a series of questions and answers, for example (although he and Marx subsequently decided in favour of a fuller text). And Engels was similarly concerned about the importance of theory, as it has already been suggested. Reflecting on German history, he opined that German workers had had important advantages over others in Europe because of their theoretical sense, without which 'scientific socialism would never have entered their flesh and blood as much as is the case'[10]. Workers' education needed to be theoretically rigorous, as well as engaging, by implication, a view that has been less actively promoted by more populist approaches to popular political education in recent times, approaches whose critics have included Paulo Freire himself. Educators should be engaging learners in processes of critical dialogue in his view; rather than simply accepting and so re-enforcing their initial premises (and prejudices) in populist ways, failing to move beyond the lowest common denominator of theoretical understanding, as a result.

This takes the discussion on to the nature of Engels' contributions to 'popular' as distinct from 'populist' education, starting with his contributions to making Historical Materialism widely accessible.

Making Historical Materialism accessible

The Communist Manifesto has already been referred to as evidence of Engels' commitment to making Marxist theory accessible. Between them, Marx and Engels succeeded in producing the most extraordinarily compelling call to political action, starting from the proposition that 'The history of all hitherto existing society is the history of class

9   F. Engels, 'Letter to J. Bloch, London, September 21, 1890', in Marx Engels Selected Works, London: Lawrence and Wishart, 1968), 682-683.
10   F. Engels, 'Supplement to the preface of 1870 for the Third Edition of 1875: The Peasant War in France' in Marx Engels Selected Works (London: Lawrence and Wishart, 1968), 246.

struggles', as they explained on the first page.[11] The Manifesto provided the basis for developing a theoretical understanding of Historical Materialism, as this was developed in their subsequent writings – and further elucidated by Engels in Socialism: Utopian and Scientific, as well as in a number of letters, providing further clarification. Whilst these texts were central to Engels' contributions as a popular political educator, they were far from representing the full range of his work, in these respects, as it has already been suggested. The Communist Manifesto had already introduced another aspect in addition, the question of the development of man's consciousness 'which changes with every change in the conditions of his material existence, in his social relations and in his social life'.[12] Before coming on to this dimension, though, Engels' writings on Historical Materialism need to be summarised – and appreciated in their own right.

Engels' preface to the English edition (published in 1892) explains the origins of Socialism: Utopian and Scientific.[13] The pamphlet originally formed part of a more extensive series of articles - subsequently brought together as a book - rebutting the arguments that a certain Dr Duhring had been mobilising against 'all previous philosophers and economists in general, and against Marx in particular'.[14] It was Engels' friend, Paul Lafargue, who had persuaded him to arrange three chapters of this Anti-Duhring book to stand on their own as a pamphlet (originally published in French in 1880).

The English language edition in 1892 followed translations into ten other languages – even more than the translations of the Communist Manifesto itself, as Engels himself reflected, providing, as it does, such an accessible explanation of the principles of Historical Materialism. This, Engels defined as

> that view of the course of history which seeks the ultimate cause and the great moving power of all important historic events in the economic development of society, in the changes in the modes of production and exchange, in the consequent division of society into distinct classes, and in the struggles of these classes against one another.[15]

Quite a summary – which Engels then illustrated with reflections on British history for his English language readership.

Far from representing an economistic account of the development of capitalism, the preface interweaves this with accounts of the ways in which ideologies have impacted, whether as barriers to - or indeed as facilitators of - bourgeois class interests. Religion emerges as a key factor here, as Engels explained, starting from the Reformation, which undermined the ties between the Catholic church and feudalism, ties which had served as barriers for the emergence of capitalism. But religion had had its uses for the bourgeoisie too, with different forms of Protestantism serving to keep the 'lower orders' down.[16]

Despite the 'religious stolidity' of the British and the shackles of traditions of various kinds working people had begun to rise again, however. 'It moves, like all things in England,

---

11   K. Marx, and F. Engels, 'Manifesto of the Communist Party', in Marx Engels Selected Works, London: Lawrence and Wishart, 1968), 31-63.

12   Marx and Engels, Manifesto, 17.

13   F. Engels, F. 'Socialism: Utopian and Scientific' in Marx Engels Selected Works, London: Lawrence and Wishart, 1968), 375-428.

14   Engels, Socialism: Utopian and Scientific', 376.

15   Ibid., 382-3.

16   Ibid., 386.

with a slow and measured step'... 'now and then with an overcautious mistrust of the name of socialism, while it gradually absorbs the substance: and the movement spreads and seizes one layer of the workers after another'. 'It has now shaken out of their torpor the unskilled labourers of the East End of London' he continued, 'and we all know what a splendid impulse these fresh forces have given it in return' with the grandsons of the Chartists 'bid fair to be worthy of their forefathers'.[17]

In summary then, the preface to the English edition exemplifies Engels' contributions as a popular political educator. The preface's summary of the key principles of Historical Materialism is followed with illustrations from British history, bringing Marxist understandings home to readers in the process. The preface then concludes by linking Historical Materialism with contemporary class struggles – evidence of Engels' contributions as an activist as well as an educator, as Lenin has already been quoted as describing him.

Socialism: Utopian and Scientific moves on in similar vein, outlining the limitations of Utopian Socialism before setting out the principles of Historical Materialism, 'a method found of explaining man's "knowing" by his "being" instead of, as heretofore, his "being" by his "knowing"'. Having summarised the materialist concept of history, Engels goes on to provide illustrations, showing how the capitalist mode of production developed from feudalism as the spinning wheel, the handloom, and the blacksmith's hammer were replaced by the spinning machine, the power-loom and the steam hammer, accompanied by the accumulation of great wealth alongside the growth of misery.[18]

Engels went on to show how the capitalist mode of production 'contains the germ of the whole of the social antagonisms of today'.[19] The development of machinery becomes 'the most powerful weapon in the war of capital against the working class', as Marx had already explained, replacing human labour, establishing 'an accumulation of misery, corresponding with (the) accumulation of capital' with increasing competition and periodic crises, followed by increasing centralisation and the emergence of monopolies.[20] Eventually the state is forced to intervene – as with the post office, the telegraphs and the railways – (ironic examples given more recent experiences in Britain). But the contradictions of capitalism continued to develop until the proletariat seizes political power, he argued, abolishing all class distinctions and class antagonisms, along with the state as an instrument of the exploiting class - leading to the 'ascent of man from the kingdom of necessity to the kingdom of freedom'.[21]

At this point Engels sums up his sketch of historical evolution for his readers, from medieval society to the development of capitalism and its inherent contradictions, paving the way for proletarian revolution. 'To accomplish this act of universal emancipation is the historical mission of the modern proletariat' he concludes. And this requires political education:

> *'To thoroughly comprehend the historical conditions and the very nature of this act, to impart to the now oppressed proletarian class a full knowledge of the conditions and of the meaning of the momentous act it is called upon to accomplish, this is the task of the theoretical expression of the proletarian movement, scientific socialism'.*[22]

17	Ibid., 392-3.
18	Ibid., 410.
19	Ibid., 415.
20	Ibid., 418-9
21	Ibid., 426.
22	Ibid., 428.

Before moving on to Engels' contributions to the understanding of human consciousness, it's worth noting his understanding of the nature of science in general and scientific methodology more specifically. This was absolutely not based on a dogmatic view of science as providing absolute answers, as some critics have suggested[23]. On the contrary, Engels approached scientific methodology as providing systematic ways to test hypotheses – and then to adjust them or indeed to refute them, if necessary, in the light of the subsequent evidence. The proof of the pudding was in the eating. Engels applied this approach to his reflections on The Class Struggles in France, 1848-1850 for example.[24] Marx's early optimism about the prospects for class struggles had proved premature Engels argued; proletarian aspirations had been unripe, at that time. Since then, the situation had changed however, reducing, although by no means eliminating, the scope for street fighting whilst opening up new spaces for struggle (including parliamentary spaces with the extension of the franchise). Long persistent educational work was required if the masses were to understand what was to be done in these changing circumstances – which was just the work that was being pursued, he argued, and with a success that was driving the enemy to despair.[25]

The Part Played by Labour in the Transition from Ape to Man

Engels' writings themselves have parallel time limitations. So much has changed since he wrote The Housing Question for example. Anthropological knowledge has similarly moved on since he wrote The Origin of the Family, Private Property and the State and 'The Part Played by Labour in the Transition from Ape to Man'.[26] But these publications raise theoretical questions with continuing relevance all the same.

The unfinished essay, 'The Part Played by Labour in the Transition from Ape to Man', was written in the spring of 1876, as part of Engels' work on The Dialectics of Nature, explaining the interrelationships between humanity and nature, mind, body and labour, over time. Through this essay the reader can grasp the principles of materialist dialectics, 'foundational to Marx and Engels' entire world view, as Jonathan White's Making Our Own History: A User's Guide to Marx's Historical Materialism explains 'a theory of what exists, a theory of our knowledge of what exists, and a theory of the relationship of this knowledge to practice action in the world'. And 'it's also revolutionary because it recognises that thought is a moment in a process of human action, in a constant dialectic with practical activity'.[27]

'The Part played by Labour in the Transition from Ape to Man' opens with the proposition that labour is the source of all wealth, although 'next to nature, which supplies it with the material that it converts into wealth. But it is even infinitely more than this, Engels continues. 'It is the prime basic condition for all human existence, and to such an extent that, in a sense, we have to say that labour created man himself'.[28] This leads him into the discussion of how man developed from his hairy ancestors, learning to walk on two legs as his hands evolved, making tools – and so enabling him to make more complex tools.

23   D. McLellan, Engels, Hassocks: Harvester, 1977).

24   F. Engels, 'Introduction to Karl Marx's Work on the Class Struggles in France, 1848 to 1850' in Marx Engels Selected Works, London: Lawrence and Wishart (1968), 640-658

25   Engels, 'Introduction to Class Struggles in France', 556-573.

26   M. Davis 'Engels Memorial Lecture: Women's oppression, the origin of the family and the condition of the working class,' Theory and Struggle, Number 122, (2021), 190-199.

27   J. White, J. Making Our Own History: A User's Guide to Marx's Historical Materialism, (Praxis Press, 2021), 11.

28   F. Engels, 'The Part Played by Labour in the Transition from Ape to Man' in Marx Engels Selected Works, London: Lawrence and Wishart, 1968), 354.

This was an interactive process of change, as Engels went on to explain. 'The hand', he argues, 'is not only the organ of labour, it is also the product of labour'. Through labour, adapting to new operations, he continued, the human hand developed 'the high degree of perfection required to conjure into being the pictures of a Raphael, the statues of a Thorwaldsen, the music of a Paganini'. Far from emerging from an automatic process of evolution, the human hand developed as the result of human interactions with nature – through labour.[29]

Engels went on to explore the implications for the rest of the human body – including the human brain and the capacity for language. The development of labour brought members of society closer together by increasing cases of mutual support and joint activity, he continued. 'In short, men in the making arrived at the point where they had something to say to each other. Necessity created the organ; the undeveloped larynx of the ape was slowly but surely transformed by modulation to produce constantly more developed modulation, and the organs of the mouth gradually learned to pronounce one articulate sound after another'. And through speech – and labour - 'the brain of the ape gradually changed into that of man'.[30]

Humans developed from there, Engels continued, harnessing fire, domesticating animals and adapting to live in different climates. 'By the combined functioning of hands, speech organs and brain, not only in each individual but also in society, men became capable of executing more and more complicated operations and were able to set themselves, and achieve, higher and higher aims'.[31] Unlike the animal, 'who merely uses its environment and brings about changes in it simply by his presence: man by his changes makes it serve his ends, masters it. This is the final, essential distinction between man and other animals, and once again it is labour that brings about this distinction'.[32]

This was far from a triumphalist account of evolution, however. On the contrary, Engels pointed to the downsides of human victories over nature, the impact of the destruction of forests to obtain cultivable land, for example. Far from standing outside, human beings are part of nature. We need to understand and to control the potentially destructive consequences of productive activities – more relevant than ever in the context of the contemporary climate crisis. And we need to understand the social effects of our actions in the field of production, the ways in which slavery received a new lease of life with the 'discovery' of America, through to the ways in which social relations were revolutionised with the creation of the steam engine and the development of industrial production, inherently dynamic processes of change. Wealth became concentrated in the hands of a minority as a result, dispossessing the huge majority - eventually giving rise to 'a class struggle between bourgeoisie and proletariat which can end only in the overthrow of the bourgeoisie and the abolition of all class antagonisms'.[33] So, Engels concludes his explanation of materialist dialectics with a summary of the implications for political practice – political education exemplified.

'The Part Played by Labour in the Transition from Ape to Man' has continuing relevance for political education today then. There have been subsequent developments in anthropological research, of course. But despite some such details, the broad outlines of his arguments hold good; providing such a clear explanation of Dialectical Materialism through his discussion of human beings' interrelationships with nature and society – and the

29   Engels, 'Part played by Labour', 355.
30   Ibid., 356.
31   Ibid., 359-360.
32   Ibid., 364.
33   Ibid., 363.

dynamics of change. This approach dispels what he described as 'the senseless and unnatural idea of a contrast between mind and matter, man and nature, soul and body, such as arose after the decline of classical antiquity in Europe and obtained its highest elaboration in Christianity'[34]

There is no such thing as 'human nature' then or 'economic man' in neoliberal terminology. People are neither inherently greedy, self-serving individuals nor inherently co-operative and compassionate social beings – although they have the capacity to be either or both, depending, at least in part, on their formation and socio-economic circumstances. The human brain develops over the lifetime in any case, responding to different stimuli, as contemporary biologists such as Steven Rose and others have demonstrated[35]; neither the product of their genetic heritage nor over-determined by their environment but by the ways in which these interact together, over time.

There are significant implications for political education here. People's consciousness develops in the context of their material situations, mediated by the prevailing common-sense ideologies of the status quo. Previous patterns can be disrupted, and critical consciousness can be promoted as a result. All of which takes the discussion into the ways in which Engels' work has been influential in more recent times.

Continuing relevance

As John Foster's Languages of Class Struggle so clearly explains, 'The Part Played by Labour in the Transformation from Ape to Man' was a major influence on Soviet theorists of language and society, such as Vygotsky, Luria and Leontiev in Moscow along with Volosinov, Baktin and later Medvedev in Leningrad.[36] Drawing on Engels' work on the interconnections between speech, language and labour in society, they developed applications for educational psychology, along with applications with particular relevance for the study of class consciousness and social change. Without going into further detail here, the point is simply to summarise the general assumptions that underpin this approach. Language is inherently dialogic. Speakers and listeners each bring their own understandings to a situation, reflecting wider understandings of society at large. But these understandings can be disrupted and especially so in situations of class conflict, as John Foster illustrates with the case study of class mobilisations on the Clyde in 1971-72.

> In a key mass meeting that determined whether the occupation of the shipyards would continue, the shop stewards exposed the "sensible compromise" advanced by both the government and right-wing trade union leaders. To accept any closures would, they argued, cripple workers' ability to defend wages and conditions in all the yards. And they did so with a blunt humour that was particular to the yards – as deployed, among others, by Billy Connolly.[37]

Meanings were being contested then, as speakers sought to decompose established meanings, using 'humour specific to the time and place – to interrogate the public "meaning" of the government and expose a deeper and more sinister class significance'.[38]

34   C. Woolfson, The Labour Theory of Culture: A Re-examination of Engels's Theory of Human Origins, London: RKP, 1982); F. Engels, 'The Part Played by Labour in the Transition from Ape to Man' in Marx Engels Selected Works, London: Lawrence and Wishart, 1968), 362.

35   R. Lewontin, S. Rose and L. Kaon, Not in our genes, London: Penguin Books, 1990).

36   J. Foster, Languages of Class Struggle (Praxis Press, 2024).

37   Foster, Languages of Class Struggle, 7.

38   Ibid., 9.

The decomposition of established meanings had been precisely what Eisenstein had sought to do through visually clashing images in film, John Foster points out, just as Brecht sought to do, through engaging his audiences in the clashing realities portrayed in his plays and his use of the absurd. Or as John Heartfield or Peter Kennard sought to achieve through the use of photomontage, juxtaposing contrasting images to challenge previously established meanings (think of Kennard's portrait of Queen Victoria with the face of Margaret Thatcher, for instance).

There would seem to be parallels here with the writings of Antonio Gramsci and his concerns with the importance of disrupting the prevailing 'common sense' - the framework of ruling class ideas that needed to be challenged. Or indeed to Paulo Freire's writings about the need to displace the oppressor within the heads of the oppressed, the battle of ideas that have been so central to debates on popular political education.

Engels subsequently reflected on the material circumstances in which such disruptions might occur, as John Foster also points out. Writing in 1889, Foster explains, Engels outlined the possibilities that were being presented by the growth of trade union organisation among the unskilled in working-class London, in response to deteriorating economic conditions, at that time. In further letters and articles he went on to focus on 'the importance of how interventions were made, of how real socialists and false ones posed their arguments and the critical role of a new cadre of trade union organisers', including Tom Mann and Eleanor Marx, who understood the need to combine organisation with political explanation and frame it in terms that could be readily understood *(Ibid. 4)*. Political education as a function of leadership, rather than being confined to those with 'political education' in their job title.

Languages of Class Struggle goes on to provide compelling case studies, illustrating the ways in which the arguments for action were won. As Collins, among others, have concluded – on the basis of community struggles, in Collins' case – this process needs to start from people's own realities and meanings, together with the ability to present alternatives that change meanings, challenging the use of language and its use/misuse as part of wider strategies of social control.[39]

This very brief summary offers no more than a caricature of the ways in which Engels has informed subsequent Marxist theoreticians, focusing on the study of class struggles and language. There is not the space to go into further detail here. Rather the point is simply to demonstrate the relevance of Engels' contributions in general and 'The Part Played by Labour in the Transition from Ape to Man' more specifically - contributions that are particularly timely right now.

Until relatively recently, popular political education theorists have tended to focus on the writings of Gramsci and Freire – interpreted and often misinterpreted in a variety of ways, as it has already been suggested. This is beginning to change with the emergence of writings based upon a wider range of theoretical sources[40] including sources drawing

---

39   C. Collins, Language, Ideology and Social Consciousness, Farnham: Ashgate, 1999).
40   P. Westoby, P. and V. Harris, 'Community Development 'yet-to come' during and post the COVID-19 pandemic: from Derrida to Zuboff', Community Development Journal, 55, 4 (2020), 553-569 P. Westoby, E. Day, F. Hawthorne, M. Toon, and K. Oldham, 'A community development story and portrayal of phenomenological reflective practice in the social field of paediatric palliative care', Community Development Journal, 58. 3 (2023), 402-418

upon libertarian socialist approaches[41]. Engels' writings have so much to contribute to these widening debates, particularly his work on language and the development of class consciousness in specific socio-economic, political and cultural contexts.

More relevant than ever

The question of meanings would seem to be more contested than ever in the context of contemporary culture wars. Battles over meanings are being waged from the Far Right of the political spectrum, part of strategies to divert popular anger and fear, focusing on blaming the 'other', the asylum seeker, the migrant, and most specifically the Muslim migrant for people's frustrations – in the face of continuing austerity, the cost-of-living crisis, and the deterioration of public services, starved of public funding despite rising social need.

There have been so many examples of contested meanings in recent years. Those dependent on welfare benefits, including the long-term sick, have been demonised, and continue to be demonised as workshy scroungers. And asylum seekers continue to be depicted as invading hoards, swamping the country, undermining British values and culture in the process. These contestations represent so much more than word games, the demonisation of asylum seekers having been used to trigger the violence that erupted in a number of places in the summer of 2024, just to refer to one recent example.

Meanwhile 'transformation' used to be a term that was applied to progressive forms of social change. Yet, in my own experience, the decimation of entire departments, through a programme of mass redundancies, has been described as part of the university's strategy for 'transformation', cuts that have been particularly targeted at departments that have been most concerned with the promotion of critical thinking. These Far-Right narratives present major challenges for political education in Britain then, in parallel with the challenges posed by Far-right narratives elsewhere, internationally. These narratives do indeed have meanings, including emotional meanings, tapping into frustrations that do need to be addressed. And these frustrations have material bases, rooted in people's daily experiences.

Social democracy is not delivering for the many rather than the few and this is becoming increasingly clear. Britain is becoming more and more polarised, with increasing precarity in employment, along with increasing homelessness. And there is no immediate prospect of improvement, with austerity Mark 2 under the current Labour government, as cuts in benefits for children and pensioners are set against the background of freebies for those in power. No wonder that there is evidence of alienation and distrust. These should be circumstances in which critical consciousness develops by leaps and bounds.

But political educators are also facing challenges of their own. Political education in the labour movement has been under threat for some time already, too often marginalised, whether as the result of funders' priorities or as a result of the need to focus on learning to enable officials and activists to undertake their roles effectively [42]– or both. There have been parallel threats from the increasing marketisation – and the increasing instrumentalisation - of higher, further and adult education. The effective demise of Ruskin College, Oxford provides just one example of this wider trend, affecting universities and colleges alike.[43]

41   A. Angelopoulos, 'Uniting threads: The dual dimension of Mutual Aid: Perspectives from Greece' in CONCEPT Vol. 15, No 2 (Autumn 2024), http://concept.lib.ed.ac.uk/

42   M. McGrath, 'Back story: a Unite approach to political education', in ed. M. Seal, Trade union education, Oxford: Workable Books, 2017), 100-114

43   M. Bailey, and D. Freedman (eds), The assault on universities, London: Pluto, 2011); S. Collini Speaking of Universities, London: Verso, 2017).

But this is so far from representing the whole story. Political education is surviving and even thriving in some ways, despite the challenges. Marx Memorial Library and Workers' School (MML) is an outstanding example here, along with others, making significant contributions of their own. MML's programme of lectures and classes engages with a range of topical subjects as well as providing opportunities to study Marxism theoretically, exploring both Historical and Dialectical Materialism in ways that are both popular and accessible. MML has been providing education for trade unions directly as well as undertaking participative research, working with Unite the Union to explore their own history through the Unite History project[44]. And MML has been providing opportunities for young people and for communities to engage with their histories and cultures in new ways, exploring different meanings and narratives through viewing items from MML's unique collections.

There are evident parallels here with the writings of Engels, along with the contributions of those who have drawn upon his writings subsequently. Political education can be more effective by being more targeted, as well as being more theoretically informed, engaging people both formally and informally, in their communities as well as in their trade unions. These contributions need to be more fully recognised among political educators, along with the contributions of Gramsci, Freire and others – educators who have recognised their debts to each other and indeed, at least in the case of Gramsci, to Engels himself. Which takes the discussion back to the starting point, Lenin's description of Engels as a great fighter but also as a great teacher of the proletariat.

---

44   M. Davis, J. Foster, M. Mayo, R. Seifert, and A. Weir, (2021-2023) The Unite History, Volumes 1-6, Liverpool: Liverpool University Press.

TOM BUCHANAN, "SPAIN MAD": BRITISH ENGAGEMENT WITH THE SPANISH CIVIL WAR
(LIVERPOOL UNIVERSITY PRESS, 2024)

JIM JUMP

Jim Jump is the son of a Spanish Republican exile who married a British International Brigader. He is the chair of the International Brigade Memorial Trust and has edited and written several books on the Spanish Civil War.

There was 'something unique' about the impact of the Spanish Civil War on Britain, Tom Buchanan tells us in his latest study of the topic. Most people familiar with the war know about the 2,400 Britons who volunteered to join the International Brigades. Less well-known is the popular mobilisation of support that took place.

The scope of activities undertaken, the amounts raised (an estimated £180 million in today's money) and the multitude of organisations that sprang up were truly remarkable. People organised street collections, sent food ships to Spain, looked after child refugees or marched in favour of 'Arms for Spain'.

As the police informant said of his colleagues at the Royal Aircraft Establishment in Farnborough, which in the 1930s was a hotbed of political radicalism, they had all gone, as the title of this book says, 'Spain mad'.

The book's first and longest chapter offers an overview of these collective and individual efforts in support of the Republic. The other ten chapters are essentially biographical.

Two are dedicated to groundbreaking historians Hugh Thomas, author of the magisterial The Spanish Civil War (1961) and Jim Fyrth whose The Signal Was Spain (1985) first documented the breadth and depth of the Aid Spain movement.

In other chapters we meet Philip Jordan, a News Chronicle Spanish Civil War correspondent who became a press secretary in the postwar Attlee government. Another figure rescued from obscurity is Anglican priest E.O. Iredell, who visited Spain four times as part of his campaigning.

The writer and Labour politician G.T. Garrett stood unsuccessfully in a parliamentary by-election in Plymouth Drake in June 1937 on a platform critical of the Conservative-led government's 'non-intervention' policy towards Spain.

Five chapters are given over to combatants, including two former commanders of the British Battalion in Spain: Wilfred Macartney, who was perhaps accurately described in police files as 'an unscrupulous adventurer', and Fred Copeman, who later converted to Catholicism and spent time as a leading figure in the Moral Re-Armament movement.

The other volunteers profiled include Frank Whitfield, an English-born Canadian killed near Zaragoza in March 1938, and artist Felicia Browne, who was killed as a militiawoman in Aragón early in the war. She shares a chapter with her friend, the Hungarian-born journalist Edith Bone.

Under his real name of Eric Blair, George Orwell was also a soldier in Spain. He spent six months in the militia of the revolutionary POUM (Partido Obrero de Unificación Marxista), serving on the Aragón front before being caught up in the fighting in Barcelona in May 1937 between government forces and the POUM. The spark was the move by the authorities to take over the city's telephone exchange, which was being run by a workers' committee. Support came from all the parties in the Popular Front government: communists, socialists, left-liberals and Basque and Catalan nationalists.

Orwell's account of his experiences in Spain, Homage to Catalonia, has been criticised by historians both for its accuracy and its misleading and narrowly-focused view of the war.

Buchanan portrays Orwell as a political innocent who is appalled by the 'vendetta' waged against the POUM. The party was banned and vilified as a Trotskyist fifth-column and its leader, Andreu Nin, was murdered by Soviet agents.

Buchanan argues that the importance of Orwell's testimony is that it shows how in later works his experiences 'had been transmuted into the basis of his new thinking about the dangers of totalitarianism'.

However, by framing the May Days, in Buchanan's words, as a 'moral rather than political' issue, Orwell was holding the Spanish Republic to a standard no other government fighting for its survival would be expected to live up to. Censorship, mendacious propaganda and the repression of internal enemies are sadly not uncommon in wartime.

Would any other government have tolerated the telephone exchange of its main city being held by political opponents who prioritised their revolutionary ambitions above the war effort? Any other government would also have taken urgent steps to incorporate the militias into the national army and to assert centralised control over arms and food production.

Barcelona was already in crisis, its population swollen by starving refugees. The war was going badly for the Republic. Málaga, which had been defended by militias, had not long ago been overrun by the enemy with barely a fight but followed by an orgy of violence inflicted on its population. In the north, Guernica had just been flattened by Hitler's Condor Legion. Bilbao was under siege and was weeks away from falling.

Buchanan, like Orwell, ignores this wider context. For an alternative perspective see the chapter 'Lights and Shadows in George Orwell's Homage to Catalonia' in Paul Preston's Perfidious Albion: Britain and the Spanish Civil War (The Clapton Press, 2024).

JOHN FOSTER, LANGUAGES OF CLASS STRUGGLE: COMMUNICATION AND MASS MOBILISATION IN BRITAIN AND IRELAND 1842-1972

(PRAXIS PRESS, 2024)

ROGER SEIFERT

Roger Seifert was professor of Industrial Relations at Keele (1993-2008) and at Wolverhampton (2008-2018). He specialises in strikes, public sector industrial relations, trade unions, the role of the state and labour history.

This study of the importance of class consciousness in class struggle takes us straight into some of the major debates on historical materialism rooted in revolutionary theory. We are invited into a world of struggle and conflict in which the working-class movement can achieve significant victories over the powerful array of the forces of organised capitalism. The point, however, is to transform such moments of practical success into something more by changing the entire world outlook of those involved. Defeating the linguistic and therefore ideological spin offs from an alienated workforce 'estranged' from their own interests through an obsessive cash nexus requires both an organised class-based political movement and self-aware need to take state power as a concrete realisation of such shifts in consciousness. This approach builds on Cohen's masterful work on ideology and exploitation (G. Cohen 1988, History, Labour and Freedom, Clarendon Press) and supports the contentions of Amartya Sen (The idea of Justice, 2009, Penguin) of the need for mass discussions to make sense of notions such as a 'just war' and an 'unjust peace'.

Five case studies across the years, in different parts of the United Kingdom, and with separate causes and legacies are explored. The focus is on the debates held within the arenas of the main protagonists starting with two examples from Clydeside: 1971-2 and 1919. These internal debates are couched in terms of splits inside the Conservative governments as between different sectional interests of finance and industrial capital and as between London-based and Scottish interests. The labour movement remained divided on tactics and strategy as its activists sought to come to terms with changes in the objective realities of everyday management practices (productivity bargaining) within a broader spectrum of external pressures on the profitability of firms. Despite the different time periods and given all that happened in between 1919 and the early 1970s, nonetheless the workers' struggles reflected the intense schism as between communists seeking betterment now in order to build a movement for fundamental change after, and those social democrats seeking improvements through accommodation with the management and their political backers.

We then move across the Irish sea to Belfast in 1919 and then a cross country phenomenon in proto-revolutionary Councils of Action 1919-1920. Quoting from the Workers' Bulletin in Belfast we are shown the importance of framing the argument for the strike in terms of wider class interests and dismantling the propaganda on offer from the owners and their political allies. The Councils of Action reflected both the powerful example of the Russian revolution and the desperate needs of the hour of those sections of the working-class betrayed and berated by the so-called national government -- no country for young men and women. In all of this the battle for the heart and soul of the labour movement was fought through the Labour Party and TUC, but more importantly in the day-to-day debates and activities surrounding actual struggles and their efforts to deliver a common cause solution through untied revolutionary grass roots.

The book ends with the case of the 1842 General Stike and the involvement of Marx and Engels in the struggles of their own age. It provides a detailed study in the dialectics of theory building and how only through the material experiences of fighting the class enemy, face to face, can a sustainable alternative to the dominant ideology of the ruling class be forged. The conclusion is that 'socialism, as a social system depends on that silence having been broken. It requires voices, many, many voices, exposing how the engine of exploitation works and how to end it' (p. 182).

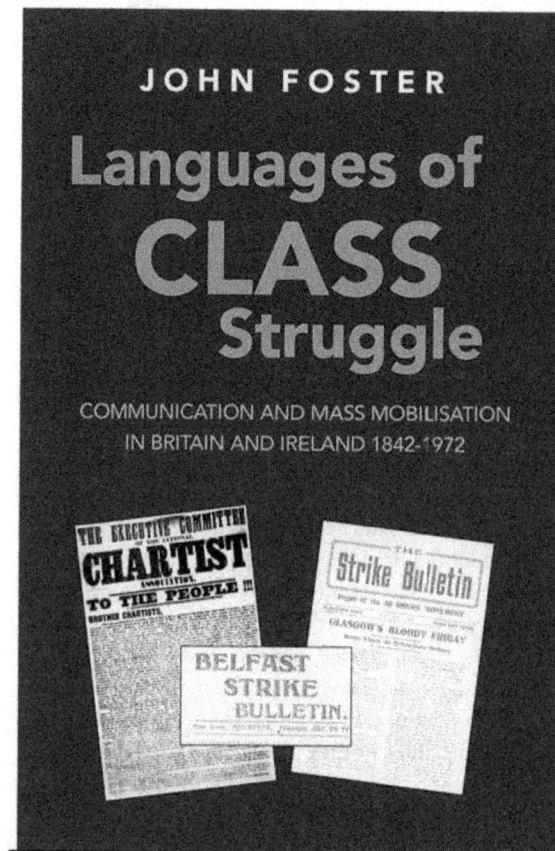

JOHN FOSTER

Languages of CLASS Struggle

COMMUNICATION AND MASS MOBILISATION IN BRITAIN AND IRELAND 1842-1972

'WESTERN' MARXISM: DIALECTICS, CAPITAL, CLASS AND OUR PLANET

RICHARD CLARKE

Richard taught ecology, conservation and science studies at London University where he directed the Birkbeck Centre for European Protected Area Research. He currently works as consultant to Lottery-funded environment schemes, is a Visiting Scholar at the University of Westminster, and edits a fortnightly 'Marxist question-and-answer' feature in the Morning Star newspaper.

Domenico Losurdo, Western Marxism: How It Was Born, How It Died, How It Can Be Reborn. Edited by Gabriel Rockhill.
(New York: Monthly Review Press, 2024)

John Bellamy Foster, The Dialectics of Ecology: Socialism and Nature.
(New York: Monthly Review Press, 2024)

These two important texts - both at first sight with little in common apart from their publication by Monthly Review Press – are linked. Both address the retreat of 'Western' Marxism from practice into theoretical debates which side-line imperialism and ecology. Dialectics of Ecology rescues dialectics from 'Western Marxists' (who if they considered it at all, denied its relevance to non-human nature) and Western Marxism critiques their self-referential 'defeatism, utopianism, and anti-communism'.

First published in 2017, a year before his death, this first English translation of Italian communist philosopher, historian and politician Domenico Losurdo's text, is a trenchant criticism of a school of intellectual discourse – from the Frankfurt School of the 1930s onwards. Losurdo begins by documenting the separation of 'Western' from 'Eastern' (sometimes 'classical' or 'orthodox') Marxism especially in relation to the latter's development after the 1917 October Revolution. Following the failure of revolution to spread throughout Europe some left intellectuals were unable to come to terms with the contradictory realities of building a state capable of resisting its encirclement by imperialism.

Academics and political dissidents associated with the Frankfurt Institute for Social Research (founded in 1923) including Max Horkheimer (from 1930 its director, who relocated it to the US during the Nazi period), Theodor Adorno, Walter Benjamin, Herbert Marcuse, and Jürgen Habermas, retreated into an analysis of the social and political superstructure of western European society. Through selected quotes their work, together with that of other luminaries such as Michel Foucault and Antonio Negri, is subject to a sustained critique for its Eurocentric blinkers and its dismissal (or ignorance) of the way that the consolidation of power in what became the USSR inspired anti-colonial revolutions elsewhere, not least in China, Vietnam and Cuba as well as Africa and Latin America.

The common thread, argues Losurdo, is their inability to understand or accept the realities of building a state capable of withstanding the military and economic aggression of imperialism;

a '...diffidence toward power, seen as a source of intellectual and moral contamination. The bifurcation between Eastern Marxism and Western Marxism comes down to a contrast between Marxists who exercise power and Marxists who were in opposition and concentrated increasingly on "critical theory," "deconstruction" and denouncing power and power relations as such.'

A particular target is Hannah Arendt, in her move from the left to her Cold War identification of the USSR under Stalin with Hitler's Germany as equal in 'totalitarianism'. Another is Slavoj Žižek whose (fading) popularity among students new to Marx and Marxism is sometimes held to be a revival of Western Marxism but which Losurdo declares is - together with Žižek's support for NATO's proxy war against Russia and his dismissal of Cuba's difficult task of building socialism - its 'last gasp'.

Losurdo's critique is summarised by the book's editor Gabriel Rockhill in an introduction written together with Jennifer Ponce de León. They assert that the whole of Western Marxism represents a withdrawal from action, to change the world into the academy; a shift away from political and economic issues (especially those of class and imperialism) in favour of philosophic and aesthetic concerns characterised by 'Eurocentric social chauvinism [...] the dogmatic rejection of actually existing socialism [...] a celebration of marketable novelty at the expense of practical relevance, and self-promotional opportunism that perpetuates cultural imperialism and disdain for Marxism in the Global South'. For its exponents, they argue, 'the exchange value of Marxist theory', augmented by 'Western Marxism's novelty and originality, is more important than its use value for human liberation.'

Rockhill himself has done significant work in uncovering the CIA's recruitment of intellectuals as instruments - whether they knew it or not - of America's role in the 'Western' development of Marxism itself, producing a 'version of Marxism that is ultimately compatible with capitalist interests'. The Frankfurt School was funded by the Rockefeller Foundation and some of its most prominent representatives moved directly into the employ of the US government, their springboard into academia. 'Western Marxism is not just an organic outgrowth of the imperial superstructure, it has been directly fashioned and promoted by the world's leading imperialist state and its capitalist ruling class.'

However, Losurdo's scattergun approach has some faults. Much of his argument is built around an eclectic but selective paste-in of quotations, for many of which (as pointed out by his editors) no sources are given. He rightly criticises Western Marxists for appropriating the work and names of György Lukács and Antonio Gramsci, both of whom were committed communists. But he also dismisses Perry Anderson, editor of the New Left Review who popularised the term 'Western Marxism' and whose critique of its development anticipated (in gentler terms) some of Losurdo's own condemnation. Importantly, Losurdo largely ignores those western (little 'w', including British) communists – including those who risked their own lives (in Spain from 1936 to 1938 to South Africa in the 1960s and 1970s) and other Marxist intellectuals as well as radical physicists, chemists, biologists and polymaths whose work engaged with the 'base' as well as its 'superstructure' and whose political commitment was manifest in practice as well as in theory.

It is those natural scientists – from J.B.S. Haldane, J.D. Bernal et al to Barry Commoner, Richard Lewontin, Richard Levins, Stephen Jay Gould, Steven Rose and others who have fed into today's radical environmentalism as well as building on the 'ecological' Marx and Engels – who feature prominently in the works of John Bellamy Foster. The Dialectics of Ecology returns to Foster's recognition in his Marx's Ecology (2000) that what is commonly held to be 'Western Marxism' ignores a parallel current in the West that very much adopted a 'dialectical' approach – to history, to economics and, most significantly, to nature.

There were two 'negations' of dialectical materialism – both in relation to Engels' Dialectics of Nature which as Foster points out in his preface 'has long divided the Marxist tradition'. One is what Foster calls 'official Marxism' in the Soviet Union (of which the Lysenko period had the most damaging physical impact) which reduced dialectics to a catechism, whilst what is often called the 'Western' Marxist philosophical tradition (principally academic 'social scientists' often disconnected from political action altogether) simply rejected it all together; 'a dual negation of the dialectics of nature emanating from the Cold War antagonism between East and West.' But, as Foster declares, that 'dual negation' 'has been increasingly transcended in recent decades as material conditions have changed'. Central to that change, along with (as Losurdo argues) the transcendence of 'Western Marxism' in general, is a recognition of the centrality of Marxist theory – and practice – to the growing environmental crisis.

Ironically, some of those like Kōhei Saito who, along with Foster, have helped to rescue the 'ecological Marx' have in the process, along with 'Western' Marxists in general, also rejected Engels. Foster challenges Saito for his argument that Engels helped '"to make Marx's ecology invisible" with disastrous effects for later Marxist theory'. In this, argues Foster, Saito attempts 'to reinforce the notion within the Western Marxist philosophical tradition that Engels' dialectics of nature, with its wider materialism, was antithetical to Marx's own historical materialism'. Foster, by contrast, asserts that there is no evidence for a 'methodological break' between Marx and Engels, concluding that 'rather than perpetuating old divisions within the left' their analyses are 'integrally related. The object should be to unite the first and second foundations of Marxist thought, providing a broader material basis for the critique of the capitalist mode of production as the essential ground for a revolutionary ecosocialist praxis in the twenty-first century.'

A second challenge is to Saito's claim in Marx in the Anthropocene that Marx's Eurocentrism in Capital assumes that 'all countries everywhere had to follow the same linear European path'. Foster asserts that Marx makes it clear in his preface to Capital that it 'was directed solely at conditions in Western Europe, and specifically at the significance of the British developments for what was later to come in Germany' and that Marx himself was clear that 'fundamentally different lines of development were possible in Russia and in other non-capitalist societies'. In this, of course anti-colonial struggles have been, and will remain, central.

The 10 chapters rehearse previously published material so there is some duplication – not a bad thing, because it means each chapter can be read, as Foster declares, as a 'totality' in itself. One of the shortest, on China, complements Losurdo's own censure of Western Marxists for their dismissal of the difficult post-revolutionary task of building socialism and of China's survival - longer than any other socialist state – and modernisation in the face of economic and military encirclement. Foster recounts the work of Joseph Needham's 1976 'thesis of the correlative development of organic materialism both East and West, with Marxism as the connecting link' and his assertion that 'China has in her time learnt much from the rest of the world; now perhaps it is time for the nations and the continents to learn again from her.' Foster calls for a vision of – and programme for 'degrowth communism' based on Marx and Engels' own vision of sustainable human development, focused on the production of use value rather than exchange value. His final chapter, 'Planned Degrowth: Ecosocialism and Sustainable Human Development' is in many ways the most important – and the most challenging. This argues for a shift, in 'wealthy societies' to 'net zero capital formation' with 'replacement investment' to deliver steady qualitative advances in production while exploitative labour conditions and reduced working hours. 'coupled with global redistribution of the surplus product and reduction of waste would allow for vast improvements in the lives of most people. Planned degrowth, which specifically targets the most opulent sectors of the world population, is thus directed at the enhancement of the living conditions of the vast majority while maintaining the environmental conditions of existence and promoting sustainable human development.' This, declares Foster, would involve creating a 'whole new stage of ecological civilization based on the creation of a society of substantive equality, of ecosocialism'.

The question, of course, is how that 'new stage' can be achieved. Losurdo argues that anti-colonial struggles will be critical; Foster that these will involve a growing 'environmental proletariat' increasingly challenging capitalism's expropriation of nature as well as its exploitation of labour. Western Marxism's subtitle (and its final section) addresses the possibility of Western Marxism's rebirth. That 'rebirth' (if one were needed) is well under way and is in no way restricted to the 'west'. As Foster argues here and in his 2022 Engels Memorial Lecture (published in this journal) the reuniting of our growing understanding of the dialectics of nature with that of the dialectics of society; 'the critique of political economy with the ecological critique of capitalism' including its global threat to our planet and its peoples, represents an ongoing 'second foundation' of Marxism.

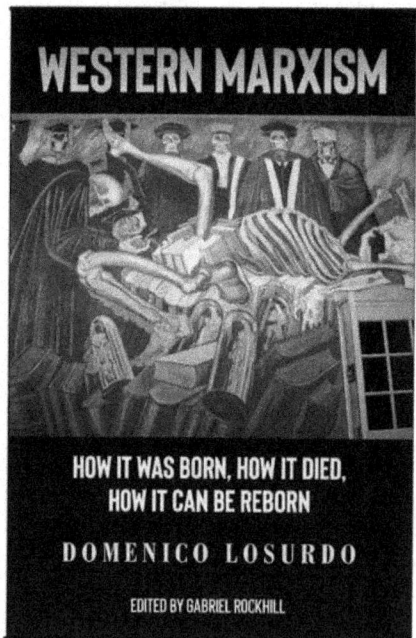

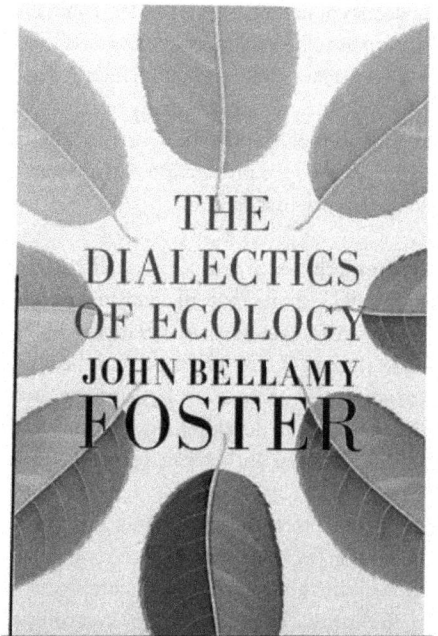

NOTE   Foster's 2022 Engels Memorial Lecture 'Engels and the Second Foundation of Marxism' can be viewed on the Marx Memorial Library's website https://bit.ly/2022EngelsLecture

KOHEI SAITO, MARX IN THE ANTHROPOCENE – TOWARDS THE IDEA OF DEGROWTH COMMUNISM
(CAMBRIDGE UNIVERSITY PRESS, 2022)

ARVINDER SINGH

Arvinder Singh is a member of the Communist Party of Britain.
He works as a Community Pharmacist.

This is a fascinating contribution to the debate on the relationship between Marxism and ecology. Saito builds his case for Degrowth Communism on the premise that after the publication of the first volume of Capital, Marx's research led the latter to develop a theory of 'metabolism' and its 'relationship with ecology' which conflicted with Engels's understanding of dialectics. These notebooks, Saito suggests, signal a transformation of 'Marx's idea of communism' and his abandonment of Historical Materialism, with its Eurocentric and productivist baggage. Towards the end of his life, Marx's serious engagement with non-Western society led him to acknowledge the 'revolutionary potentialities' of societies based on communal landed property.

Saito contends that a critical difference between Marx and Engels is that whereas Engels believed that once capitalism was transcended, ecosocialism would fully emancipate productive forces for the sake of the working class, the late Marx 'distanced himself from the endorsement of endless growth and pointed to the need for social equality and sustainability based on the problems of "communism in living."'

The book provides an elucidation of the concept of metabolic rift and a useful overview of the philosophical controversies surrounding it. Saito confronts an array of monist philosophical challenges to the theory. Along the way, notions such as 'luxury communism' are effectively debunked. In perhaps the most interesting section of the book, Saito engages with the work of György Lukács, who, Saito claims, 'called for establishing a new dialectical science that takes into account both dimensions [the social and natural] for the sake of establishing a more sustainable society.'

Saito sets himself the task of contributing 'to the practical task of providing solutions to the ecological crisis.' What might a post-capitalist, communist, society look like? He provides a list of five reasons that communism increases the chance of repairing the metabolic rift compared with capitalist production, the implementation of which he can't imagine as feasible without degrowth. There's little to disagree with, but it reads like a wish-list rather than the promised solutions.

One only has to switch on the news to see that the world is indeed on fire, as Saito declares at the beginning of his book. If 'Pandemic, war and climate breakdown are all symptomatic of the end of history', then Saito lays the blame firmly at the door of the triumph of neoliberal globalisation. Having worked so hard to free Marx and himself of any perceived association with the 'past dogmas of Orthodox Marxism', it is perhaps unsurprising that Saito seems unwilling to speak of imperialism. If we consider the practical objective to be the uprooting of capitalism and its insatiable thirst for profit, there's no way around Engels and the struggle against imperialism. It is difficult to imagine that one simply needs to choose between productivism and degrowth communism.

Saito's book, in my view, serves as a useful overview of the debates and controversies within Marxist approaches to ecology. He does, though, expend much effort in absolving Marx of any responsibility for the 'technocratic productivism of Engels and his Promethean' descendants', and his charge of Eurocentrism against Marx is hardly new.

None of this should prevent anyone from reading this book. With the increasing realisation that capitalism now constitutes an existential threat to humanity, Saito shines a light on the enduring relevance and power of Marxism.

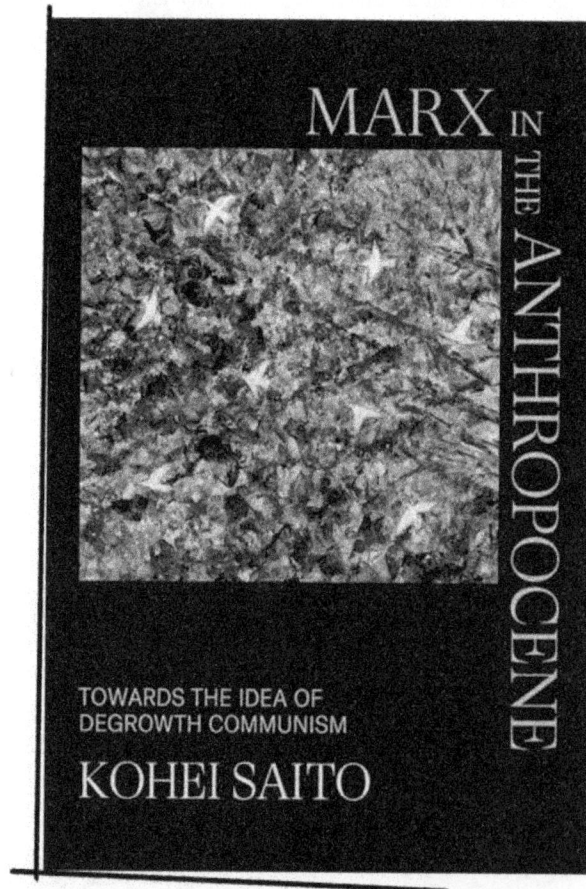

MARX IN THE ANTHROPOCENE

TOWARDS THE IDEA OF
DEGROWTH COMMUNISM

KOHEI SAITO

KOHEI SAITO, SLOW DOWN: HOW DEGROWTH COMMUNISM CAN SAVE THE WORLD
(WEIDENFELD & NICOLSON, 2024)

RICHARD MURGATROYD

Richard Murgatroyd is a historian, teacher and landscape gardener.

This is an ambitious book about the most important issue facing humanity today. It is also well-written, lively and accessible. Saito, a Marxist economist, first published Slow Down in Japan, where it became an instant best seller. His starting point is the environmental and resource crisis, in what he calls the age of the 'Anthropocene'. This background is well known, and the focus is very much about what we can and must do to secure the future health, prosperity and even existence of humanity. He claims that 'a new Marx for a new era' shows us the way.

Why new? Saito argues that in later life Marx came to revise or even reject some of his earlier ideas in light of research undertaken into imperialism, ecology and the dynamics of communal society. As a result, he abandoned Eurocentrism and the epochal historical materialism of the Communist Manifesto. Now he believed that there could be multiple roads to socialism. Building on his studies of communes and communal living, he came to reject 'productionism' and instead moved towards a vision of a 'degrowth communism' that emphasised internationalism, equality, regulation, sustainability and a steady-state economy.

This late-Marx approach is clearly at odds with most twentieth century Marxists who strove to build on the industrial and technological means of production created by capitalism. Clearly the urge for profit dramatically boosted the productive forces. The socialist imperative was to collectivise, plan and fairly distribute them. Saito argues this productionism had a number of adverse effects for the socialist project.

Firstly, it required an industrial work regime that mimicked capitalism, prevented workers' self-management and more sustainable, community-rooted forms of production. Instead of bottom-up mutual aid, socialist state planners created top-down bureaucratic systems with strong divisions of labour built around economic 'growth'. Just as under capitalism, the ensuing targets took little account of the environment, while stifling equality and democracy Secondly, the pursuit of commodity production to sustain what Saito calls the 'Imperial Mode of Living', with all its empty, consumerist excesses, is quite simply environmentally unsustainable. The earth cannot carry endless growth and the impact on species, resources and climate that it inevitably entails.

Thirdly, shifting the socialist struggle away from productivist demands opens space for things that really can make us happy, creative, socially connected and fulfilled. So, while Saito continually emphasises that he does not oppose technology and industry in favour of a return to an agrarian 'good life', neither communism nor a sustainable world can be achieved by authoritarian 'Climate Maoism', with its rule by bureaucrats and experts.

As Saito acknowledges, for many Marxists this is controversial, but argues that the shift in Marx's later thought is evidenced in the surviving writings. He points out that only volume one of Capital was published in Marx's lifetime, while volumes two and three were edited and revised by Engels after his death. Crucially, this didn't reflect the unpublished work undertaken by Marx after the publication of volume one which not only deepened his understanding of capitalism's relationship to the natural world, but also the shape of any future communist society.

Saito goes further and argues that degrowth communism is 'a project that might truly topple European capitalism'. For, he claims, Marx came to understand that the struggle for internationalism, social equality, democracy and authentic 'abundance' was inextricably linked with the need to create a 'metabolic relationship' between humans and nature. Not only would this vision address the alienation and destructiveness of capitalism but also offer something immeasurably better for working people across the world. Indeed, unless humanity turns away from capitalist productivism, we are in serious trouble as a species. As Saito puts it, this 'book is [therefore] meant to be a version of Capital for this new era, a thorough critique of capital illuminating the bright future to come'.

This is obviously big picture stuff, but his argument is closely supported by numerous detailed examples that thoroughly debunk any claims for a sustainable 'green' capitalism. Saito also effectively critiques existing alternatives put forward by eco-socialist thinkers which envisage technology unlocking 'luxury automated communism'. Less convincing, for this reviewer at least, was the textual evidence in support of Marx's late-life shift in thinking, which was rather sparse. But in a real sense that didn't matter. For an understanding of the true limits and possibilities of the natural world and its proper relationship with humanity are central to historical materialism. Marx and Engels certainly understood the damage capitalism was doing to the planet. But ultimately, they were men of their age and could only extrapolate from the evidence before them. We don't have that excuse. As our scientific knowledge of the climate emergency deepens, it's hard to disagree with Saito's argument that degrowth communism is now firmly on the agenda.

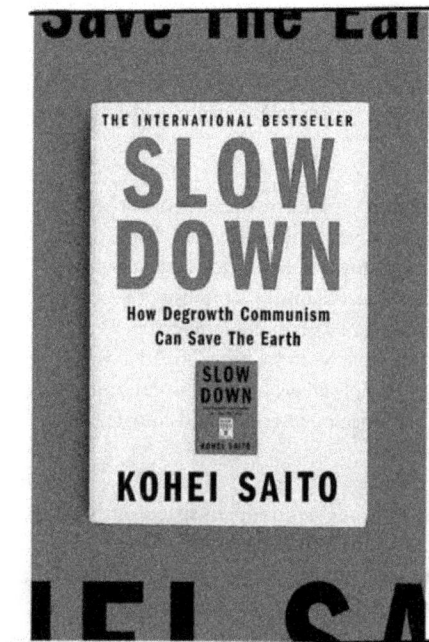

ROGER MCKENZIE, AFRICAN UHURU: THE FIGHT FOR AFRICAN FREEDOM IN THE RISE OF THE GLOBAL SOUTH
(MANIFESTO PRESS, 2024)

LUKE DANIELS

Luke Daniels is President of Caribbean Labour Solidarity

African UHURU is a work rooted in the author's experience as a trade unionist and pan-African advocate, bringing us back time and again to the importance of black self-liberation, while acknowledging the support of white allies in the fight to defeat racism and fascism. There is much food for thought for academics and activists alike, as Roger McKenzie explores race and class consciousness. He is unflinching in his analysis of the issue of racism, unafraid to apply critical thinking where merited. The Labour Party and trade union movement come under severe scrutiny, and not unfairly so; yet McKenzie speaks as only a friend can, particularly about the trade union movement, where he has had considerable first-hand experience.

He chronicles British working-class struggles, including race riots and challenges to the colour bar leading to Black self-organisation to resist oppression not only in the workplace but in public spaces. He charts the invaluable history of black workers' struggles in the trade union movement and believes 'that it is in the vital interests of the working class to unite against racism'.

We learn about the numerous practical applications of Black self-organisation - Black used as a term to embrace all non-white peoples, drawing on the experience of enslavement and colonialism to organise against racism - as in the Indian Workers Association. Tribute is paid to founding members of the Labour Party Black Sections such as Diane Abbott, Bernie Grant, Paul Boateng and Keith Vaz.

McKenzie is mindful of the shoulders we stand on in the fight for liberation. His broad sweep of the black radical tradition at times reads like a Who's Who of radical thinkers, from W.E.B. DuBois to Malcolm X and beyond, touched on but not necessarily looked at in depth – which would require a book at least twice the size – though he leaves the reader with a number of works to revisit or discover. We are reminded of the roots of the Pan African movement, and its centrality in challenging white hegemonic supremacist power. He links Africans and their descendants in the struggles for self-actualisation. Marcus Mosiah Garvey and his UNIA movement comes in for special attention.

McKenzie sees the intersection of race and class as crucial; African UHURU is rooted in local experience but is internationalist in outlook. It takes us to the heart of the insurgencies that have left an indelible mark on the world, including the Russian and Cuban revolutions.

We go on a roller-coaster ride with grass-roots activists and the black intelligentsia from every region of the Caribbean, USA, and Africa. We hear from Marcus Garvey to Walter Rodney, C.L.R. James, Eric Williams, Cheikh Anta Diop, Angela Davis, Claudia Jones, George Padmore and Richard Hart, to mention a few, whose works are still relevant to the solutions of black empowerment today.

He sees central to ending racism is winning the white working class to the movement. Trade unions have a key role to play. Although, historically, there was open resistance to black workers in what were seen as traditional white working-class jobs, there has been a shift in attitude, because of activism and leadership shown by white allies.

McKenzie not only charts historical resistance via theory and practice but sees solutions to ending the capitalist divide-and-rule era. Above all, this is a book of hope that systems of oppression will change, and that Africans have a key role in making change for a peaceful world a reality. A must-read for experienced activists and emerging black and white leaders, fighting oppression in all its forms. This is a timely contribution to the body of work challenging racism and fascism the world over.

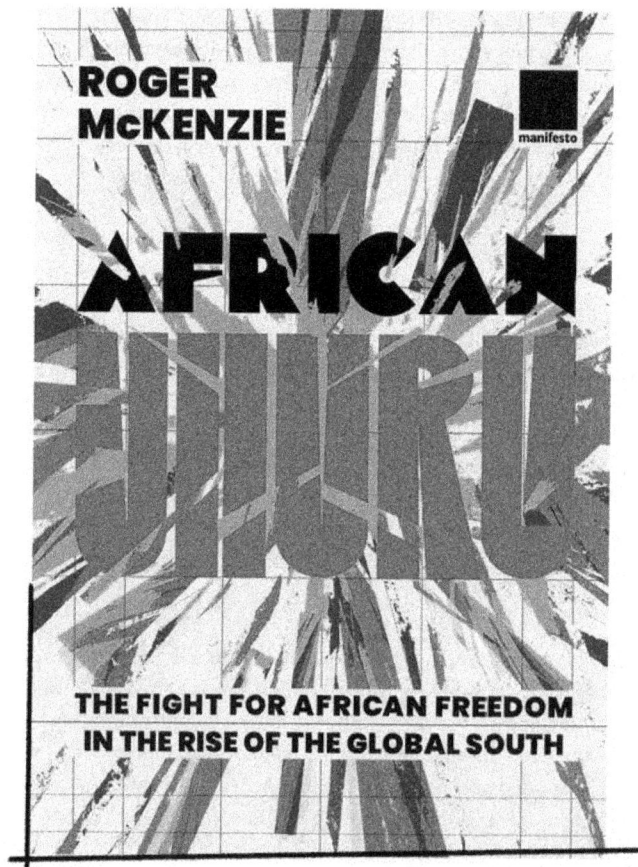

DAVID LANE, GLOBAL NEOLIBERAL CAPITALISM AND THE ALTERNATIVES: FROM SOCIAL DEMOCRACY TO STATE CAPITALISMS

(BRISTOL UNIVERSITY PRESS, 2024)

KENNY COYLE

Kenny Coyle is a writer and publisher with specialist knowledge of China and elsewhere in Asia

David Lane's latest book Global Neoliberal Capitalism and the Alternatives: From Social Democracy to State Capitalisms, is a concise yet comprehensive overview of the doctrines and practices of neoliberalism.

Lane examines the historical development of neoliberal capitalism, its global impact, and the challenges it poses to equality, democracy, and sustainable development. He looks critically at the two major historical alternatives to capitalism which came to the fore in the first half of the twentieth century: social democracy, particularly in its post-1945 format, and the state socialist nations that spread out worldwide following the October 1917 Revolution in Russia. Lane believes the exhaustion of both these alternatives in the last period of the twentieth century has been a major factor in what appeared to be the apparent definitive triumph of neoliberalism, the 'end of history' in what now appears to be an embarrassingly inaccurate prediction.

The book begins by tracing the rise of neoliberal capitalism, which emerged in the twentieth century as counter to Keynesianism and a variety of state-led economic models.

Lane's second chapter 'Global Neoliberalism and What it Means' outlines the theoretical and political origins of neoliberal ideology from Ludwig von Mises and Friedrich Hayek to Milton Friedman and the Monetarist school. This chapter, one of the most comprehensive outlines of neoliberalism, is highly recommended even as a standalone piece. During the last quarter of the twentieth century, neoliberalism went from a fringe academic current to become the dominant global paradigm, embraced by governments from Washington to London and promoted by institutions such as the International Monetary Fund and the World Bank.

Despite its intellectual pretensions, Lane argues that fundamentally 'neoliberalism' is predicated on a simplistic economic of human behaviour. Lane argues that this system has had devastating social consequences, exacerbating inequality, undermining social welfare, and concentrating power in the hands of transnational corporations and financial elites. He shows that neoliberal policies have led to economic instability, environmental degradation, and erosion of democratic institutions. The author explores the social and political consequences of neoliberal capitalism, particularly its impact on labour, public services, and global inequality.

He highlights how the commodification of public goods, such as healthcare and education, has affected marginalised communities. Lane discusses the rise of populist movements and political polarisation as reactions to the failures of neoliberalism, suggesting that these trends reflect widespread dissatisfaction with the status quo.

In the second part of the book, Lane examines alternatives to neoliberal capitalism. First, he considers social democracy, which sought to balance market economies with social welfare systems and progressive taxation. While acknowledging some successes in reducing inequality and providing social welfare, Lane believes that social democracy has faced challenges, including pressure to deregulate and privatise. He argues that a renewed social democratic model, adapted to contemporary global conditions, could offer a viable alternative.

More contentiously, Lane also analyses 'state capitalism' which he sees as being practiced in countries such as China and Russia. In his view, these countries combine state control over key industries with market mechanisms, allowing for rapid economic growth and poverty reduction. However, he dislikes this system's authoritarianism, limited freedoms, and corruption. Even so, Lane suggests that this 'state capitalism' represents a significant challenge to neoliberal orthodoxy and offers lessons for nations seeking to assert greater control over their economies. Nonetheless, some critics may find Lane's combination of Russia and China under a single 'state capitalist' system unsatisfying, although he does offer certain nuances. Even for those who question some of his concepts, Lane has assembled a truly impressive amount of data and sources to buttress his arguments.

The author has lectured in China and knows the country well, yet it's a little disappointing that his stimulating discussion of China's 'socialist market economy' relies so heavily on Western interpretations without including Chinese-based debates. Admittedly, the currently available English-language material on the topic is still frustratingly sparse. The Chinese concept of the 'primary stage of socialism', a major and fundamental rethinking of socialist development and the path and stages that takes societies from capitalism to socialism, is not addressed. This is a pity since it possibly provides a useful counterpoint to some interpretations of China's transition from 'state socialism'.

These points aside, Global Neoliberal Capitalism and the Alternatives, is an invaluable contribution to debates on the future of the global economy and yet another impressive work to add to Lane's lifetime fascination with post-capitalist, and post-socialist transitions.

JIM WHISTON AND ELAINE MCFARLAND (EDS.), WHAT HISTORY IS FOR? ESSAYS IN HONOUR OF PROFESSOR JOHN FOSTER
(MANIFESTO PRESS, 2024)

GAWAIN LITTLE

Gawain Little is general secretary of the General Federation of Trade Union

This slim volume is a treasure trove of dialectics and historical materialism. A collection of short essays by a range of authors in honour of Marxist historian and educator Professor John Foster, it is as wide-ranging as the work of its dedicatee. From Marxist historiography to community organising, from public health to the role of imperialism today, there is plenty here for anyone with an interest in Marxist approaches to understanding the world we live in – and changing it.

The diverse range of authors leads to a combination of different writing styles, structures and approaches. All eleven chapters are lively and engaging, and the variation in style and subject makes the book as a whole a refreshing and rewarding read.

As the authors note, Professor Foster has had an impact on a huge number of different disciplines, from his first published book – on the Class Struggle and the Industrial Revolution in 1974 – onwards. This first publication, praised by Eric Hobsbawm as 'strikingly original and lucid 'technically sophisticated' and overall 'a remarkable book', broke new ground in explaining the dilution of working class militancy in the first half of the 19th century, as detailed in Mary Davis' opening chapter. Davis looks at Foster's defence of the Marxist approach to history, and of historical materialism specifically. In doing so, she gives a useful summary of key tenets of the approach.

Next up, Chick Collins looks at the contribution Foster has made to understanding Scotland's 'excess mortality'. For someone with no background in public health, this was a fascinating and very readable account, that demonstrates not just the unique contribution made by Foster but the way in which a Marxist approach can illuminate problems by applying a more comprehensive and yet more critical lens. This is replicated in subsequent chapters on workplace struggle; class, culture and nation; anti-capitalist resistance; community organising; the recent strike wave; imperialism; religion; the role of Black communists; and psychological trauma. Whilst covering a huge breadth of subjects, each individual piece is accessible to a non-specialist, develops understanding of the subject matter and demonstrates the way in which historical materialism enables us to understand the world as a dynamic totality, as opposed to the static and fragmented approaches of much of academia. As the title suggests, it does indeed provide a snapshot of 'What history is for'.

In spite of its brevity, there is much here to educate about the specific subject matter and to develop the reader's understanding of Marxism and its application to understanding and changing the world we live in. There could be no more fitting tribute to a giant of Marxist theory and practice.

AGUSTÍN LAGE DÁVILA, *THE KNOWLEDGE ECONOMY AND SOCIALISM: SCIENCE AND SOCIETY IN CUBA*
(MONTHLY REVIEW PRESS 2024)

JOHN GREEN

John Green is a writer, former trade union official and television journalist. He has written several political biographies including a well-received one on Friedrich Engels.

The term 'knowledge economy' has come to characterise the increasing importance of knowledge in the present stage of global economic development.

Industries that have moved to the centre of our economies in the last half century have as their business the production and distribution of knowledge and information rather than, as in the past, the production and distribution of objects. That is a paradigm shift.

As a result of the vindictive boycott by the USA, socialist Cuba has been forced to become increasingly self-reliant. Here, Cuban immunologist Dr. Agustín Lage Dávila compares Cuba's approach to utilising knowledge for the public good, rather than solely for commercial gain.

This book is a compilation of articles, published by him between 1994 and 2013, so there is some overlap, but each chapter holds useful nuggets of information and insight. The author is attempting to capture a conceptual elaboration that crystallises those two decades, based on his own practical experience and more generally to examine science's role in the construction of socialism in Cuba.

'Each chapter,' Dávila writes, 'can be read separately with relative independence from each other. Seen as a whole, what you read describes a social experience of constructing links among science, economy and culture, a creative experience of which we Cubans feel justly proud.'

The very idea of privatising intellectual property had been, until recently, unthinkable. Until the twentieth century, the accumulation of knowledge was viewed as a process belonging to all of us. Investigations and discoveries were in the public domain and free to be used by society as a whole. Science evolved and built on the work of others; knowledge was freely exchanged and built upon by others.

In the past, scientific papers were freely circulated, but today are invariably only accessible on payment of hefty fees. Up until the late nineteenth century, scientific research was carried out in home-based laboratories, often by dilettantes, or in public institutions of higher education. During the twentieth and twenty-first centuries, such research has become increasingly separated from the public sphere and attached or beholden to capitalist interests in private research centres. This has led to the development of scientific ideas almost exclusively within commercial contexts. With the increasing importance of electronics and associated software, as well as the development of chemical and pharmaceutical wares, intellectual ideas have come to be treated in just the same way as industrial fixed assets and physical labour, as exploitable.

In Cuba, the challenge of a knowledge economy has been taken up in a very different way from the capitalist world. Between 1959 and 2002 the number of schools in Cuba increased from 7,679 to 12,717, teaching personal increased ten-fold from 22,800 to 258,000; higher education centres increased from three to fifty-four (today sixty-five). The country has 221 research centres, employing more than 31,000. It has the world's highest ratio of doctors and teachers per inhabitant. This would have been impossible in a country run on capitalist lines and it has been achieved despite vindictive US embargoes and boycotts. This focus has enabled Cuba to compete globally. It makes complete sense for it to develop to the full the educational potential of its citizens and make full use of their knowledge potential.

The country has spent more than twenty years building a new sector of the economy: biotechnology. It currently operates more than a thousand patents in the biotechnology sector. It is 'knowledge property' Dávila says, but 'in different hands and with a different social meaning. Its meaning cannot be dissociated from the social (state) character of scientific research.'

As a result of its emphasis on bio-technical research, Cuba has been able to develop a whole range of medicines and vaccines, including a recent one for Covid. This research and development has had a huge impact not only on the health of the Cuban people themselves but also worldwide, as Cuba offers these products at affordable prices to other nations.

Today, in expanding industries and entire branches of the economy, it is not land, raw materials or even capital that have become the 'limiting resources' but knowledge. In the software industries, for example, raw materials play no role, everything is knowledge.

Between 1976 and 1996, the portion of world trade classified as 'high technology' (i.e. largely knowledge-based) doubled from eleven to twenty-two per cent, while that of primary products decreased significantly.

In a knowledge-based society like that emerging today, Cuban experience differs fundamentally from that of the capitalist market. In a knowledge-based economy the failure of market mechanisms and the contradiction under capitalism between the social character of production and the private character of appropriation – a contradiction that only socialism can overcome – becomes ever more evident,' Dávila argues.

In his concluding chapter, he answers questions posed by Cubans about the country's economy and the difficulties it faces. An informative and thought-provoking read.

DAVID MATTHEWS, THE CLASS STRUGGLE AND WELFARE: SOCIAL POLICY UNDER CAPITALISM

(MONTHLY REVIEW PRESS 2025)

RICHARD CLARKE

Richard taught ecology, conservation and science studies at London University where he directed the Birkbeck Centre for European Protected Area Research. He currently works as consultant to Lottery-funded environment schemes, is a Visiting Scholar at the University of Westminster, and edits a fortnightly 'Marxist question-and-answer' feature in the Morning Star newspaper.

An ongoing debate within the trades union and labour movement and within the left more generally, concerns the 'social wage' – collective provision of public goods and services ranging from education and health care through public libraries, parks and playing fields, public toilets, roads and pavements, to state regulation of food standards and environmental quality. All are funded in the last resort, through the value created by labour – via income taxes, VAT on the goods you buy, local rates and (yes, even) taxes on profits. Most hardly existed in Marx's day, except perhaps through charitably funded schools and hospitals – and workhouses.

David Matthews focuses on welfare and specifically (despite the American spelling) of 'labor' on the British 'welfare state' that emerged following the Second World War and which from 1979 has been increasingly under attack. He begins with a short primer on Marxist political economy, in particular regarding the state. The state under capitalism, he declares, is "ultimately a capitalist state, having the primary purpose of enforcing and protecting the conditions of accumulation, including labor's reproduction" with welfare "the dominant form of institutional provision outside of the informal care provided by the family." At the same time the state is itself "a location for the class struggle, having the conflict between capital and labor stamped upon it, resulting in it embodying contradictory values." "A Marxist understanding of social policy is to be aware of its duality" – including "state welfare as social control" enhancing national efficiency and labour productivity at the same time as alleviating the condition of the working class.

With chapters on social security, disability, health, housing and education, Matthews shows how welfare provision within capitalism is ultimately a product of class struggle – a dialectical phenomenon, the outcome of popular campaigns, tolerated and moulded by the state to suit the interests of capital.

Matthews' analysis starts with social security, declaring "the reproduction of labor power is a preeminent function of the welfare state" together with "maintaining the labor power of future members of the labor force." with its second core function "the maintenance of non-laboring groups [...] such as children, the elderly, individuals with disabilities, the long-term sick, those with caring responsibilities, and the unemployed who are not part of the labor market." "Social security exists as an institution of a capitalist state whose objective is the long-term preservation of capitalism" he declares. Today, as illustrated by the introduction of Universal Credit (UC) and the Employment Support Allowance (ESA), social security functions not as a 'safety net' but as an instrument of social control; physical and ideological.

On health, Matthews returns again to Marx and Engels who argued that the root cause of poor health was capitalist production, Marx writing of the "victims of industry, whose number increases with the increase of dangerous machinery, of mines, chemical works etc., the mutilated, the sickly." Today we would add personal and financial services – from healthcare to call centres. Healthcare under capitalism is, he argues, itself ideology, reducing health overwhelmingly to an individual, biological problem, which fits well with its increasing marketisation. Couched in the language of 'consumer choice' and with the opportunity for the private sector to be represented on them, these expose the English NHS "to an unprecedented threat of privatisation." By contrast, in Wales "the overall organisation and planning of healthcare remains the direct duty of the Welsh government, which delegates responsibility to regional state organisations in the form of Local Health Boards" and "there is very little market-driven distinction between purchaser and provider".

Along with the NHS, council housing was one of the most radical elements of the British welfare system. Housing today is much less a focus of welfare provision. In 1872, commenting on the attempt by 'enlightened' capitalists to facilitate home ownership by sections of the working class, Engels suggested that their motivation was that through the acquisition of house property, workers would also "lose their proletarian character and become once again obedient toadies." That – plus the opportunities for private profit it presented – was certainly the objective of Margaret Thatcher's 'Right to Buy' policy from the 1980s. Supposedly to advance the concept of a 'property owning democracy' it led to the collapse of investment in new social housing and a new 'generation rent' with over 40% of right-to-buy homes now privately rented, many from landlords with multiple properties.

Quoting Marx and Engels, Matthews argues that education involves the reproduction of labour power; in any society it is itself a form of commodity production. But under capitalism, it also involves the reproduction of the relations (as well as the forces) of production, via the acquisition of technical and intellectual skills, and through its ideological function, with children "a captive audience from their formative years." At the same time, there is a degree of autonomy in the educational system which allows for the development of politically conscious education professionals and also produces 'misfits and rebels.' Education itself is a "terrain of class struggle." The reversal of early hopes for a truly inclusive comprehensive education system was followed by neoliberal incursions. From the turn of the century, central government funded academies were introduced, removed from local authority control and managed by boards of directors (by whom their teachers are directly employed) to compete with comprehensive schools, both sectors placing increased emphasis on 'work readiness.'

Most readers will have some knowledge of issues raised in at least one of these chapters. But their assembly in one text, contextualised within a Marxist framework, is hugely valuable. Welfare provision - "a genuine productive gain for labour" - has been steadily eroded in recent decades, under both Labour and Tory administrations. Its defence has largely involved rearguard action, led by the workers and users most directly affected.

Rather than focusing on how such defensive action can be advanced, Matthews concludes with a vision of what collective action might be aimed at securing. His final chapter argues that "a socialist system of welfare, under the authority of the working-class, will have to look beyond the state." Quoting from Marx: "within the old form are the first sprouts of the new, although they naturally reproduce all the shortcomings of the existing system" he asserts that rather than reflecting only the needs of capital, welfare provision contains institutions and practices that are already in opposition to capitalism, representing foundations upon which a more equal and democratic economic and social life can be organised. Alongside state provision – including that of the local state 'mutual aid' will be important and can feed into a movement, not only to protect and extend what exists, but to fight for something better, including "an alternative society to capitalism, one which has at its heart equality, democracy, solidarity and love."

Matthews' analysis has been given yet greater urgency with Labour's determination to cut the welfare budget to fund preparations for war. This is an important text and should provide significant input to ongoing theoretical analysis and practical action to defend public services.

PATRONS OF THE MARX MEMORIAL LIBRARY & WORKERS SCHOOL

Patrons of the Marx Memorial Library & Workers' School are valued supporters whose contributions help us to secure a thriving future for our work as the leading education and research centre on Marxist and socialist history.

Contact Meirian Jump, MML Director, to find out more:
m.jump@marx-memorial-library.org.uk

- Kevin Acott
- Dyal Bagri
- Michael Bailey
- Bill Bowring
- Philip Brown
- Pauline Bryan
- Tony Burke
- Christine Child
- Mark Daniel
- John Deighan
- Ann Field
- Alex Gordon
- David Grove
- Lord John Hendy
- Michael Howells
- Michael Ironside
- Edward Keith Jerrome
- Chris Kaufman
- Sean Kettle
- David Lane
- Aleksei Logachev
- David McLoughlin
- Rob Machin
- Emil Maschner
- Caroline Michie
- Manuel Moreno
- Hank & Jean Roberts
- Alan Tait
- Claire & Len Weiss
- Penny Welch
- Robert West
- Dave Wetzel
- Barry White

MARX MEMORIAL LIBRARY & WORKERS' SCHOOL

Leading research and education centre on Marxism and socialist history in London's Clerkenwell

VISIT our historic building and displays including the Lenin Room on weekly tours and regular open days

ENGAGE in our dynamic education and events programme including lectures, panels, launches, online courses and more

EXPLORE our unique archive and library collections by booking a reading room appointment or bespoke workshop

VOLUNTEER with our fantastic team to play your part in our work

JOIN us and become a member or affiliate for as little as £15 per year for benefits including online annual journal subscription and special invites

☞ *37A Clerkenwell Grn, London EC1R 0DU, United Kingdom*
☞ **marx-memorial-library.org.uk**

Photography © **Karl Weiss**

MARX MEMORIAL LIBRARY
& WORKERS' SCHOOL

DON'T BE LEFT WITHOUT THESE TITLES

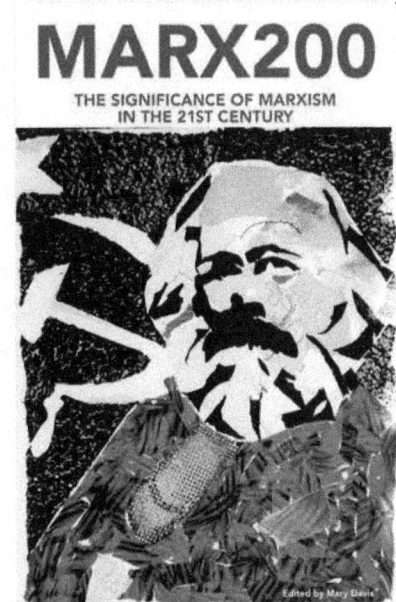

www.ingramcontent.com/pod-product-compliance
Lightning Source LLC
Chambersburg PA
CBHW080425270326
41929CB00018B/3162